The Problem of Force

THE PROBLEM OF FORCE

Grappling with the Global Battlefield

Simon W. Murden

LYNNE
RIENNER
PUBLISHERS

BOULDER
LONDON

Published in the United States of America in 2009 by
Lynne Rienner Publishers, Inc.
1800 30th Street, Boulder, Colorado 80301
www.rienner.com

and in the United Kingdom by
Lynne Rienner Publishers, Inc.
3 Henrietta Street, Covent Garden, London WC2E 8LU

© 2009 by Lynne Rienner Publishers, Inc. All rights reserved

Library of Congress Cataloging-in-Publication Data
Murden, Simon W.
 The problem of force : grappling with the global battlefield / by Simon W. Murden.
     p. cm.
 Includes bibliographical references and index.
 ISBN 978-1-58826-649-1 (hardcover : alk. paper)
 1. Military art and science—United States—History—21st century. 2. War on Terrorism, 2001– I. Title.
  UA23.M896 2009
  909.83'1—dc22
                                                             2009002535

British Cataloguing in Publication Data
A Cataloguing in Publication record for this book
is available from the British Library.

Printed and bound in the United States of America

 The paper used in this publication meets the requirements
of the American National Standard for Permanence of
Paper for Printed Library Materials Z39.48-1992.

5 4 3 2 1

Contents

List of Figures	vii
Acknowledgments	ix

	Introduction	1
1	War and Warfare in the Early Twenty-First Century	5
2	Mapping Contemporary Insurgency	25
3	Mapping Contemporary Intervention	45
4	The Origins of the War on Terror, 1991–2001	59
5	The War in Afghanistan	81
6	Planning the Iraq War	115
7	What Went Wrong in Iraq?	135
8	The Surge Experiment in Iraq	169
9	Whither the War on Terror?	189

Bibliography	211
Index	223
About the Book	233

Figures

1.1	The Spectrum of Warfare	8
1.2	The Operational Art of Fourth-Generation Warfare: Focusing Persuasive Power Through Local and Global Audiences	20
2.1	The Dynamics of Basic Types of Organization	30
2.2	The Specialized Functionaries of the Constellation Network	31
2.3	Map of Al-Qaida Affiliates and Potential Allies	36
2.4	Schematic of the Main Gravities in the Militant Islamic Movement in the Afghan-Pakistan Milieu	38
2.5	The Networks and Narrative Gravities of the Militant Islamic Movement	42
3.1	The Nexus of Force, Reconstruction, Reconciliation, and Assimilation, and Long-Term Governance in the Management of Conflict in Complex Social Settings	48
3.2	The Track of Emphasis in the Management of the Malaya Emergency, 1948–1960	49
3.3	Potential Tracks of Policy Emphasis in the Management of Conflict in Complex Social Settings	54
3.4	Progressing Through the RRA Zone: Closing the Reconciliation and Assimilation Gap	56
5.1	Map of the War in Afghanistan, 2001–2002	84
5.2	The Expedited Move to Governance in Afghanistan as Embodied in the Bonn Process	89
5.3	The Bonn Political Process in Post-2001 Afghanistan	90
5.4	Expansion of NATO (ISAF) in Afghanistan, 2004	104
6.1	Map of the Iraq War, 2003	126
7.1	Potential Alternative Tracks of US Policy Emphasis in the Management of Occupied Iraq	141

7.2	Map of the Coalition Occupation of Iraq, September 2003	143
7.3	The Actual Track of the US Occupation of Iraq, 2003–2006	144
7.4	Map of the Ethnic Landscape of Iraq	151
8.1	The Surge and Closing the Reconstruction, Reconciliation, and Assimilation Gap, 2006–2008	170

Acknowledgments

In early 2002 I moved to Britannia Royal Naval College in Dartmouth to join a growing team that included Geoff Sloan and Tim Benbow. Under Geoff's leadership, the Department of Strategic Studies and International Affairs briefly expanded its range of activities. Together Tim and I did quite a bit of thinking about both contemporary warfare and events unfolding in the Middle East. Talking over issues with Geoff and Tim was of great value, and I continued to benefit from discussing matters with them even after they took new assignments. Many parts of this book are improved thanks to their input.

As ever, I thank my parents, especially my father for pointing out the work of Donald A. Schon from the 1960s and 1970s. I'd also like to express my appreciation to the anonymous referees who offered many helpful comments and suggestions.

—*Simon Murden*

Introduction

Looking back at the US war on terror since its inception in 2001, it is difficult not to think about what went wrong. When then–President George W. Bush initiated the use of US military power in Afghanistan, it was an understandable response to the 9/11 terrorist attacks. But his subsequent decision to expand the conflict into Iraq sent its objectives and effects sprawling. The decision to conquer Iraq was a truly historic one, made all the more extraordinary because it was so poorly thought out beforehand. After a promising start, the operation in Afghanistan undertaken by the United States in association with the North Atlantic Treaty Organization (NATO) ran into a resurgent Taliban and had to face a renewed struggle for the future of that country. Meanwhile, Al-Qaida's mission continued to seep across the world, sporadically manifesting itself in the sort of murderous terrorism seen in Madrid, London, and Algiers. Few can have expected the war on terror to have been such a fraught experience. Indeed, by February 2006 one of the doyens of British journalism, Simon Jenkins, writing in *The Sunday Times,* even had some cause to wonder: "Is OBL [Osama bin Laden] winning after all? Until recently, I would have derided such a thought. How could a tin-pot fanatic who is either dead or shut in some mountain hideout hold the world to ransom for five years? It would stretch the imagination of Ian Fleming. . . . Bin Laden is not going to win and never was. But Bush and Blair are giving him an astonishing run for his money."[1]

Bush's war on terror did not seem to be working very well. Beyond the confines of the initial war on terror, the Iraq War demonstrated the limits of US military power and the pitfalls that came with unleashing it.

So why was the greatest power in the world unable to subdue countries the size of Afghanistan and Iraq or engineer anything approaching a desirable endstate in either? Why were the United States and its allies unable to decisively turn the tide on Al-Qaida and its ilk? This book will explore these questions and seek to explain the general and particular reasons as to why the use of force has been so problematic in the war on terror. Clearly, the particular circumstances of the Iraq War especially negated the accomplishment of US objectives. Iraq was always dogged by insufficient legal backing, a dysfunctional planning process, and sheer ineptitude. Beyond the particular shortcomings, it could also be argued that the utility of force was undercut by more general factors in the contemporary context. The advent of the world of liberalized globalization had led to a new generation of warfare—if not of war itself—in which novel kinds of diffuse actors were capable of sustaining what can be termed a *glocal* insurgency (a global-level mission and movement, locally networked and conducted) against great states. Indeed, the failure of US forces in Iraq after 2003 represented a failure to understand the changing nature of warfare almost as marked as the failure of most European militaries in 1914 and 1940.

The conflicts in Afghanistan and Iraq were the two great laboratories of warfare in the early twenty-first century, and studying them is the first place to go in order to gain insights into contemporary practice as well as into more theoretical questions about the nature of war. Of course, whether it is actually possible to disentangle the general from the particular when making assessments about the difficulty in making force work during the war on terror is likely to remain debatable, but setting out the factors will provide a basis upon which better judgments can be made about some of the big questions of the day: To what extent have war and warfare changed? How can highly diffuse globalized actors such as Al-Qaida be contained or defeated? Was the faltering of the Iraq project the result of particular mistakes, or was it inevitable? To what extent have developments in tactical and operational practice during the war on terror conquered the problems of contemporary warfare? And does war have a future?

An enormous amount has been written about 9/11 and the war on terror, especially the wars in Afghanistan and Iraq. Many of the accounts are very well sourced, and it would be difficult to add much to the narratives already produced by the likes of Bob Woodward, Michael Gordon and Bernard Trainor, L. Paul Bremer, Thomas E. Ricks, Ahmed S. Hashim, and Rajiv Chandrasekaran.[2] Although this book will provide a succinct account of relevant events, its principal purpose is not to add new facts to the history—that would be difficult to do in any substantial way now—but rather to offer some new insight into the mass of information and argument that is already out there. The analytical offerings come from two directions: first, to put the war on terror in the context of the broader practice of war in the early twenty-first century; and second, to model the particular battles of the war on terror by referring to social network theory as well as to present a new triangular map of waging warfare in complex social settings. With such analytical elements, I hope to explain why it was so difficult to make force work in the war on terror.

The book begins by assessing the nature of contemporary war and warfare, especially the way in which the purpose and practice of war have become increasingly diffuse. Chapter 1 examines some of the causes of this diffusion. Some causes, notably the advent of nuclear weapons, have existed for many years. Other diffusing factors stemmed from the expansion of the world of liberalizing globalization following the end of the Cold War. The military superiority of the United States and its Western allies also meant that it was scarcely rational for adversaries to challenge them on the conventional battlefield. The outcomes of these developments have been examined by the advocates of Fourth Generation Warfare (4GW); and even though the concept is not without its problems, the chapter argues that it does describe a new kind of diffuse war-practicing actor, requiring a new operational art to engage it. Chapter 2 goes on to analyze the phenomenon of the glocal insurgency, and drawing on organizational theory from the business and sociological studies provides a new conceptual map of the narratives and networks of Al-Qaida. Chapter 3 examines contemporary Western intervention, especially through a series of post–Cold War conflicts, and proposes another conceptual model to help understand the dynamics of waging warfare in a complex social setting.

In moving toward the case studies of Afghanistan and Iraq, Chapter 4 describes the particular strategic context for the outbreak of the war on terror, arguing that it can only really be understood in terms of the rise and fall of a US-constructed security architecture in the Middle East in the 1990s; this security architecture was based on a number of pillars, including the Arab-Israel peace process, the "dual containment" of Iran and Iraq, and the garrisoning of the Persian Gulf. Although this security architecture had great potential for bringing peace and order to the region, it was flawed, and its decay in the second half of the 1990s primed renewed conflict not only between the United States and Iraq but also between the United States and the Islamic militants led by Osama bin Laden. America's decaying security architecture in the Middle East finally went critical on 11 September 2001, and the subsequent war on terror would be synonymous with the attempt of the Bush administration to undertake an extreme makeover of it.

Chapter 5 examines the opening shots of the war on terror. In Afghanistan, the United States was initially able to deploy a startlingly efficient model of warfare and a follow-on political process that also appeared to work well. The Taliban regime was unseated more easily than anticipated, and a major defeat was inflicted upon the Al-Qaida organization. The apparent efficiency of force was impressive—but it was a false dawn. As the United States and its allies turned toward Iraq, they left unfinished business in Afghanistan. A disgruntled local population and political tendency was not reconciled to what the war of 2001–2002 had done, and this allowed militant jihadists to seep back into the game.

The decision of the Bush administration to invade, conquer, and transform Iraq was a historic moment for the Middle East, but it would also highlight the fact that in contemporary circumstances insurgency was the dominant idiom of warfare, and the US armed forces were not particularly well equipped, organized, or attuned to deal with it. Chapters 6 and 7 examine why the world's most powerful state found its Iraq project so difficult to execute. Although the political and legal context was never an auspicious one, the tactical and operational approach of US forces was found wanting. After bitter experience, US policymakers and commanders would put their minds to the problem and come up with powerful new approaches. Chapter 8 examines the concept and execution of the so-called surge in Iraq in 2007–2008 and assesses to what extent it provided a route to "victory" as well as a cutting-edge model for future military operations. Had the surge restored the utility of force?

The defeat of the Taliban and Al-Qaida in Afghanistan and regime change in Iraq may have offered most Afghans and Iraqis the chance for a better life, but what was done in both cases was not unambiguously good in either a moral or practical sense. US prestige in the world was grievously damaged. The international systems in the Middle East and South Asia were destabilized. The ongoing wars in both countries were a tremendous boon to militant Islamists across the world. Chapter 9 assesses the state of the war on terror by 2007–2008 and, deploying the conceptual map of the war proposed in Chapter 2, outlines what kind of "effects" could be seen as tactical, operational, and strategic in the war. In this way, it may be possible to glean how, one day, Al-Qaida might be disempowered and deactivated and the war on terror brought to a conclusion. The chapter concludes with some comments about the likely future of warfare.

Notes

1. Simon Jenkins, "Comment: Bush and Blair Have Brilliantly Done bin Laden's Work for Him," *The Sunday Times,* 19 February 2006, 18.
2. Bob Woodward, *Bush at War* (New York: Simon and Schuster, 2002), and Bob Woodward, *Plan of Attack* (London: Simon and Schuster UK, 2004); Michael Gordon and Bernard Trainor (Lieutenant General, USMC), *Cobra II: The Inside Story of the Invasion and Occupation of Iraq* (London: Atlantic Books, 2006); L. Paul Bremer with Malcolm McConnell, *My Year in Iraq: The Struggle to Build a Future of Hope* (New York: Simon and Schuster, 2006); Thomas E. Ricks, *Fiasco: The American Military Adventure in Iraq* (London: Penguin Books, 2006); Ahmed S. Hashim, *Insurgency and Counterinsurgency in Iraq* (London: C. Hurst, 2006), xxviii; Rajiv Chandrasekaran, *Imperial Life in the Emerald City: Inside Baghdad's Green Zone* (London: Bloomsbury, 2006).

1
War and Warfare in the Early Twenty-First Century

By the year 2001, our dominant image of war was still that which had been forged in the twentieth century. During that century the world witnessed conflict on an epic scale shaped by several factors: the centrality of the European-type territorial state as the principal actor in world affairs; the inherently competitive nature of the state system that those states inhabited; and the increasing capacity of the state to mobilize people and technology into military organizations for the pursuit of national interests. War among the world's major powers got bigger, and the ends for which war was pursued escalated. This escalation toward ever bigger wars had been predicted by the great nineteenth-century Prussian strategist Carl von Clausewitz (1780–1831). For Clausewitz, although war might be pursued for any number of political objectives and by any number of means, it was such a costly, dangerous, and unpredictable business that it was probably best waged with the intent of overpowering the "will" and "capacity" of the enemy to resist—literally "to disarm the enemy in order to subject it to one's will."[1]

But war is not what it used to be. During the last decade of the twentieth century, the kind of wars that had preoccupied major powers no longer seemed so pressing. The sight of massed armies battling one another with the intent of achieving some decisive victory was now a rarity. Instead, in the aftermath of the Cold War the major powers were at peace, and the proliferation of local wars and insurgencies appeared to mark the beginning of new era of war. The near disappearance of conventional warfare—or the threat of it—was described by a number of thinkers, notably William S. Lind, Martin van Creveld, Edward N. Luttwak, Mary Kaldor, Colonel Thomas X. Hammes (USMC), and General Rupert Smith (British Army).[2] For some contemporary theorists, if Clausewitz was not exactly rendered useless, what must now most interest the scholars of strategy was the dynamics of limited war and conflicts other than war, kinds of conflict that in Clausewitz's writing were overshadowed by his thinking on escalation and full-scale war. The dominant reading of Clausewitz as *the* apostle of conventional war no longer seemed so relevant. By the late twentieth century, war was not really about decisively *disarming* the enemy in order to subject it to one's will but instead about *persuading* or *inducing* it to give up or come to terms.

Whether humankind had really seen an end to conventional war as we knew it remained to be seen. In his book *Another Bloody Century* (2006), Colin S. Gray—defending the continuing relevance of interstate war and Clausewitz—sought to debunk much of the new theorizing. Setting the terms of reference, Gray recalled Clausewitz's distinction between the "nature" and "character" of war. The objective nature of war embodied its basic definition. War could be defined by three timeless elements: first, it is fought for political objectives; second, it is a reciprocal duel conducted with the aim of imposing one's will on another; and third, it has a distinctive climate of violence, uncertainty, and chance.[3] Meanwhile, the subjective character of war related to how it was practiced. The objective nature of war was timeless—it would always be defined by the three basic elements—but the practice, or grammar, of warfare was liable to change according to particular time and circumstance. So for Gray, war remained part of the human condition, and whatever changes were evident were in the secondary realm of practice (i.e., about warfare rather than war itself). Claims that war was an anachronism were wrong, even dangerous, and any attempts to conceptualize a new era of war were really overblown fads. In any case, limited and insurgent-type wars were hardly new, and neither were the things that were getting some contemporary strategists excited, such as the importance of psychological pressure and the role of the media in warfare.

Clearly, the practice (and threat) of warfare was different after the end of the Cold War. Interstate war was rare and improbable, and the dominant idiom of warfare did seem of a more limited nature. Beyond describing radical changes in the practice, though, a number of contemporary theorists, notably Lind and van Creveld, did take the bolder line by arguing that war itself was being transformed. War had not only lost its utility for the state; the changing nature of the actors involved, of their political objectives, and of the duel of war itself were fundamental. Small, internally chaotic actors pursued objectives that were often ambiguous and changeable. For such actors, the act of practicing warfare might be as important as any distant and implausible political objective; this certainly seemed to be the case for some Islamic-inspired jihadists. Moreover, the nature of the duel itself was different: less rapiers at dawn, more Spanish tomato festival. Certainly, if the War on Terror was any measure, wars were now fought by a myriad of small nonstate groups, each with different objectives and modus operandi, repeatedly swooping in and out of conflicts for all sorts of reasons, and sometimes it was not just about trying to impose one's will on a clearly defined adversary. Thus, it was arguable that changes in the nature of the actors, the political objectives, and the duel pointed to a new era not only of warfare but also of the institution of war itself.

How fundamental these changes in war actually were would continue to be debated by academic strategists. Yet even if it was too early to declare a transformation in the institution of war, the changes in practice were much less debatable. For realist theorists like Colin Gray, the inclination was to downplay the significance of these changes in warfare: The older types of warfare, Gray speculated, "may well be resting rather than declining in an irreversible obsolescence."[4] Maybe so—but not in this world! The reality of the post–Cold War world was that realist assumptions about the persistence of interstate rivalry had been largely overpowered by the interaction of several factors that determined—as they always have determined—how warfare is practiced. These *factors of warfare* include the nature of the actors practicing war; the kind of international system that exists, especially the structuring of community relationships within it; and the state of the technology of warfare (material and social). In the second half of the twentieth century, a series of developments came into play that acted to make war and warfare more diffuse and more difficult to make work as a policy option. The greatest military power of the day, the United States, would struggle to win its wars even as its superiority in practicing them remained unrivaled. The particular historical and technological developments at play in the post–Cold War world were the advent of nuclear weapons and disutility of general/total war; the effects of liberalizing globalization in the late twentieth century; and the effect of US military superiority and its impact on the contemporary battlefield. Each of these developments is discussed below.

The Advent of Nuclear Weapons and Disutility of Total War

The development of nuclear weapons at the end of World War II was among the most important factors that limited the practice of twentieth-century warfare. If the invention of the atomic bomb threatened a ruinous new level of strategic bombing, the subsequent development of the hydrogen bomb threatened to extinguish human civilization altogether.[5] Such weapons simply made it too dangerous for nuclear powers to go to war against each other. Risking an apocalyptic exchange was not a rational act of policy, because the likely scale of destruction would surely usurp any political objective. Avoiding war became more important than actually waging it, and partly for this reason it was expert civilians—people like Bernard Brodie, Herman Kahn, Henry Kissinger, Thomas Schelling, Robert Osgood, and Robert McNamara—who formulated much US Cold War strategy. Although the theorizing and design of deterrents were the order of the day in the standoff between the United States and Soviet Union, both superpowers tacitly accepted that the use of war was still possible as long as it was limited by certain rules of the game—that the armed forces of the superpowers were not to clash directly or be unduly provoked, and that limited wars were to take place only outside areas of vital interest. War was sent off to the third world, where it mattered less. The era of limited wars and proxy wars had been born, with the conflict in Vietnam being the definitive example. Although a great deal of violence was applied in Vietnam, it was limited in terms of means and ends. It was a persuasive war characterized by a US attempt to bomb North Vietnam to the negotiating table, with a countereffort by North Vietnam to inflict such pain on the United States as to persuade it to go away. The persuasive bombing war remains among the most important tools of US warfare today.

In short, nuclear weapons sent warfare down a spectrum from decisive conventional war toward the persuasive asymmetric war or the symmetric proxy war (see Figure 1.1). In his book *The Utility of Force*, General Rupert Smith (echoing authors like Martin van Creveld) went as far as to argue that nuclear weapons had produced a "paradigm shift" in war, leading to a new condition that he called "war among the people."[6] The last genuinely competitive tank battle—the iconic practice of twentieth-century warfare—was fought in the Arab-Israel War of 1973; this type of battle was not likely to be seen again.[7] The last strategically successful "industrial-type war" was the Falklands War of 1982.[8] The Gulf War of 1991 was much less strategic than it looked. The idea of conventional war continued to have tremendous inertia, but the reality was that it had lost its utility. Industrial-age war was no longer the great deciding event that it had been.

For Smith, despite the repeated efforts of Western militaries to reinvent conventional war in a different context, the new condition of "war among the people" was really fought by and among populations, and it was won or lost in that context.[9] War among the people was largely a series of tactical-level and propaganda events that rarely reached any kind of culminating point. Thus, the aim of decisive victory—and the operational art designed to achieve it—must eventually be superseded by the practice of political-type warfare

Figure 1.1 The Spectrum of Warfare

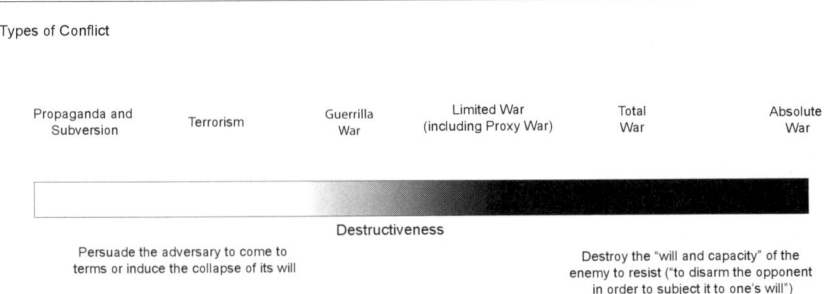

among the populations of contested areas. When it came to the Iraq War of 2003, for instance, Smith thought that getting rid of Saddam Hussein's regime was an operational-level objective, but the whole enterprise had quickly and inevitably receded to tactical-level skirmishing with insurgents. The strategic objective was the creation of a democratic Iraq, but the US-led coalition could not really reach the strategic level, because any political settlement had to be decided among Iraqis—not by Americans—and very few of them were genuinely inclined to do America's bidding.[10] In other words, the use of force was applied substrategically. Even if things had gone to a plan, the strategic outcome would be decided by the occupied people, not by the occupier. At the end of the Cold War, war among the people was already the dominant paradigm of warfare, but it would be some years before this fact was widely recognized.[11] Iraq would play a major part in this.

The Effects of Liberalizing Globalization

Today, it is not just the hydrogen bomb that prevents the recurrence of war between major powers; it is the nature of the liberal international order that emerged from the end of the Cold War. During the Cold War, the United States forged the Western world. It was an alliance of Western states that evolved into a security community, that is, an international community in which the extent of mutual interests, political, economic, and military cooperation and interdependence, and collective institutions made violent conflict between its members inconceivable. The United States was the ultimate arbiter and guarantor of the Western security community, but the system was governed in a law-based way. The West won the Cold War with this system and, in its aftermath, would globalize the Western security community. Many states were soon integrated into the world of liberalizing globalization, and the other major powers—Russia, China, and India—offered a place. A new era of consensus-generating international institutions and a truly global marketplace became possible.

Creating a Global Security Community and the Major Power Consensus

The world order that emerged in the 1990s was organized in a relatively inclusive way, with many collective decisions being formulated and implemented through multilateral institutions. Thus, at a time of tremendous change, the international community was stabilized and successfully reordered. As one of the leading US thinkers on globalization, G. John Ikenberry, succinctly put it, "American power did not destabilise world order—it helped create it. The creation of rule-based agreements and political-security partnerships were both good for the United States and for a huge part of the rest of the world. The result by the end of the 1990s was a global political formation of unprecedented size and success—a trans-oceanic coalition of democratic states tied together through markets, institutions and security partnerships."[12]

Integration into the system offered advantages that significantly altered the costs and benefits of going to war. Whereas China and Russia remained politically illiberal, for instance, they adopted broadly cooperative strategies. Selfish power-seeking no longer seemed necessary, normatively acceptable, or practically viable. Thus, Russia, China, and India learned to make their way in the world within the context of the West's global system, and the imperatives of operating as rival imperial monopolies were superseded by the rule of law, a consensus about acceptable practice, and a relatively open global trading system. Indeed, China soon started accumulating many tens of billions of dollars as it consolidated its position as the workshop of the globalizing world, and it was not long before China and the United States were locked into a kind of economic mutually assured destruction. As one of the world's principal repositories of oil and raw materials, Russia—if it so chose—could take a somewhat more independent or autarkic line, but it too was immersed in international trade. As long as the global trading system remained reasonably intact, the resort to war—even limited or proxy war—between major world powers simply did not seem to be a rational way of maximizing national interests (although that did not exclude the possibility of irrational or ideological decisionmaking, or that stemming from internal political-bureaucratic contests). Meanwhile, for the leaders of states who did still believe in the utility of war, what happened to Iraq and Serbia in the 1990s served as examples.

Thus, if nuclear weapons had sent conflict between major powers off into the realms of the limited and proxy wars, then the advent of the world of liberalizing globalization *ended* even that kind of behavior. To the extent that there was conflict between powerful states, it was largely political, economic, and cultural. To the extent that limited or proxy war might take place, it was most likely to involve a few states outside the globalized security community—perhaps involving pariahs of the international community, the so-called rogue states like Iran and North Korea. Within the global security community, as David Held and Anthony McGrew observed in the *Review of International Studies* in 1998,

> although the discourse of national security dominates political and popular debate about military matters, it acts more as a simplified representation or legitimating device than a reflection of the actual behaviour of states. For many states the strategy for achieving 'national security' has become almost indistinguishable from an international security strategy. . . . Pollution, drugs, human rights and terrorism are amongst an increasing number of transnational policy issues which cut across territorial jurisdictions and existing political alignments, and which require international co-operation for their effective resolution. Defence and security issues no longer dominate the global

agenda or even the political agendas of many national governments. These developments, accordingly, challenge the conventional Westphalian (and realist) principles of world political order.[13]

Although the unleashing of US military power during the war on terror shook confidence in the rules and institutions of the globalized security community, and may have primed some maneuvering among major world powers, the system remained intact.[14] The vast majority of the international community simply benefited too much from the security, prosperity, and predictability that the globalized security community provided. And despite transgressions by the United States, most of the international community accepted that for the time being the world order had no other relatively benign hegemonic organizer. Even as the United States faced increasing levels of resentment, few states really wanted a world without the public international goods that it supplied.

The Limiting Effect of Liberalism on Western War-Making

If Western stewardship of international security was externally limited by the need to maintain the global security community, especially to keep the other major powers on board, it was also internally limited by the nature of liberal democracy and the belief shared by most Westerners that the use of force was legitimate only if it was proportionate, governed by rules, undertaken in the last resort, and done only after some sort of consensus had been achieved across the international community. The US administration of President Bill Clinton (1993–2001) accepted the logic of this multilateralism, and as the 1990s went on it became possible to talk about the emergence of a multilateralized Western hegemony over the world order, rather than a simple US hegemony.[15] Of course, the subsequent administration of President George W. Bush (2001–2009) was to alter the prevailing understandings, although not in a fatal way. Notwithstanding Iraq, the rule of law was one of the historic foundations of Western democracy, and to varying degrees all Western states continued to be constrained by national laws as well as international legal conventions; these were also in the interests of Western states to preserve.

Western-led management of international security after the Cold War would be torn by two impulses: the so-called solidarist impulse to assume more responsibility in managing international security, including safeguarding human rights everywhere; set against the old sovereignty principle (as set out in the United Nations Charter of 1945) and an aversion to being involved in violent conflict. In the 1990s, these contradictory impulses would be played out among politicians and publics to a background of the globalized news media. The outcome was something of a paradox: Although Western states gradually became more inclined to intervene across the world, Western publics and politicians were liable to recoil from the implications of doing so. The very idea of a liberal war, the scholar Lawrence Freedman observed, was an oxymoron.[16]

The ambiguous attitude of the West toward intervening and engaging in war could be seen in the light of what Colin McInnes referred to as the advent of "spectator-sport war."[17] The West waged wars of choice that were fought for limited objectives, in a limited way, and that elicited only limited commitment. Moreover, with the enemy's now being defined by Western policymakers as errant leaders and their evil cohorts rather than as whole nations—that would be too arbitrary for the law-loving liberal—it was incumbent on Western commanders to use as minimal and targeted force as possible.[18] Spectator-sport war was largely the business of a few highly professional soldiers, and although the citizenry could watch from the sidelines, it was neither likely nor desirable that they become too involved in the play. For McInnes, spectator-sport war was a pageant and—rather like wrestling—it was important that the good guys not disappoint themselves or their audience by failing to live up to their reputation lest they be redesignated as the villain.[19]

The other limiting aspect to wars of choice related to the willingness of Western peoples and their politicians to persevere when the going got tough. Although containing the overall level of disorder in the world was vital to the maintenance of liberalized globalization, it remained difficult to make the case for going to war without defining a direct national interest. Politicians and publics in the United States remained very wary of committing forces unless Americans were at risk or national security at stake. If the national interest was not clear, then the preparedness to persevere in the face of losses was liable to be limited, with Somalia in 1992–1993 standing as the definitive example of a weakly supported intervention that quickly passed the perseverance tipping point.

Following Somalia, it was widely assumed that Western aversion to casualties was a serious limitation. In an article in *Foreign Affairs* in 1995, Edward Luttwak observed that the need to use "military force collide[d] with the general refusal of the American public to sanction interventions in place after place without end."[20] Luttwak argued that the rise of a "post-heroic" culture in the West was related to the intense individualism of Western societies and the higher value put on young people when families produced only one or two offspring. Moreover, an asymmetry of willpower had emerged between the "professional, salaried, pensioned, and career-minded" soldiers of the West and their various adversaries who were "inflamed by nationalism or religious fanaticism."[21] Although it is possible to overstate Western sensitivity to casualties, the assumption does have some validity. Western politicians do find it difficult to justify losses in the context of wars of choice, and even where national interests are powerful—as for the United States in Iraq—it was a struggle to keep a viable proportion of the voting public on board once casualties mounted. Of course, managing the asymmetry of will between the small professional army and the energized horde is hardly a new problem, and, as Luttwak observed, the response of the US military was essentially the same as that of the Roman army. Despite the cult of decisive victory that pervaded both forces, the reality was that most of the time they sought to minimize risk. The best bet for the highly valued and technologically superior force was the set-piece battle rather than the fluid battle, with the trade embargo and armed blockade of US forces standing as the equivalent to the Roman siege.[22]

The Empowerment of Small Nonstate War Makers

While the new world order fostered peace among states, social-level forces were at work that led to the proliferation of small violent groups and enabled them to project force across the world. These small groups were empowered by the new technologies and open borders of liberalized globalization. The relative weakening of the state, and its complete failure in a few places, also opened more space for nonstate actors. It was increasingly difficult for states to control the kinds of people, information, goods, and services flowing in and out of their territory. With many tens of millions of people on the move and the ongoing development of globalized communications and financial systems, the opportunities to engage in truly transnational subversion were growing. The emergence of various post-Soviet mafias, notably from Russia, Chechnya, and the former Yugoslavia, were the kind of threats that dogged the expansion of globalization. An organization like Al-Qaida, too, really could not have existed amid the highly bordered world of the Cold War. The Internet—especially the introduction of broadband and other high-speed communications technologies—provided such groups with another powerful tool for propagation, recruitment, and training.

Nonstate subversives could broadly be divided into *globalization-haters* and *globalization-loving deviants*. The globalization-haters encompassed a myriad of nationalists, religious fundamentalists, and other traditionalists who did not want to be part of the world of liberalized globalization; they tended to see the liberal idea as morally and socially banal and Western leadership as pernicious. Instead, they often sought to preserve a more traditional vision of the world that they believed (probably rightly, from their perspective) to be under threat. By contrast, the globalization-loving deviants included actors involved in transnational criminal activities like narcotics trafficking, arms sales, and human smuggling as well as those subverting the trustworthiness of the Internet for the purpose of profit, politics, and fun.

Although the globalization-haters and globalization-loving deviants were ostensibly different beasts, they often networked with each other for contingent reasons. Nationalists and religious fundamentalists did deals with transnational organized crime and embraced the new technologies and openness to create extensive networks themselves. The globalization-haters were the most dangerous to international security because they were inherently political and thus more likely to engage in war. However, according to John P. Sullivan, the increasing coincidence of crime and politics had produced what he called the "third generation" criminal gang, which was interested not only in providing "conflict services" for profit to politically inspired groups but also in shaping national and transnational governance issues.[23] It was often in the interests of the third-generation gang to foster governance black spots to facilitate their domestic and transnational operations. With the advent of the war on terror, the organizers and mercenaries of third-generation gangs in Asia would become more entangled with globalization-hating insurgents.

The rising challenge of substate actors was to become synonymous with the idea of what was referred to as the "asymmetric" threat—a term coined in US defense documents during the mid-1990s.[24] Threats became asymmetric not only because such actors were of a different size to Western states but also because they were likely to adopt weapons, tactics, and values specifically designed to negate the advantages of the powerful state. Western states had vulnerabilities: dependency on infrastructure and high-tech communications networks; sensitivity to casualties by virtue of public pressure; the desire to live up to their own moral and legal norms; and the unity of Western alliances.

The ultimate concern about asymmetric actors was that one day they might acquire a weapon of mass destruction (WMD), either by manufacturing it themselves—as the Aum Shinrikyo cult infamously did for its sarin nerve-gas attack on the Tokyo subway system in March 1995—or by acquiring it from a failing post-Soviet state or rogue regional power. It was possible to imagine a whole range of scenarios whereby a troubled state, or elements within it, might pass a WMD or WMD technology to a substate group. Such a possibility was particularly disturbing because many asymmetric actors were unlikely to pay much attention to deterrents. Attacks might be untraceable, and even if the perpetrators could be identified they might prove difficult to find and access—or else be totally indifferent to the danger they were in. Thus, the asymmetric threat—especially the potential nexus between the terrorist group and the rogue regional power—became one of the principal security issues in the post–Cold War world. Moreover, while asymmetric actors individually represented only a limited challenge to Western states, collectively they threatened to debilitate the world of liberalized globalization. If the world order was not to sink under a mass of small-scale geopolitical conflicts, sociocultural resistance, and deviant activity, then all of it had to be managed. The level of disorder in the world had to be contained.

In sum, liberalized globalization had empowered a new kind of small transnational actor that was capable of practicing war. Indeed, the principal frontier of international security after the Cold War would pit the managers of globalization—the United States and its key allies—against the stragglers and deviants in the system. Other kinds of conflict might surface as a result of irrationality, ideology, and the persistence of preexisting regional conflicts, but if these old-style conflicts took place it would be in spite of the main forces operating in the international system rather than because of them. Interstate warfare was not an incipient function of the world of liberalized globalization. Asymmetric warfare was.

The Effect of US Military Superiority and Its Impact on the Contemporary Battlefield

The United States was a military colossus by the end of the Cold War, and in the 1990s its superiority was extended as it massively outspent all the other major states combined. The US defense budget moved to more than US$300 billion a year by the end of that decade, and the George W. Bush administration would oversee its increase to around US$500 billion a year.[25] New technologies and planning techniques significantly enhanced the ability of the US military to reach, understand, and dominate the conventional battlefield. In particular, airpower was made much more precise and useable, and the coercive air war—aerial bombing to persuade adversaries to alter their behavior or face further consequences—was to become the strategy of choice for US policymakers. US aircraft carriers and forward bases cast a shadow almost everywhere in the world, and US military power was the ultimate arbiter of local balances in conflict zones such as the Balkans, the Middle East, South Asia, and the Korean peninsula as well as the Persian Gulf, South China Sea, and Taiwan Strait.

But the possession of preeminent military power is rarely straightforward—and such was the US lot. The sheer extent of US superiority on the conventional battlefield was to further reinforce the changing practice of warfare. Although the idea was not without its problems, the effect of US military superiority was perhaps best encapsulated in the idea of fourth-generation warfare (4GW). The 4GW concept was primed by an astonishingly forward-thinking article in *Marine Corps Gazette* in October 1989 by William S. Lind, Colonel Keith Nightengale, Captain John F. Schmitt, Colonel Joseph W. Sutton, and Lieutenant Colonel Gary I. Wilson.[26] The article tried to make sense of what seemed to be contradictory trends acting to shape the future of warfare. To do this, the authors contended that the development of warfare since Napoleon could be seen in terms of three generations.

The first generation of warfare (1GW) was conditioned by the limitations of the smoothbore musket and cannon. The 1GW battlefield involved drawing men up into linear formations to conduct attritional battle. The second generation of warfare (2GW) stemmed from technological developments in the nineteenth century—new weapons, railways, and the telegraph (there were developments in leadership and doctrine, too)—which led to a change in firepower and enabled larger maneuvers aimed at altering the terms of trade before the final attrition. The third generation of warfare (3GW) arose from the development of technologies such as the tank, aircraft, and radio. More important, 3GW was driven by new concepts, especially the ideas of combined arms and deep battle aimed at incapacitating or decapitating the enemy as distinct from simply overwhelming it. 3GW was not necessarily linear, and the focus of the operational art shifted from mastering space to mastering time and tempo. The Wehrmacht (German army in World War II) was the first to realize 3GW with its *blitzkrieg*—deep tank and airpower penetrations at lightning speed—at the beginning of the war, but it was the United States that would bring 3GW to its apogee by the end of the twentieth century as it synchronized combined arms, deep battle, effects-based planning, and the networked battlefield.

As the Cold War came to an end, Lind and his fellow authors perceived that warfare might be on the verge of another shift—toward a fourth generation. Why? The US military had made itself such a master of 3GW that adversaries would have no option but to disperse and devolve; those who didn't would simply be subject to the laws of natural selection. Adversaries of the US military must avoid presenting nodes of command and control and so would probably have to organize themselves on the basis of mission concept rather than on hierarchical structure. Greater diffusion might even go as far as taking on novel nonnational and transnational forms of organization. Thus, if the first three generations of warfare had led to the deployment of ever larger armies with ever more firepower and mobility, 4GW was likely to be much more dissipated. Fewer combatants would be more deeply immersed in the landscape, with future warfare less about massing to attack the enemy from the outside and more about undermining it from within.[27] The authors perceived that "psychological operations may become the dominant operational and strategic weapon in the form of media/information intervention."[28] The changes involved were likely to be truly historic:

> For about the last 500 years, the West has defined warfare . . . because the West's strength is technology, it may tend to conceive of a fourth generation in technological terms. However, the West no longer dominates the world. A fourth generation may emerge from non-Western cultural traditions. . . . The fact that some non-Western areas, such as the Islamic world, are not strong in technology may lead them to develop a fourth generation through ideas rather than technology. The genesis of an idea-based fourth generation may be visible in terrorism. This is not to say that terrorism is fourth generation warfare, but rather that elements of it may be signs pointing toward a fourth generation . . . the more successful terrorists appear to operate on broad mission orders that carry down to the level of the individual terrorist. The "battlefield" is highly dispersed and includes the whole of the enemy's society. The terrorist lives almost completely off the land and the enemy. . . . [Terrorists] can move freely within our society while actively seeking to subvert it. They use our democratic rights not only to penetrate but also to defend themselves. If we treat them within our laws, they gain many protections; if we simply shoot them down, the television news can easily make them appear to be the

victims. Terrorists can effectively wage their form of warfare while being protected by the society they are attacking.[29]

The 4GW concept initially attracted little interest, but its relevance was promoted by a number of subsequent works, most notably Martin van Creveld's *The Transformation of War* and Colonel Thomas X. Hammes's *The Sling and the Stone*. The fact that it predicted the kind of novel transnational force like Al-Qaida also made it extremely prescient after 2001.

The 4GW concept is not without its critics.[30] The concept can be taken to task in a number of ways: whether there was much new in it; the generational characterization of warfare and the time line for its evolution; whether the state was declining to the extent suggested in the iteration of 4GW proposed by Lind; and whether conventional interstate warfare has been largely superseded. Some academic strategists saw it as an attempt to kill Clausewitz.[31] Others perceived that conventional warfare and insurgent warfare were such different types that they were best represented on two completely different scales of progression.[32] In an important symposium on 4GW undertaken by *Contemporary Security Policy* in its August 2005 issue, James Wirtz, Edward Luttwak, Michael Evans, and John Ferris cued up to say that the idea that "peasant armies, guerrillas, mujahideen, terrorist networks, or individual fanatics" enjoyed some sort of universal and timeless superiority over conventional militaries could not be sustained.[33] Moreover, although the 4GW challenge might be chiefly political, such movements were not well positioned—due to their diffuse organization and nearly universal legal status as criminal entities—to turn coercive pressure into positive political outcomes.

Many of the criticisms have merit. However, 4GW was always designed as a heuristic device, in particular to be used in US military colleges to highlight the diminishing likelihood of conventional war and the increasing possibility of asymmetric warfare requiring new approaches (although, it must be said, that in this sense 4GW was a failure in that the US military remained resistant to reorganizing and reequipping itself throughout the 1990s). For all the criticisms, though, a number of important points have come out of the theorizing about 4GW that make it an essential concept in understanding contemporary warfare. These are discussed in turn below.

4GW Describes a New Kind of Glocal Insurgency

One of the principal criticisms of 4GW was that there was little new in it and that it was really just a faddish rehashing of the existing body of work on insurgency and terrorism. In charting the origins of 4GW, one of the leading 4GW thinkers, Thomas X. Hammes, certainly argued that Mao Tse-tung had pioneered the modern insurgency and that a path of development could be traced through the conflicts in Vietnam, Algeria, Afghanistan, Lebanon, and the Israeli Occupied Territories.[34] Contemporary insurgents undoubtedly owe something to their predecessors, but what the most useful 4GW thinking does—as Hammes eventually did—was go on to describe how contemporary circumstances had led to a significant evolution in insurgency. What 4GW was most concerned with—or rather what it *should* be most concerned with—was the insurgent in the age of liberalized globalization and, in particular, with the phenomenon of the glocal insurgency (a global-level mission and movement, locally networked and conducted). The glocal insurgency was an endemic feature of liberalized globalization and the principal hard security threat to its stability.

To understand this, it is probably best not to define all terrorists and insurgents as 4GW actors. Groups like Hamas, Hezbollah, and the Taliban are not really full-on 4GW actors themselves. Rather, they are more traditional social movements with a hierarchical organization and with, in reality, territorially limited aspirations, although this is not to say that they have not adopted 4GW-type techniques and are not drawn in to the networks of more developed 4GW actors. Hamas, Hezbollah, and the Taliban are perhaps better described as "sub-4GW" actors. The full-on 4GW actor is the instigator of a glocal insurgency: Its strategic objectives are pitched at the transnational and/or global level, and even though the 4GW actor might precipitate into more hierarchical forms of organization locally (where conditions allowed), its diffuse existence was truly regional and possibly global in extent. The global-level insurgency it instigates emerges from a mission concept and is propagated by such means as globalized electronic communications. In his account of what he calls the contemporary "complex insurgency," John Mackinlay observes that

> their apparent coherence is a random convergence of individual groups responding to the same impulse, a mutually experienced rage, admiration of a particular leader, the thrall of an intoxicating idea that explains the world. Its power seems to be crucial to the insurgent's momentum, so pervasive that it uniformly reaches widely separated communities of different ethnicity and so powerful that it takes men from their wives, families and otherwise normal lives to commit appalling acts against complete strangers. . . . Today the synergy of the Internet and thrall of an intoxicating idea have replaced vertical structures and elaborate campaign plans; impulse is the new strategy, the Internet the new structure.[35]

The most important thing that the glocal insurgent did was to network among older types of insurgent and deviant groups. 4GW would see global revolutionaries, third-generation criminal gangs, and local insurgents and sympathizers form diffuse and evolving networks to conduct deals and develop synergies. Iraq after 2003 was to be a definitive example: For a time at least, the 4GW insurgents of the self-proclaimed Al-Qaida in Iraq provided mission concept, leadership and violent shock on the battlefield, and organizational and brokering services; criminal mafias added logistics support and general disorder; local insurgents and sympathizers contributed personnel, intelligence-gathering, and attritional capacity. This system of synergies was described in a RAND report on Iraq as a "federated insurgency complex."[36]

Although the Al-Qaida–type model might be a relatively rare phenomenon—care is needed, Tim Benbow observes, not to overgeneralize from Al-Qaida because it might be a once-in-twenty-five-year or once-in-fifty-year phenomenon—it was possible to imagine that one day militant environmentalists, some Marxist-type movement, or even a globalized diaspora might provide the mission concept for other glocal insurgencies to develop.[37] The potential for the 4GW glocal insurgency would exist as long as there were global-level issues capable of generating sufficient friction and mission concept, related local-level grievances for global insurgents to exploit, relatively open borders, and a poorly policed Internet.

4GW Demands a New Operational Art

As the US military, during the mid-1990s, began to ponder the prospect of asymmetric warfare, it initially tried to play to *its* strengths by extending the weapons and techniques of the 3GW battlefield to the 4GW battlefield. The Revolution in Military Affairs (RMA) concept was a very American idea in that material, technological, and organizational solutions were posited as the means to achieve control over the environment. The US military did develop a fearsome model of urban airland battle that would eventually be unleashed with the clearance of Fallujah, Iraq, in 2004. But as events on the ground in Iraq demonstrated, it was not the solution to 4GW.

The fundamental problem of the 4GW battlefield was that even though it was still possible to imagine the application of decisive force at a tactical level—a village or town might be encircled and most of those insurgents presenting themselves for battle killed or captured—it was very difficult to imagine that 4GW adversaries could be defeated at an operational or strategic level by military means; they were simply too dispersed to all be found and engaged. Moreover, simply stacking up tactical-level victories with the hope of someday reaching a tipping point implied the kind of drawn-out attritional warfare that was difficult to sustain in the contemporary political context. Public opinion in Western countries and beyond was not likely to support Western militaries' applying the kind of force required to subdue 4GW insurgents who might be immersed across entire cities or societies. The scale of force applied by US forces in Fallujah in 2004, for instance, not only risked vital ongoing political talks but also prompted a backlash that probably brought more insurgents into the battle in Iraq and primed Islamist activism farther afield.

Assuming that Western policymakers were not sanguine about engaging in endless and irresolvable conflict with 4GW adversaries—as a kind of unavoidable yet tolerable price of running the world of liberalizing globalization—the bottom line was that if 4GW adversaries could not be decisively defeated by military means, then they had to be persuaded to give up or their networks induced to fail. Thus, the operational art in the era of 4GW was less about maneuvering forces in time and space than about focusing persuasive power through various bodies of opinion (e.g., of supporters, the undecided, and enemy sympathizers) against the diffuse networks of enemy decisionmakers and functionaries (see Figure 1.2). In short, 4GW was the era of the asymmetric bargaining war.

The changing nature of the 4GW-type battlefield would increasingly be recognized in US thinking, especially after the faltering of the US military in Iraq. Reflecting the new mood in a widely cited article in the US Naval Institute magazine *Proceedings* in October 2004, Major General Robert Scales (US Army, ret.) recognized that

> so far, we have spent billions to gain a few additional meters of precision, knots of speed, or bits of bandwidth. Some of that money might be better spent improving how our military thinks and studies, to create a parallel transformation based on cognition and cultural awareness.... War is a thinking man's game. A military too acculturated to solving warfighting problems with technology alone should begin now to recognize that wars must be fought with intellect. Reflective senior officers returning from Iraq and Afghanistan have concluded that great advantage can be achieved by outthinking rather than out-equipping the enemy. They are telling us that wars are won as much by creating alliances, leveraging non-military advantages, reading intentions, building trust, converting opinions, and managing perceptions—all tasks that demand an exceptional ability to understand people, their culture, and their motivation.[38]

Thus, various types of information operations (IO—encompassing intelligence collection and related actions, public affairs work among various audiences, and psychological operations against the enemy and its sympathizers) came to the fore on the 4GW battlefield.[39] 4GW was warfare by virtue of marketing, and even though the United States and its allies had powerful capabilities

Figure 1.2 The Operational Art of Fourth-Generation Warfare: Focusing Persuasive Power Through Local and Global Audiences (highly simplified)

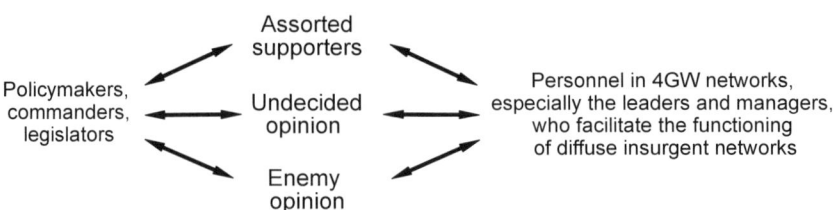

in these respects, it was a form of warfare in which their material and technological superiority was much reduced. The playing field was also not level. For some Islamic jihadists, for instance, the practice of suicide bombings, kidnappings, and videotaped beheadings were an extreme form of persuasion, a stark representation of their politico-cultural ideas, and a demonstration of superior willpower vis-à-vis the enemy. However, it must be said that such techniques were apt to be as counterproductive as useful in that they repelled great swathes of Muslim opinion. Al-Qaida operations in Iraq after 2003 would eventually alienate enough opinions among local sympathizers and the undecided as to completely undercut its position within the country.

The marketing techniques of Western states had to be much more limited—or rather it was better if that was so! The fact that 4GW opponents were not constrained by the same norms and laws might rankle some Western policymakers, but such asymmetry of will and ruthlessness was a fact of life in the political context. The Bush administration was soon making the mistakes to prove the rule. The creation of a US gulag archipelago (Bagram, Guantánamo, Abu Ghraib, and elsewhere) during the early years of the war on terror may have delivered intelligence-gathering and intimidation effects, but it was a colossal marketing disaster. It damaged the persuasive power of the United States among almost all relevant audiences and provided a powerful counternarrative for 4GW insurgents to network among local Muslims. It was really no good for Western policymakers to complain about the limitations. Western politicians could not expect to suppress the workings of Western democracy indefinitely or ignore the limitations of the rules of the game in the liberalized international system. If Western states could not out-terrorize or out-persevere some 4GW opponents, they had to develop other more nuanced ways to defeat them.

When the Bush administration embarked on the war on terror in 2001, it did not fully appreciate how contemporary circumstances had limited the utility of conventional military force. It would be a tough learning curve. What it required were more sophisticated understandings of the glocal battlefield and a new operational art to act more effectively on it. Above all, the key task was to deploy military and other means for the purposes of persuading the enemy to give up or to induce its failure. Chapters 2 and 3 present two different conceptual maps that describe and simplify the new battlefield—and point to more effective approaches on it.

Notes

1. Carl von Clausewitz, "End and Means in War," chapter 2 in *On War,* edited and introduced by Anatol Rapoport (London: Penguin Books, 1982), 123 (*Vom Kriege* [On War] was originally published in 1832).

2. See Martin van Creveld, *The Transformation of War* (New York: Free Press, 1991); Thomas X. Hammes, *The Sling and the Stone: On War in the 21st Century* (St.

Paul, MN: Zenith Press, 2004); Edward N. Luttwak, "Toward Post-Heroic Warfare," *Foreign Affairs* 74, no. 3 (May–June 1995): 109–122; Mary Kaldor, *New and Old Wars: Organized Violence in the Global Era* (Palo Alto: Stanford University Press, 1999); Rupert Smith, *The Utility of Force: The Art of War in the Modern World* (London: Penguin Books, 2005).

    3. Colin S. Gray, *Another Bloody Century: Future Warfare* (London: Phoenix Paperback, 2006), 30–31.

    4. Ibid., 36.

    5. For further discussion see Robert Jervis, *The Meaning of the Nuclear Revolution: Statecraft and the Prospect of Armageddon* (Ithaca: Cornell University Press, Cornell Studies in Security Affairs, 1990); Richard Rhodes, *Dark Sun* (New York: Simon and Schuster, 1996).

    6. Smith, *The Utility of Force*, 3.

    7. Ibid., 1–2.

    8. Ibid., 273.

    9. Ibid., 297.

    10. Ibid., 271.

    11. Ibid., 267.

    12. G. John Ikenberry, "Liberalism and Empire: Logics of Order in the American Unipolar Age," *Review of International Studies* 30, no. 4 (October 2004): 609–630, 622.

    13. David Held and Anthony McGrew, "The End of the Old Order? Globalization and the Prospects for World Order," *Review of International Studies* 24, Special Issue (December 1998): 219–243, 226 and 232–233.

    14. See Ikenberry, "Liberalism and Empire," 609–630.

    15. See Josef Joffe, "Clinton's World," *Washington Quarterly* 24, no. 1 (Winter 2001): 141; Fred Halliday, *The World at 2000: Perils and Promises* (Basingstoke, UK: Palgrave, 2001), xii, 103–107.

    16. Lawrence Freedman, *The Transformation of Strategic Studies,* Adelphi Paper 379 (London: International Institute for Strategic Studies, 2006), 36.

    17. Colin McInnes, *Spectator-Sport War: The West and Contemporary Conflict* (Boulder: Lynne Rienner, 2002), vii.

    18. Ibid., 56, 65, and 73.

    19. Ibid., 151.

    20. Luttwak, "Toward Post-Heroic Warfare," 109–122.

    21. Ibid., 115.

    22. Ibid., 115–117.

    23. See Gary I. Wilson and John P. Sullivan, "On Gangs, Crime, and Terrorism," 28 February 2007, available at the website of Defense and the National Interest, www.d-n-i.net/fcs/pdf/wilson_sullivan_gangs_terrorism.pdf; and "As Gangs and Terrorists Converge," 16 March 2007, available at the website of Military.com, www.military.com/forums/0,15240,128818,00.html; John P. Sullivan, "Fusing Terrorism Security and Response," chapter 17 in Peter Katona, Michael D. Intrilligator, and John P. Sullivan, eds., *Countering Terrorism and WMD: Creating a Global Counter-Terrorism Network* (New York: Routledge, 2006), 272–290 (John P. Sullivan served as a lieutenant in the Los Angeles Sheriff's Department and was cofounder of the Los Angeles Terrorism Early Warning Group).

    24. First explicit mention of the concept of asymmetric warfare was in the 1995 Joint Doctrine of the United States. It also appeared in the 1997 Quadrennial Defense Review. *Report of the Quadrennial Defense Review,* presented by William S. Cohen, US Secretary of Defense (May 1997), esp. section II: The Global Security Environment. Available at http://www.defenselink.mil/pubs/qdr/archive.

25. The *CIA World Factbook* (2006) estimated respective defense expenditures of the United States at US$518 billion (FY2004); China at US$81.48 billion (2005); France at US$45 billion (FY2006); Germany at US$35 billion (2003); India at US$19 billion; Japan at US$44.3 billion (2005); Russia (N/A); and the United Kingdom at US$42.8 billion (2003). Figures available at www.cia.gov/cia/publications/factbook/index.html.

26. William S. Lind, et al., "The Changing Face of War: Into the Fourth Generation," *Marine Corps Gazette* (October 1989): 22–26, http://www.d-n-i.net/fcs/4th_gen_war_gazette.htm.

27. In ibid., 3, the authors observed that "fourth generation warfare seems likely to be widely dispersed and largely undefined; the distinction between war and peace will be blurred to the vanishing point. It will be nonlinear, possibly to the point of having no definable battlefields or fronts. The distinction between 'civilian' and 'military' may disappear. Actions will occur concurrently throughout all participants' depth, including their society as a cultural, not just physical, entity. . . . Success will depend heavily on effectiveness in joint operations as lines between responsibility and mission become very blurred."

28. Ibid., 4.

29. Ibid., 4 and 5.

30. For a discussion of the debate see Tim Benbow, "Talkin' 'bout My Generation? Assessing the Concept of 'Fourth Generation Warfare,'" *Comparative Strategy* 27, no. 2 (April–June 2008): 148–163.

31. Gray, "Grand Narratives of War, 1800–2100," chapter 4 in *Another Bloody Century*, 131–167; see also Antulio J. Echevarria II, "Deconstructing the Theory of Fouth-Generation Warfare," chapter 7 in Terry Terriff, Aaron Karp, and Regina Karp, eds., *Global Insurgency and the Future of Armed Conflict: Debating Fourth Generation Warfare* (London: Routledge, 2008), 58–66.

32. Freedman, *The Transformation of Strategic Studies,* 21. See also Lawrence Freedman, "War Evolves into the Fourth Generation: A Comment on Thomas X. Hammes," chapter 10 in Terriff, *Global Insurgency,* 78–86.

33. James Wirtz, "Politics with Guns: A Response to T. X. Hammes' 'War Evolves into the Fourth Generation'" (chapter 4), Edward Luttwak, "A Brief Note on 'Fourth Generation Warfare'" (chapter 5), Michael Evans, "Elegant Irrelevance Revisited: A Critique of Fourth Generation Warfare" (chapter 8), and John Ferris, "Generations at War?" (chapter 9), in Terriff, *Global Insurgency,* 47–51, 52–53, 67–74, and 75–77 (quote by James Wirtz, 49).

34. Thomas X. Hammes, "War Evolves into the Fourth Generation" (chapter 3) and "Response" (chapter 14), in Terriff, *Global Insurgency,* 21–44 and 105–111; see also Hammes, "Insurgency: Modern Warfare Evolves into a Fourth Generation," *Strategic Forum,* Institute for National Strategic Studies, National Defense University, no. 214 (January 2005). Available at http://www.ndu.edu/inss, 2.

35. John Mackinlay, *Defeating Complex Insurgency: Beyond Iraq and Afghanistan* (Whitehall Paper 64, London, Royal United Services Institute, 2005), xii, 26–27.

36. Ibid., 23–24.

37. Benbow, "Talkin' 'bout My Generation?"

38. Robert H. Scales (Major General, ret.), "Culture-Centric Warfare," *Proceedings of the US Naval Institute* 130, no. 10 (October 2004): 32–36, esp. 32–33.

39. See F. G. Hoffman, "Combating Fourth Generation Warfare" (chapter 19) and Thomas X. Hammes, "Information Operations in 4GW" (chapter 20) in Terriff, *Global Insurgency,* 177–199 and 200–207.

2
Mapping Contemporary Insurgency

The phenomenon of the glocal insurgency (the global-level subversive mission and movement, locally networked and conducted) was a product of late-twentieth-century globalization. The post–Cold War world offered plenty of places for new insurgencies to develop. The potential was at its greatest where governance was weak—and where old and new kinds of conflict merged. As the Soviet Union disintegrated and the United States retrenched, a wave of conflict swept around the edges of the old Soviet empire and in the developing world. In such places as Afghanistan, Somalia, the former Yugoslavia, the Caucasus region, and Central and West Africa, conflicts erupted between newly emerging sovereignties over borders, as well as within states among different ethnic and religious groups. When the aggrieved promulgated a broader analysis of their predicament—especially if they had a universal or global-level mission—and sought to mobilize a wider constituency of support, the new technologies and open borders of globalization enabled more extensive propagation, mobilization, and action. Of course, the potential of where this more extensive networking might lead would first be realized with militant Islamism.

When the administration of George W. Bush declared the Global War on Terror following 9/11, it did not fully appreciate how a glocal insurgency functioned and how complex and contestable the new battlefield would be. The diffuse networks of Al-Qaida would prove robust, and any attempts to use conventional military force against them were often counterproductive. US military intervention itself was liable to create and nourish the very conditions in which glocal insurgents prospered. In subsequent years, a better understanding of the contemporary battlefield was developed, including work that sought to apply social networking theory to the 4GW-type actor.

The growing interest in social networking theory was reflected in new thinking within the US military, most notably that which led to the publication in December 2006 of *Counterinsurgency (FM 3-24/MCWP 3-33.5),* a joint field manual of the US Army and Marine Corps that outlined in detail the new US counterinsurgency doctrine.[1] Its Appendix B focused on social network analysis.[2] *FM 3-24* noted that the key terrain in counterinsurgency was likely to be centered on important political and economic structures and that

> social network analysis (SNA) is a tool for understanding the organizational dynamics of an insurgency and how best to attack or exploit it. It allows analysts to identify and portray the details of a network structure. It shows how an insurgency's networked organization behaves and how that connectivity affects its behaviour. SNA allows analysts to assess the network's design, how its members may or may not act autonomously, where the leadership resides or how it is distributed among members, and how hierarchical dynamics may mix or not mix with network dynamics.[3]

Appendix B went on to describe how social networks could be represented in diagrammatic form and what kind of analysis was important. Understanding the shape of networks by undertaking a quantitative analysis was underscored, with denser connections tending to indicate higher levels of activity and influence, although Appendix B also touched on the need to develop a more qualitative analysis of particular roles within networks. It noted that

> SNA helps units formalize the informality of insurgent networks by portraying the structure of something not readily observed. Network concepts let commanders highlight the structure of a previously unobserved association by focusing on the pre-existing relationships and ties that bind together such groups. By focusing on roles, organizational positions, and prominent or influential actors, commanders may get a sense of how the organization is structured and thus how the group functions, how members are influenced and power exerted, and how resources are exchanged.... SNA can help commanders determine what kind of social network an insurgent organization is. That knowledge helps commanders understand what the network looks like, how it is connected, and how best to defeat it.[4]

But Appendix B did not really explore the qualitative dynamics of social networks; this was a more complex task, one that was still some way from being developed. In fact, in practice the application of social networking approaches tended to focus on mapping local hierarchies (patterns of command, control, and logistics in local cells) with a view to striking at high-value targets and nodes. Such approaches undoubtedly increased the potency of tactical-level operations against local cells in such places as Afghanistan and Iraq, but they sometimes missed the broader picture that could have better informed the waging of an effective asymmetric bargaining war.

In an article in *Military Review* in 2006, Colonel Thomas X. Hammes (USMC, ret.) also pointed to the importance of mapping networks, wondering whether existing antigang computer software might be adapted to place individuals in networks and visualize their extended interactions.[5] Hammes also urged the need for more qualitative analysis, noting that by mapping the human connections in insurgent networks and then applying cultural knowledge and network theory to the networks, we can understand them more clearly. . . . [We] can use the network map of the insurgency and its environment to develop a plan for victory. The network map provides important information about the nature of the interaction between the key hubs and smaller nodes of the insurgency. While the hubs and nodes are the most visible aspects of any network, it is the nature of the activity between them that is important. We must understand that well to understand how the network actually functions. This is difficult to do, and what makes it even more challenging is that one cannot understand the network except in its cultural context. Therefore, we must find and employ people with near-native language fluency and cultural knowledge to build and interpret our map. . . . In counterinsurgency, we still want to move speedily, but the focus must be more on accuracy (developed in the observation-orientation segment of the Observation-Orientation-Decision-Action [OODA] loop). The government must understand what it is seeing before it decides what to do. To date, network-centric concepts have focused on shortening the sensor-to-shooter step (Boyd's decision-action segment). Now, we must focus on improving the quality of the observe-orient segment. Even more important, the OODA loop expands to track not just our enemy's reaction, but how the entire environment is reacting—the people, the host-nation government, our allies, our forces, even our own population.[6]

The research agenda was clear. More work was needed to understand the qualitative dimensions of insurgent networks, as well as the interplay between networks and narratives in particular cultural and community settings.

The following section aims to add to the understanding of the 4GW-type glocal insurgency in two ways. First, it will present a more nuanced account of 4GW's diffuse networks by drawing on the organizational theory of Donald A. Schon, an American sociology and business systems theorist who did important work on social networks during the 1960s and 1970s and who wrote about the counterculture movement of that era. Second, it will chart the interplay between the networks and the narratives of glocal insurgency, concentrating on the case of Al-Qaida. The contemporary glocal insurgency of Islamic militants is not monolithic. It is composed of individuals and groups of differing perspectives that can be broadly grouped into three gravities of story and struggle. The interplay between these three gravities has hitherto been overlooked in understanding the war on terror.

Understanding Diffuse Organizational Forms

Within both business and sociological theory, a considerable body of literature exists upon which strategists can draw when thinking about modern insurgent networks. Some of the most relevant stems from the 1960s and 1970s, when business-oriented theorists began to recognize and chart the evolution of industrial/corporate organizations in the West. The early phase of industrial development had been characterized by patrimonial (hierarchical and personalized) structures, with all rights and powers within organizations defined and ceded by the boss. But this form of organization had increasingly been superseded by bureaucratic (hierarchical and rule-based) systems of ownership and management that produced economies of production and scale as well as organizational growth (including horizontal and/or vertical integration). However, as J. K. Galbraith had foreseen in *The Affluent Society* (1960), the maturing of markets (where the supply of goods outstripped the demand) meant that businesses had to be increasingly competitive and dynamic; thus they needed to be much more responsive to technological developments and embrace the advantages of market research, repeated restyling, and advertising.[7] The new, more competitive context required higher levels of expertise, innovation, and commitment from individuals working within the organization and that the organization as a whole was more agile.

The imperatives that stemmed from a highly changeable/unstable operating context led to the evolution of what Tom Burns and George M. Stalker called in their seminal work, *The Management of Innovation* (1961), the "organismic" organization as distinct from the more hierarchical/bureaucratic "mechanistic" form.[8] In fluid and unstable conditions, the most agile forms of organization were those that gave problem-solving (whoever could best do that) precedence over hierarchical position. According to Tom Burns,

> [In changing and unstable conditions] the definitive and enduring demarcation of functions becomes impossible. Responsibilities and functions, and even methods and powers, have to be constantly redefined through interaction with others participating in common tasks or in the solution of common problems. Each individual has to do his job with knowledge of overall purpose and situation of the company as a whole. Interaction runs laterally as much as vertically, and communication between people of different rank tends to resemble "lateral" consultation rather than "vertical" command. Omniscience can no longer be imputed to the boss at the top. . . . For the individual, the important part of the difference between the mechanistic and the organismic is in the degree of his commitment to the working organization. Mechanistic systems tell him what he has to attend to, and how, and also tell him what he does not have to bother with, what is not his affair, what is not expected of him—what he can post elsewhere as the responsibility of others. In organismic systems, such boundaries disappear. The individual is expected to regard himself as fully implicated in the discharge of any task appearing over his horizon. He has not merely to exercise special competence, but to commit himself to the success of the concern's undertaking as a whole.[9]

The study of more devolved and diffuse organizations would be taken on in the later 1960s and 1970s with development of the idea of "learning systems" by a group of business and sociological theorists, notably Donald A. Schon, Raymond Hainer, and Chris Argyris. The work done by Schon for the BBC's Reith lecture in 1970, which he subsequently wrote up in his important book *Beyond the Stable State* (1971), appears to have particular explanatory power for today, especially in his recognition of a new kind of diffuse subversive movement that was evident in the so-called counterculture of the late 1960s.[10]

In *Beyond the Stable State,* Schon charted how hierarchical and coreperiphery types of organization had evolved in the twentieth century into more diffuse "constellation" business and social systems (see Figure 2.1). Such evolution occurred when a "top" or "center" was no longer the most natural or appropriate way of "managing" geographically or functionally diverse "subordinate" or "peripheral" elements.[11] Changes in the relationship between topto-bottom or center-and-periphery elements were key to understanding the evolution of an organization, notably the relative balance between who and how "leadership" (the provision of inspirational idea, mission concept, entrepreneurial or social culture, etc.) and "management" (the provision of organizational structures, command and control processes, logistics, training, etc.) was provided. In a hierarchical system of organization, leadership tended to be highly bureaucratized in a management-heavy system of rules from top to bottom. In a core-periphery organization, leadership and management functions were shared between center and periphery, but with the center retaining some control of leadership and management by deploying a centrally directed monitoring and implementation staff. In a constellation system, the center's relationship with the periphery was heavy on leadership but light on management. The center might set political objectives and mission concept, but most of the management was undertaken almost completely autonomously by subordinate units.

Schon could see that the reorganization of business firms or social groups into more diffuse networks took place when a constellation of specialized functionaries emerged to facilitate it, describing the essential roles played by what he called the System Negotiator/Leader, Network Manager, Underground Manager, Facilitator, Project Broker, and Maneuverer (see Figure 2.2).[12] Moreover, although not all the functionaries of the system were in direct contact with each other or with the center, as the various functionaries popped up and did things, the knowledge that they generated tended to seep around the entire system of its own accord (horizontally from periphery to periphery elements) rather than having to be actively disseminated by a center via a more formal communications systems; thus the constellation could be seen as "learning system."

Indeed, in cases where a constellation system emerged from a crisis at the center, Schon noted that the center

> no longer formulates and promulgates a central message. Instead, it picks up the policy themes around which peripheral messages develop as variants. Peripheral messages are no longer instances of central policy but variations on central policy themes. Central sets out to help peripheral systems transform themselves and to connect them with each other. It goes "meta" with respect

Figure 2.1 The Dynamics of Basic Types of Organization

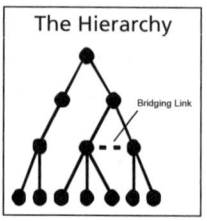

The Hierarchy

The apex of the hierarchy defines aims and distributes functions and powers accordingly. Hierarchies sometimes originate as systems of personalized rule that become bureaucratized (impersonal and rule-based). Individuals in the hierarchy concern themselves with their specialized function only. Those at the bottom are most specialized and least knowledgeable. Most information travels vertically, but operational imperatives may prompt horizontal bridging links to speed observation-decision-response, although these work at the discretion of those above. "Mechanistic" systems are most appropriate where control and predictability are key values, and they work best in a relatively stable environment.

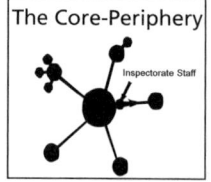

The Core-Periphery

The center defines common aims and outputs, but management responsibility is devolved to subunits because they are the most efficient/expert locations to undertake particular tasks. While subunits may manage their own affairs largely autonomously, the center may seek to enforce its leadership and a degree of management control with the use of a central inspectorate; this may involve the dispatch of inspectorate staff to ensure a minimum degree of discipline and coordination. The capacity of center-periphery communications links (the "spokes") as well as of the inspectorate staff is a key factor in maintaining the long-term coherence of such organizations.

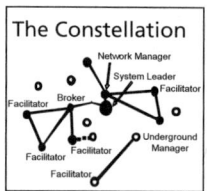

The Constellation

Less a formal organization than a collection of individuals and groups that put themselves forward to fulfill functions that collectively contribute to a common aim or purpose. The constellation may emerge from the failure of a more formal organization or when a system leader articulates a mission around which others cluster. The system leader (acting as or through a network manager) may manage an extensive network, but the constellation may also include those with no formal links (the hollow circles); they simply subscribe to the common mission. Although facilitators may maintain local hierarchies, operational-level "policy" emerges from lateral (often very informal) consultation. In such "organismic" systems, few have clearly defined job descriptions, with individuals/groups often embracing whatever function they are capable of discharging.

---

to these discovered systems, prodding them to develop evaluative processes conducive to learning and linking them in learning networks.[13]

The constellation-type network was potentially very dynamic, with its very structure quickly responding to circumstances. Where there was an opportunity or need to provide a function to the whole system, new functionaries might simply emerge in a rather organic way. Schon noted that "the constellation form displays peculiar capabilities for adaptation. Each semi-autonomous unit may be discarded when it gets into trouble, and new units brought into being, without disturbing the other units and without requiring major shifts in the nucleus of the firm."[14]

Clearly, in relation to a diffuse insurgency movement, although a constellation-type system might lack the coherence to seriously challenge more organized

Figure 2.2 The Specialized Functionaries of the Constellation Network (according to Donald A. Schon)

Network Role	Enabling Function
System negotiator/leader	Inspirational guide, ultimate ombudsman. Serves as the key reference point others cluster around.
Network manager(s)	Executive administrator for the system negotiator/leader. Oversees the network: monitoring flows of information, the process of review, and the provision of resources.
Maneuverer	Operates on a project basis, and through personal networks may persuade or coerce people and organizations to assist. Often operates as a freelance (and ephemeral) facilitator and broker.
Broker	Connects sellers and buyers (in an insurgency, network manager(s) to maneuverers and facilitators as well as maneuverers and facilitators to footsoldiers). By virtue of superior knowledge and attention to detail, the broker channels information and often clears blocks to connection. A potentially risk-laden role. The position is established and maintained by personal skills, protecting contacts, successfully enabling the flow of reliable information and resources, and finding common values and interests with both sellers and buyers.
Facilitator (local/regional leader)	Inspires a local/regional group and manages their connection to the network, although the group may significantly vary from the central mission. Facilitators manage aims, resources, and training of the devolved group, with the best facilitators acting as enablers rather than monitors/enforcers.
Underground manager	Maintains and operates an informal underground network that cuts across established organizations to pursue deviant aims from within them.

Note: "These roles are essential to the design, creation, negotiation, and management of ad hoc and continuing networks." Donald A. Schon, *Beyond the Stable State*, 197–200.

forces, it was likely to be quite effective in generating and propagating subversive messages as well as robust in managing losses. Of course, the development of the Internet (which Schon could not appreciate at the time) was to further boost the potential for constellation-type networking, because it increased the potential for leadership without formal systems of management to support it. At the same time, it was possible to imagine that a particular insurgent movement might evolve back and forth between hierarchical, core-periphery, and constellation types of organization as circumstances dictated or allowed.

Schon's work is also useful because in *Beyond the Stable State* he went on to give an analysis of the counterculture movement of the late 1960s. What Schon called the Movement was arguably a putative 4GW-type actor. Certainly, it was the most significant transnational constellation movement of dissidence/insurgency since the anarchists of the late nineteenth century. The Movement was composed of a great number of personalities and campaign groups. In the United States alone, it included Martin Luther King Jr., the Student Non-Violent Coordinating Committee (SNCC), the Council on Racial Equality (CORE), the Black Panthers, the Southern Christian Leadership Council (SCLC), the Urban League, the National Association for the Advancement of Colored People (NAACP), Students for a Democratic Society (SDS), the Peace and Freedom Party, Awareness for Democratic Action (ADA), as well as a host of local student action groups. There was a similar myriad of leftist and progressive groups across Europe, too. The Movement was characterized by a number of features:

1. It had no stable, centrally established message, objective, or doctrine. The Movement loosely subscribed to various Marxist-derived ideas about society. Those involved tended to sympathize with the same progressive ideas and campaign causes, as well as read the same kind of books and writers (such as Antonio Gramsci, Noam Chomsky, Susan Sontag, Saul Alinsky, Herbert Marcuse, Jean-Paul Sartre).
2. Centers of dissident activity popped up on a shifting, ad hoc basis, with multiple leaders appearing to press multiple, if overlapping, agendas. For instance, a local group of militant students might assume the limelight for possibly only a few days, later to be eclipsed by another. However, as groups came and went, they imparted new knowledge about techniques as well as new narratives and mythologies to the Movement.
3. It was shaped by the infrastructure of new communications technology and often further primed by changes in that capacity. The telephone, television, transistor radio, tape recorder, and jet airliner enabled the Movement to network overseas. Television became a system of global witness, propagation, and mobilization. Schon also noted that groups promoting black power in the United States developed relations with third world factions in Algeria and Cuba when new communications links, especially direct telephone links, were established.

Writing in 1969–1970, Schon thought that the constellation network of the Movement was likely to be very robust, noting that "the learning system of the Movement is survival-prone because of its fluidity and its apparent lack of structure. Its ability to transform itself allows it to continue to function with vitality as issues and situations change around it. Its lack of a single fixed center makes it difficult to attack. Its scope is no longer limited by the energy or the resources at the fixed center, nor by the capacity of the 'spokes' connecting the primary center to secondary ones."[15]

In fact, the reality was that by 1970 the best days of the Movement had already passed (arguably, they'd passed by the second half of 1968), and within a few years the constellation that Schon described had almost completely dissolved. Why? The potential problem with core-periphery and constellation networks is that they are vulnerable to a loss of coordination and even unexpected dissolution. Schon himself highlighted the potential limitations of devolved systems: the limits of infrastructure (personnel and technology); the death, imprisonment, and discrediting of key functionaries (King, Malcolm X, and others); the kind of competence needed to create networks was different from that of maintaining them; motivations (means and ends) across the network diverging in response to internal and external change; and ideological evolution or impasse causing friction between center-periphery and periphery-periphery.[16] Many of these problems afflicted the Movement. At the same time, attempts by particular functionaries to increase coherence—implying the relative centralization of leadership and management functions—were also capable of producing internecine conflict. Internecine conflicts were sometimes rationalized in ideological terms, and members of the Movement were prone to bickering about petty ideological differences.

When thinking about the failure of the Movement with the luxury of hindsight, however, what seems most crucial was not the failure of the constellation network as such but the loss of two colossal campaign causes—or narratives—that acted as the medium across which the networking could take place. It was the narratives that kept the constellation together. The two campaign causes were civil rights and the Vietnam War, and together they provided powerful stories (or narrative gravities) that first drew in a broader constituency of sympathizers and, second, provided a more plausible mission concept (i.e., things to actually protest about). For the leftists and anarchists of the Movement, civil rights and Vietnam were stories that they could contextualize in terms of a much broader analysis of the oppressive character of American modernity with its exploitative capitalism and imperialism. But when civil rights and the Vietnam War were essentially resolved, the aggrieved mainstream drifted away from the constellation movement and its ideological broader analysis, and there was a critical loss of gravity. In the absence of civil rights and Vietnam—real political and geopolitical conflicts—a generalized angst against capitalism or modernity was not enough to sustain the Movement. The leftists that remained became isolated and, ultimately, began to consume themselves in internecine disputes.

The Power of Narrative in Diffuse Systems: The Case of Al-Qaida

Compelling narratives (stories) of oppression, struggle, and hope are among the foundation stones of insurgency movements. Such stories are especially important to diffuse movements, because in the absence of real systems of command and control they create a common purpose. The narratives of oppression and struggle were important to the counterculture during the late 1960s, and they would also be important to the diffuse constellation network of Al-Qaida beginning in the 1990s.

The Al-Qaida idea and its supporting stories had roots in the failure of the Qutbist Muslim Brotherhood. Before his execution by Gamal Abdul Nasser's regime in Egypt in 1966, Sayyid Qutb developed a political theory arguing that Muslim societies had been reduced to a state of *jahiliyya* (ignorance) by Muslim rulers seduced and corrupted by foreign powers and secular ideologies. For Qutb and his followers, there were now so few proper Muslims that it was up to an elite of true believers—a vanguard—to seize back Muslim societies by means of political revolution. Once the Islamic vanguard had overthrown the corrupted elites, Muslim societies could be re-Islamized from above, that is, returned to the *salafi* path (the right path) through the implementation of a proper version of *sharia* law by an Islamic state. The cadre of the Qutbist Muslim Brotherhood perhaps could be seen as Islamic Leninists, and in such places as Egypt, Jordan, Syria, and Algeria they embarked on a revolutionary struggle against the secular state. However, by the latter 1980s the struggle in most Muslim countries was deadlocked: Islamists could not overthrow the secular state, but neither could the secular state finally defeat the Islamists.

Eventually, the Qutbist challenge faltered. In what the French author Olivier Roy describes as the evolution of political Islamism into neofundamentalism, some of the activists abandoned their grand dreams of seizing the state and instead opted to re-Islamize Muslim society from below.[17] The neofundamentalists redirected their energies toward neighborhood and village life and adopted a more traditionalist kind of Islam. The threat to the secular Muslim state subsided, but the threat of chronic violence within Muslim societies increased as Islamists sought to take back neighborhoods. A few political Islamists took a different path. Some were literally turned out of prisons in Algeria, Egypt, Jordan, and Syria to be packed off to Afghanistan to wage jihad against the Soviet invader. After the Afghan jihad, an Islamic international group continued to make its way around the Muslim world's trouble spots, with the war in Bosnia being an important formative experience, as well as to a number of Islamist refuges such as in Afghanistan, Pakistan, and Sudan. By the mid-1990s the Saudi jihadist Osama bin Laden, and the leader of the Egyptian *Al-Jihad* group, Ayman al-Zawahiri, had made their way back to Afghanistan, where they set about designing a new Islamic narrative and mission concept.

In their Afghan refuge, bin Laden and al-Zawahiri promoted a new story. It was this: Muslim leaders like Hosni Mubarak (Egypt), Hafiz al-Asad (Syria), King Hussein (Jordan), and King Fahd (Saudi Arabia) were hopelessly corrupt and incompetent, so how had they survived? Why had Islam not triumphed over such people? For bin Laden and al-Zawahiri, the answer was obvious—it was the West, especially the United States, that was keeping them in power. Moreover, when the West imposed itself on Muslim lands, it not only acted to maintain corrupt Muslim regimes but also directly attacked Islamic doctrine and the moral fabric of Muslim society. Bin Laden was especially vexed by the continuing presence of US troops in the Arabian Peninsula after the Gulf War (1990–1991). Only when this distant enemy was humbled and sent packing could Muslim societies be re-Islamized. Thus, Al-Qaida's political Islamists revived the old Islamic formulation of a world divided between Dar al-Islam (the Realm of Peace) and Dar al-Harb (the Realm of Unbelief/War). When infidels brought their realm into that of Islam, they were literally waging unbelief/war. The presence of the West in Muslim lands, especially in Saudi Arabia, wasn't just a reason to go to war—it was already war itself.

Crucially, Al-Qaida's narrative overlapped with the concerns of other cadres of Islamists in the broader movement of Islamic militancy. Al-Qaida shared their pain. It told those Islamists involved in local geopolitical struggles that the West was behind their oppression or, at least, stood by and watched them suffer injustices. It told Islamic traditionalists that the perceived corruption of their society and the decline of traditional patterns of their neighborhood and village life was the fault of the West and its modernity. Little could be put right until the West and its Muslim puppets were purged. As Ahmed S. Hashim observed in the *Naval War College Review* in Autumn 2001, "Bin Laden has brilliantly established a nexus between those who hate the United States for what it is—the great seductress, spreading a culture and religion of material plenty around the globe—and those who despise it for what it does in the Middle East, as they see it—extending support to Israel, turning its back on the Palestinian quest for justice, continuing to punish Iraq for transgressions of a decade ago."[18]

After an initial focus on the presence of infidel troops in Saudi Arabia, Al-Qaida's agenda would snowball as it sought to co-opt other Islamists involved in the conflicts in Palestine, Kashmir, Bosnia, Somalia, Chechnya, Uzbekistan, and the Philippines (see Figure 2.3). The idea of aiding and defending beleaguered Muslims was a powerful tool for recruiting activists and raising money. The effects of the containment regime on Iraq in the 1990s also gave Al-Qaida a powerful new story; sanctions were inhumane, and US and British bombing was a humiliation for all Muslims. Thus, Al-Qaida tapped the deep frustrations in the Muslim world about the way Muslims had come under attack in the post–Cold War world and the apparent inability of anyone to do anything about it.

The new story was soon translated into mission concept. Above all, Al-Qaida set itself up to lead a jihad against the onslaughts of the so-called Zionist-crusader alliance, and this posture was central in the two key statements that declared the "distant jihad"—the "Declaration of War against the Americans Occupying the Land of the Two Holy Places" of 23 August 1996, and the "Declaration of the World Islamic Front for Jihad against the Jews and the Crusaders" on 22 February 1998.[19] The 22 February 1998 edict—published in the Arabic-language paper *Al-Quds al-Arabi* and signed by bin Laden (Al-Qaida),

Figure 2.3 Map of Al-Qaida Affiliates and Potential Allies

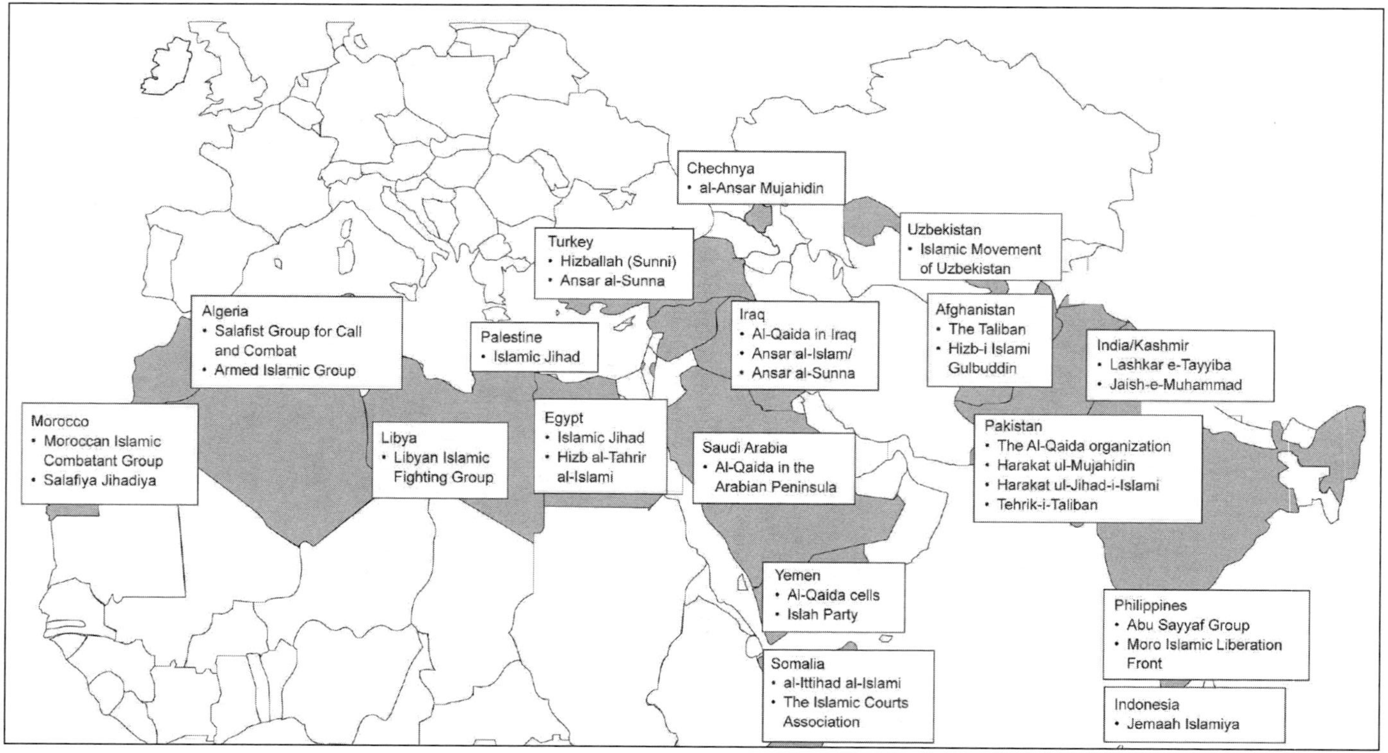

al-Zawahiri (Egyptian Islamic Jihad), Abu-Yasir Rifa'i Ahmad Taha (Egyptian Islamic Group), Shaikh Mir Hamzah (Pakistan's Jamiat-ul-Ulema-e-Pakistan), and Fazlur Rahman (Amir of the Jihad Movement in Bangladesh)—talked of the attacks being made by the United States on Muslims in its occupation of the Land of the Two Holy Mosques (Mecca and Medina), its enforcement of sanctions on Iraq, and its support of Israel. These supposed crimes constituted "a clear declaration of war by Americans against God, his Prophet, and the Muslims," and so it was incumbent on all individual Muslims to wage jihad by whatever means available. The declaration argued, "To kill Americans and their allies, both civil and military, is an individual duty of every Muslim who is able, in any country where this is possible, until the Aqsa Mosque [in Jerusalem] and the Haram Mosque [in Mecca] are freed from their grip and until their armies, shattered and broken-winged, depart from all the lands of Islam, incapable of threatening any Muslim."[20]

The mission concept was soon demonstrated by deed. On 7 August 1998, Al-Qaida militants launched simultaneous truck bombings on the US embassies in Nairobi, Kenya, and Dar-es-Salaam, Tanzania, killing more than 250 people, including nine Americans. The attacks catapulted Al-Qaida onto the global stage and enormously raised its profile and credibility within the Islamist milieu in Afghanistan-Pakistan.

By the late 1990s, the Al-Qaida leadership had proposed a plausible story of commonality between the different gravities of the Islamic militant movement and set about networking across them, especially in the context of the system of Islamist training camps that existed in Taliban Afghanistan. Although the relationship between Al-Qaida and the Taliban regime may not have been as straightforward as sometimes portrayed, by virtue of the personal relationship between Osama bin Laden and the head of the Taliban, Mullah Muhammad Omar, Al-Qaida appears to have been given a grant of authority to deploy its ideas, money, and contacts across the training camps in the country. Ultimately, Al-Qaida became a force because it was able to position itself at the intersection of what can be seen as the three gravities of interest/emphasis in the contemporary Islamist movement: Islamic globalists (the universalists and global-level counterrevolutionaries); Islamic geopoliticals (those harnessing Islam in local geopolitical conflicts); and Islamic traditionalists (see Figure 2.4). Al-Qaida was, as Jason Burke has argued, more like a venture capital firm than an all-powerful organization capable of directing the Islamist camps.[21] Thus, of the fifty or more camps in Afghanistan in the latter 1990s, perhaps only two could be described as Al-Qaida, yet the organization had become a hub of the broader Islamic internationale comprising many spokes.[22] The narrative overlap between these Islamist gravities was the fertile medium in which Al-Qaida's networks could grow.

Al-Qaida joined a number of Islamist groups that pitched their aspirations and struggles at a truly transnational level. Other such groups, notably

Figure 2.4 Schematic of the Main Gravities in the Militant Islamic Movement in the Afghan-Pakistan Milieu (circa 2001)

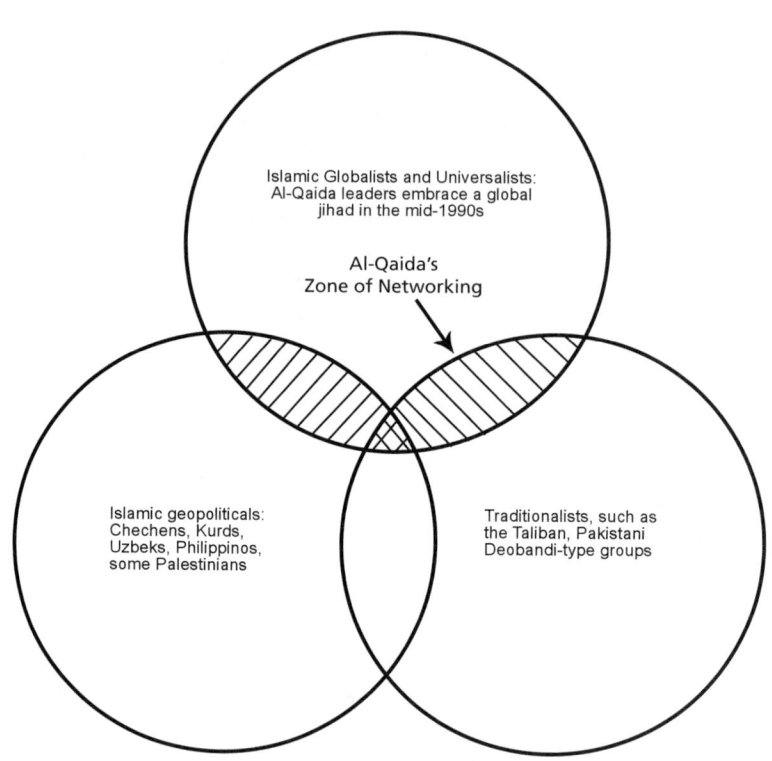

Al-Mujaharoun and Hizb ut-Tahrir, often articulated the ultimate ideal of an Islamic world order: They talked of vanquishing the *kufr* (infidel), raising the Islamic banner over every Muslim country, and working toward a universal caliphate that might aspire to bring Islamic governance to all humankind. However, the message of these universalists did not really resonate across the Muslim world, because their objectives were just too distant and unrealistic. The vast majority of Muslims were simply not interested in waging some war on the world in order to install some improbable ideal. Few Islamic militants actually aspired, however, to destroy the West and other infidel powers as a prelude to an Islamic conquest of the world. The concerns of the vast majority of Islamic militants were far more parochial.

To some extent Al-Qaida avoided this relevance problem. Although during fanciful moments Al-Qaida leaders might talk about a global revolution and universal caliphate, their focus was more commonly on means rather than ends. Whereas the likes of Al-Mujaharoun and Hizb ut-Tahrir scarcely articulated a coherent modus operandi of struggle to achieve the global revolution, Al-Qaida's overwhelming emphasis was on the struggle—jihad—against the United States and its allies everywhere. Thus, Al-Qaida did not get bogged down in endless bickering with other Islamic globalists and traditionalists about the final Islamic ideal—and avoided disengaging Islamic geopoliticals who were apt to regard talk of global revolutions and universal caliphates as distracting and irrelevant dreams. In fact, the Al-Qaida model worked best when means and ends were tailored to the local. Although only a very few Muslim people wanted Al-Qaida's final Islamic world order, far more wanted its struggle against the West and its minions.[23]

This focus on means rather than ends led some Western observers to comment that Al-Qaida's struggle looked nihilistic and pointless—it didn't have objectives that were realistic or negotiable. However, for the time being, the appeal of the struggle was enough, not least because its stories about Palestine, Kashmir, Chechnya, Afghanistan, Iraq, and other besieged Muslim lands resonated across the movement of Islamic militants as well as among mainstream Muslim opinion. The zone of overlap between the universalists/globalists and the geopoliticals was particularly important in Europe. For the likes of the young British Muslims who killed themselves and fifty others in the London bombings of 7 July 2005, for instance, it was the perceived injustices done against Muslim brethren (probably, most immediately, the pictures of the 2004 US storming of Fallujah) that appear to have driven them. It seems very unlikely that most were motivated to actually kill themselves as a function of some vast project to bring down Western civilization, or else from some culturally innate hatred of freedom and democracy. Indeed, if the suicide video of the London group's leader, Muhammad Sidique Khan, was anything to go by, then the London bombers rationalized their actions as defensive, reciting such mantras as "we will not let you live in peace, while we live in war" and "someone must pay a price for what is being done to us in your name."[24] The 7/7 group was a coalescence of individuals fired up in the moment and co-opted by an Al-Qaida missionary (Khan).

The importance of geopolitical grievances to Al-Qaida's persistence after 2001–2002 was increasingly reflected in the marketing strategy of Al-Qaida's leadership, notably in the videotaped messages of bin Laden and al-Zawahiri.[25] Indeed, bin Laden went as far as to define a bargaining position to Europeans in an audio statement on 14 April 2004 and to Americans in late 2005.[26] His message to Americans even offered a suspension of the conflict if a series of geopolitical conflicts were resolved.

Without the existence of real geopolitical grievances, it seems unlikely that the Al-Qaida phenomenon could ever have amounted to much. Thus, the violence and conflict that Al-Qaida visited upon the West was not really the manifestation of some vast and irresolvable ideological struggle between liberal modernity and Islamic opinion. Rather, Al-Qaida's real center of gravity was in older geopolitical conflicts that could, in theory, be resolved. But as long as so many of these local political and geopolitical conflicts persisted around the world, they would continue to represent a medium across which its networks could grow. A multitude of local Islamist groups involved in local conflicts and small cells of Muslim people sympathetic to Al-Qaida's mission concept, or struggle, existed across the world.

The Narratives and Networks of Al-Qaida: Toward an Effects Map of the War on Terror

In the late 1990s, Al-Qaida was already a diffuse core-periphery type of organization that spanned the various gravities of Islamic militancy (recall Figure 2.4). In 2001–2002, following the war in Afghanistan, Al-Qaida's Taliban hosts were overthrown and Al-Qaida's top leaders killed or forced into deep hiding. The capacities of Al-Qaida's system negotiator/leader and network manager (bin Laden and al-Zawahiri) to manage whatever organization existed were severely reduced. At the same time, though, 9/11 and the war in Afghanistan brought Al-Qaida to global prominence, giving it an iconic status among Islamic militants. It acquired a degree of ideational power across the world that it did not have before, and it was not long before new adherents were subscribing. The evolution of the Al-Qaida organization into a full-fledged constellation movement was further primed by the religious-ideological leadership disseminated by bin Laden and al-Zawahiri in their occasional video messages. What developed, then, was a much weakened core-periphery organization of Al-Qaida members and a new constellation network of what can be called struggle associates. Struggle associates might or might not directly communicate with the Al-Qaida organization proper, but they tended to work in sympathy by virtue of some common purpose.

In practice, the Al-Qaida constellation was now more reliant on self-appointed glocal functionaries acting as facilitators and freelance maneuverers: In post-2001 Afghanistan, it was Taliban leaders such as Mullah Dadullah and Mansour Dadullah; in Iraq, the most infamous was Abu Musab al-Zarqawi. The synapses of the network were smoothed, rather than directed, by centrally located network managers (mostly Pakistan-located) and a cadre of mobile brokers and locally located underground managers (see Figure 2.5). Brokers were often particularly important in smoothing the relationship between facilitators and groups of other local Islamists, potential recruits, and supportive criminal organizations. Local functionaries took it upon themselves to develop the recruitment, training, and logistics activities necessary to undertake a struggle. Knowledge about management techniques and operational practice could be disseminated via the Internet without reference to the center.

The Al-Qaida constellation would reach its ultimate expression in Iraq after the US occupation in 2003. All manner of deals would be done in Iraq between Al-Qaida facilitators and other local collaborators who became effectively functionaries (wittingly or not) in Al-Qaida's constellation network. Working almost organically, the network managed to provide arms and money for the struggle, generate and exchange vital intelligence, and integrate a portfolio of insurgent activities.

The Sunni insurgency in Iraq would display the facets of a learning system. For instance, as particular cells of activists (including suicide bombers) came and went, they often added information to the learning system about tactical techniques as well as leaving new inspirational mythology behind. Moreover, while the loss of important facilitators, maneuverers, or underground managers might be a significant blow for a time, if they could not be replaced directly they were likely to be superseded by other self-appointed functionaries. Indeed, maneuverers especially were sometimes encouraged to sacrifice themselves in the struggle and, in so doing, impart new jihadic inspiration (a function of local leadership) to the system.

The limitation of such a model of action was that Al-Qaida, other than in the unusual situation in Iraq between 2003 and 2006, was unable to sustain anything more than sporadic attacks. Most attacks could only be organized by an Al-Qaida facilitator or maneuverer in the places where a sufficient state of outrage existed among local Islamic geopoliticals. It was also difficult to imagine that Al-Qaida could begin to realize its ultimate political objectives without organizing itself into a more hierarchical form locally.[27] Of course, if Al-Qaida cells did try to precipitate into more hierarchical forms (a hierarchy or a core-periphery organization), they faced two problems: First, they made themselves much more vulnerable to conventional military attack; and second, they were also likely to heighten latent tensions with associates in the constellation network, specifically with local Islamists who were disinterested in Al-Qaida's global-level jihad, let alone willing to accept its management structures. On both counts, this was to be Al-Qaida's experience in Iraq between 2005 and 2008. When the Al-Qaida organization in Iraq dispatched what could be termed the "nutting squad" (Provisional Irish Republican Army parlance for its central inspectorate staff) to enforce discipline on its struggle associates—partly in an effort to consolidate its declaration of the Islamic State of Iraq—they resisted fiercely. The attempt to turn the constellation network into a core-periphery organization or hierarchy (recall Figure 2.1) led the large-scale dissolution of the constellation. The constellation system could be robust, but it was apt to abruptly fall apart.

Conclusion

The potential for glocal insurgency emerged from the kind of world that took shape in the late twentieth century. With the emergence of Al-Qaida, and the

Figure 2.5 The Networks and Narrative Gravities of the Militant Islamic Movement

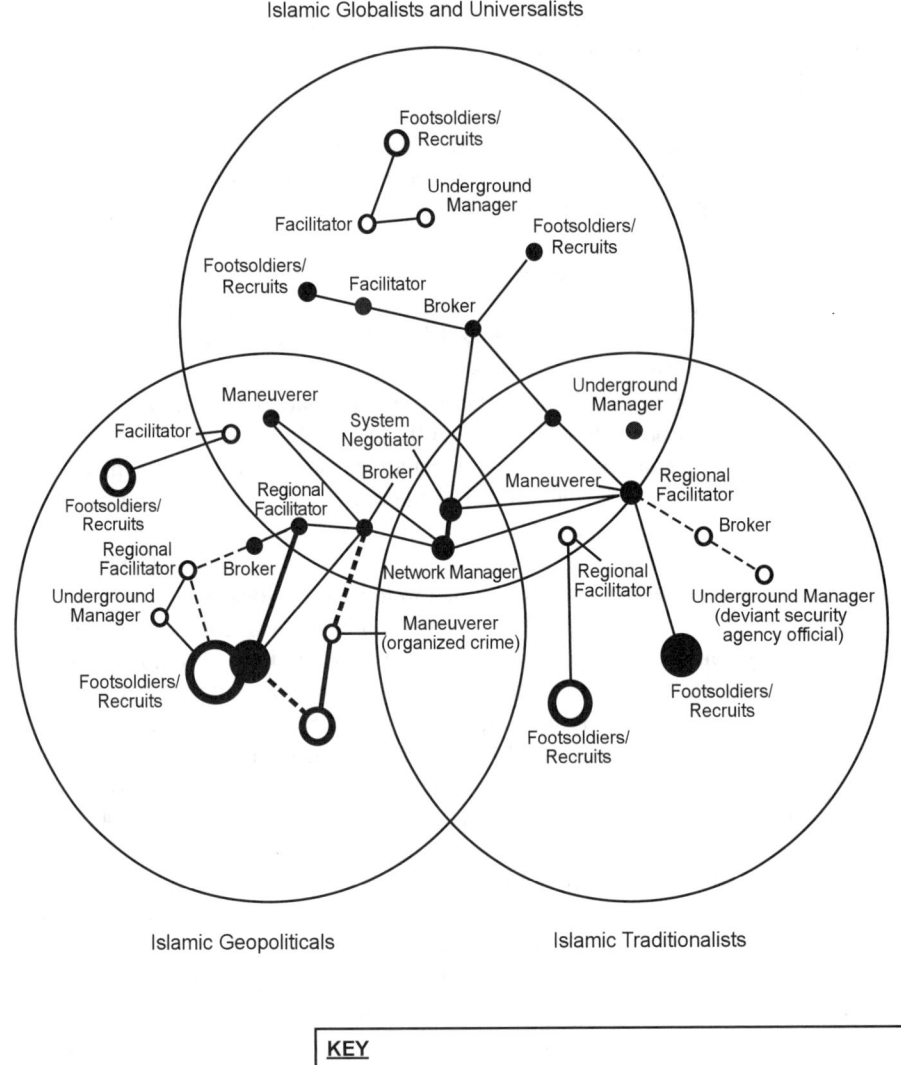

act of 9/11, the glocal insurgency would become the dominant idiom of conflict in the world of liberalizing globalization, and it would remain so for as long as the international system functioned as it did. Although Al-Qaida and militant Islamism were the first of the new glocal insurgencies, it was not hard to think of other global-level causes that might one day spawn other glocal insurgencies: The obvious possibilities were glocal insurgencies driven by militant anticapitalists and environmentalists.

Understanding the interaction of various networks and narratives was critical to fathoming the phenomenon of the glocal insurgency. For the global counterinsurgent, understanding who the specialized functionaries of the constellation network were, what they believed, and what they did was key. During the early Global War on Terror, the Bush administration and its military commanders did not appreciate the complexity of the task before them. Beyond engaging in a tactical-level battle of attrition, there was little sense about what actions and effects really counted as tactical, what as operational, and what as strategic on the glocal battlefield. The learning process would be a long and frustrating business for everyone involved.

Notes

1. Field Manual 3-24, *Counterinsurgency*, was formulated by the Doctrine Division of the Combined Arms Center, Fort Leavenworth, Kansas, under the leadership of Lieutenant General David Petraeus. For a brief account of the writing process see John Nagl, "An American View of Twenty-First Century Counter-Insurgency," *RUSI Journal* 152, no. 4 (August 2007): 12–16.

2. Doctrine Division of the Combined Arms Center, US Army and Marine Corps, Foreword by General David H. Petraeus, Lt. General James F. Amos, and Lt. Colonel John A Nagl, "Social Network Analysis and Other Analytical Tools," Appendix B in Field Manual 3-24, *Counterinsurgency (FM 3-24/MCWP 3-33.5)*, Headquarters Department of the US Army (December 2006), B1–B22. Hereafter cited as *FM 3-24*.

3. Ibid., B10.

4. Ibid., B17.

5. Thomas X. Hammes, "Countering Evolved Insurgent Networks," *Military Review* 86, no. 4 (July–August 2006): 18–26, 23.

6. Hammes, "Countering Evolved Insurgent Networks," 23 and 25.

7. Tom Burns, "Mechanistic and Organismic Structures," Extract 3 in D. S. Pugh, ed., *Organization Theory* (Harmondsworth, Middlesex, UK: Penguin Books, 1971), 43–55 (an extract from his article "Industry in a New Age," *New Society*, 31 January 1963, 17–20).

8. Tom Burns and George M. Stalker, *The Management of Innovation* (Oxford: Oxford University Press, 1994 [orig. 1961]; new edition with new preface by Tom Burns).

9. Burns, in Pugh, *Organizational Theory*, 48–49.

10. Donald A. Schon read philosophy at Yale and Harvard. He worked as an official in the US Department of Commerce during the Kennedy and Johnson administrations. He went on to become the Ford Professor of Urban Studies and Education at MIT (working with Raymond Hainer and Chris Argyris). Schon delivered the BBC's Reith

Lecture in 1970. Donald A. Schon, *Beyond the Stable State* (London: Temple Smith, 1971).

11. Ibid., 189.
12. Ibid., 197–200.
13. Ibid., 189.
14. Ibid., 67.
15. Ibid., 113.
16. Ibid., 90–94.
17. Olivier Roy, *The Failure of Political Islam* (London: I. B. Tauris, 1994), xi.
18. Ahmed S. Hashim, "The World According to Usama Bin Laden," *Naval War College Review* 54, no. 4 (Autumn 2001): 31.
19. Ibid., esp. 22–29.
20. Ibid., 27–28.
21. Jason Burke, "Think Again: Al-Qaeda," *Foreign Policy* (May–June 2004): 18–26, 18.
22. A figure given by Moazzam Begg in an interview with Jon Snow, Channel 4 News (UK), 7 P.M. news broadcast, 24 February 2005. Moazzam Begg was a joint Pakistani-British citizen who became involved in the Afghan-Pakistan Islamic milieu from the 1990s. He was detained in Pakistan following the war in Afghanistan in 2001 and spoke to Channel 4 News shortly after his release from the Guantánamo Bay detention facility.
23. Shibley Telhami, "America in Arab Eyes," *Survival* 49, no. 1 (Spring 2007): 107–122, 121.
24. "London Bomber: Text in full," BBC News, 1 September 2005, http://news.bbc.co.uk/1/hi/uk/4206800.stm.
25. For examples, see "Bin Laden Tape Urges 'Jihad,'" BBC News, 16 February 2003, http://news.bbc.co.uk/1/hi/not_in_website/syndication/monitoring/media_reports/27688; "New al-Qaeda Tape Is Released" (Ayman al-Zawahiri), BBC News, 2 October 2004, http://news.bbc.co.uk/1/hi/world/middle_east/3707550.stm.
26. Brynjar Lia and Thomas Hegghammer, "Jihadi Strategic Studies: The Alleged Al Qaida Policy Study Preceding the Madrid Bombings," *Studies in Conflict and Terrorism* 27, no. 5 (September–October 2004): 355–375, 356; "Bin Laden Tape Warns of Attacks," BBC News, 19 January 2006, http://news.bbc.co.uk/1/hi/world/middle_east/4628738.stm; "U.S. Rebuffs Bin Laden 'Truce Call,'" BBC News, 20 January 2006, http://news.bbc.co.uk/1/hi/world/middle_east/4630314.stm.
27. See Lawrence Freedman, *The Transformation of Strategic Studies,* Adelphi Paper 379 (London: International Institute for Strategic Studies, 2006), 89.

3
Mapping Contemporary Intervention

The glocal insurgency primed by Al-Qaida was apt to sporadically precipitate into violence wherever disgruntled Muslims lived, but it was amid a lengthening list of post–Cold War geopolitical conflicts that the potential for glocal networking was at its greatest. Above all, it was where non-Muslim powers—the United States, the United Kingdom, Serbia, Israel, Russia, India, Australia, the Philippines, and others—affronted Muslims in their homelands that Al-Qaida was able to seed itself. It was in the context of these geopolitical conflicts that the armed forces of the United States and its allies faced the glocal insurgent as well as the prospect of "waging war among the people." With the US interventions in Afghanistan and Iraq, major fronts in the war on terror were opened, and they were to put the United States and its allies on a long and painful learning curve as best tactical and operational practices were slowly developed.

Waging war in a complex social setting can hardly be said to be a new problem. The insurgency (a revolt against an authoritative system of government or an occupying power for some political end) is an ancient phenomenon. Throughout the twentieth century, Western states, especially Great Britain, France, and the United States, fought nationalist insurgencies in their colonial possessions as well as communist-inspired insurgents in the developing world in the context of the Cold War. A great body of counterinsurgency (COIN) thinking and practice—the work of soldiers and officials like Major General Charles E. Callwell, Major General Sir Charles Gwynn, Lieutenant General Sir Harold Briggs, Field Marshal Sir Gerald Templer, Sir Robert Thompson, General Sir Frank Kitson, David Galula, General Creighton W. Abrams, and Robert W. Komer—continue to offer an understanding of such warfare—although it must be said that the propensity of Western militaries to forget the past is something approaching an iron law.[1]

The counterinsurgent usually adopts either one of two distinct approaches. First, some emphasized an attritional approach, involving an attempt to defeat insurgents directly with the use of superior force as well as to forcibly separate insurgents from sympathizers among any host population by means intimidation, imprisonment, collective punishment, and violent reprisal. For thinker-practitioners like C. E. Callwell, for instance, the most important thing was to apply ceaseless military pressure on all insurgent refuges simultaneously. Echoes of Callwell can be traced in the war on terror and the COIN operations in Afghanistan and Iraq. Although it may well be possible to defeat an insurgency if enough violence is used, it is an approach that Western states found increasingly difficult to deploy in the twentieth century because of the restraints of domestic law, international law, democratic government, and public opinion. The end of the Cold War increased these restraints. Ugly things happened in the conduct of the war on terror, but the kinds of violent repression that had been used by Western states in even Malaya, Kenya, and Aden, much less Algeria and Vietnam, were simply not possible in the post–Cold War world. Western forces could not systematically use death squads, mass executions, torture, and grossly disproportionate collective punishments. In the age of liberalizing globalization, an attritional approach to waging war in complex social settings was very problematic, if not self-defeating.

The second basic approach to COIN emphasizes a more nuanced portfolio of political, economic, and military means that aim to persuade as much as to defeat. With the right balance of incentives and disincentives (i.e., the carrot-and-stick approach), insurgents and host populations might be persuaded to change their behavior and come to terms. What has become known as "winning hearts and minds" was to be particularly well articulated by some of the leading practitioners of British COIN, with the insurgent war in Malaya (1948–1960) against the Malay Communist Party (mostly composed of the ethnic Chinese minority) becoming the best example of the development of a more nuanced hearts and minds approach, albeit one that continued to use a great deal of the stick.[2] What Thompson, Briggs, and Templer eventually put together in Malaya was a model that encompassed the key requirements for waging nuanced warfare in a complex political and social setting. These elements were

1. A *strategic aim* that was *coherent* and *realistic*. For Western states in the twentieth century, the strategic aim was increasingly predisposed toward handing power and authority to local leaders and fostering a system of democratic governance—although such aims may not necessarily be a coherent and realistic proposition in all circumstances.
2. An *operational-level concept* for COIN operations that emphasized winning hearts and minds among the host population and some insurgents, as well as a *practical plan* to do this that blended the appropriate

political, social, economic, and military incentives and disincentives. In practice, the priority was to suppress political subversion and its causes rather than simply strike at the terrorists; thus the minimum use of force was important for the plan to succeed.
3. An *organization* that was capable of generating and coordinating the concept and the plan.
4. The *art of implementation.* It was one thing having an appropriate concept, plan, and organization; ensuring their implementation was another matter. An additional leadership element may be crucial. For instance, in Malaya it was not until the installation of Gerald Templer as a supreme political and military coordinator that a style of leadership was adopted that enabled the concept, plan, and organization to gel. Templer got around his command, reaching through the levels of command to make sure that operational-strategic level aims were implemented in the field.

Thinking more broadly about the experience of Western states with more nuanced COIN approaches, the interaction of three factors appears to be especially important. The hypothesis to be developed in this book is that warfare in complex social settings can be conceptualized in terms of a *trinity of policy emphasis* that corresponds to the key areas in which insurgents and counterinsurgents contest the future of a society. This trinity of policy emphasis embodies the application of force and provision of security; winning hearts and minds among a host population and some enemy combatants with the aim of reconciling them to a longer-term settlement (although, for reasons explained later, this is probably better described as reconstruction, reconciliation, and assimilation [RRA] activity); and the construction of a viable system of long-term governance (see Figure 3.1).

All insurgencies and interventions can be tracked on such a trinity. With respect to Malaya, for instance, British-led forces initially lacked a coherent concept and plan to progress the conflict very far from the zone of force. However, after a coherent concept, plan, organization, and leadership were pulled together, British-led forces were able to progress away from an emphasis on force. The subsequent route taken was shaped by the decision not to expedite the creation of a system of national governance but instead to implement a series of political, social, and economic measures designed to win the hearts and minds of the insurgent-hosting population and some insurgents, then develop a system of governance with bottom-up initiatives in local government (see Figure 3.2). It took time, and the formulation of the approach was done in a rather haphazard manner, but the track pioneered by Thompson, Briggs, and Templer eventually reconciled significant numbers of the hostile population and many insurgents to the status quo, thereby creating the conditions for a more stable move to national self-government.

Figure 3.1 The Nexus of Force, Reconstruction, Reconciliation, and Assimilation (RRA), and Long-Term Governance in the Management of Conflict in Complex Social Settings

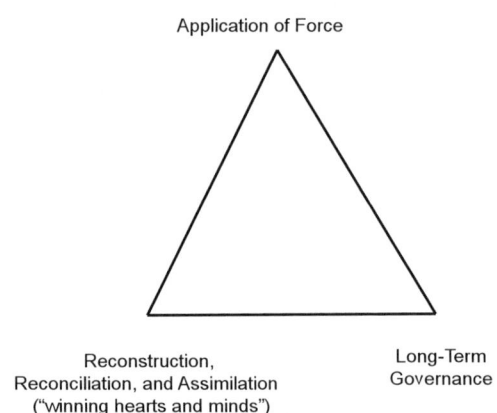

In the aftermath of the Cold War, the problems of managing conflicts in complex social settings would increase. Warlords and insurgents had new tools at their disposal, especially communications and propaganda tools, and smuggling of arms, personnel, and money became easier. Moreover, the centrality of liberal-democratic values in Western countries and the transparency brought by ever increasing media coverage meant that Western military responses came under even more intense scrutiny. Although the strategies adopted by Western interveners in post–Cold War conflicts would continue to be rather haphazard, there would be significant developments in practice. However, what would ultimately become clear, especially following the experiences of the war on terror, was that the sequencing between the use of force, RRA activities, and the development of governance was crucial—and getting this sequencing right was an inherently difficult thing to do for the liberal intervener.

The Evolution of the Liberal Intervention from the 1990s

Beside the body of COIN experience relevant to the management of conflict in complex social settings, a significant new approach would be developed after the Cold War in the form of enhanced UN peacekeeping operations. The intervention in Somalia by the United States and the international community from 1991 to 1993 saw a new kind of robust peacekeeping verging on peace enforcement. However, for a host of reasons the intervention in Somalia went

Figure 3.2 The Track of Emphasis in the Management of the Malaya Emergency, 1948–1960

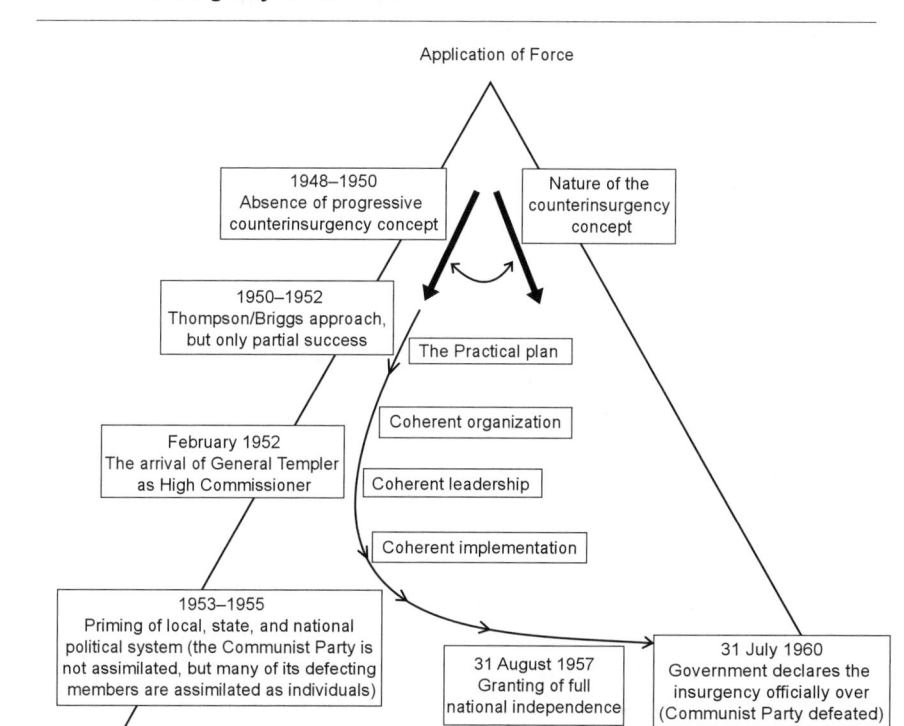

badly, and the mission was terminated before the conceptual and organizational problems with it were ironed out. What happened in Somalia slowed the development of enhanced peacekeeping, and the international community would struggle to find an effective response to the conflicts in Rwanda and the former Yugoslavia. But an important moment would come during the war in Bosnia in July–August 1995.[3] Fed up with the intransigence of the Serbian side, the US administration of President Bill Clinton would abandon impartial peacekeeping, instead opting for a strategy of picking winners and deploying packages of limited force to achieve political outcomes. The United States orchestrated a combination of NATO airpower (used largely persuasively) linked to special forces and local allies on the ground, followed by more robust peace support operations (PSO) forces and a longer-term multilateral reconstruction and reconciliation effort. Something akin to this would see the United States and its Western allies through their interventions in Kosovo in 1999 (29 March–9 June) and, in modified form, Afghanistan in 2001–2002.[4]

The evolution of so-called first-generation peacekeeping into a model linking coercive warfare techniques, more robust peacekeeping forces, and a multilateralized follow-on was an important development. The reality was that it constituted a new model for waging limited war, although it could be seen as a postmodern one in the sense that it did not look like the pursuit of selfish US national/hegemonic interests but about restoring peace and security for the benefit of the international community. This raised the legitimacy of intervention, reduced resistance to it, and cut the costs and risks for the United States itself. The multilateralized follow-on also opened the way for prolonged RRA work. In Bosnia, for instance, the Serbs were successfully bombed into accepting peace talks at Dayton, Ohio, the worst of the fighting was brought to end, and a UN High Commissioner assumed the stewardship of Bosnia pending the results of an RRA process of indeterminate duration.

The combination of high-tech airpower and new approaches to conflict management on the ground appeared to bring a *great leap* in the utility of military power in the late 1990s. But the new model was not a magic bullet, and a number of serious questions remained. The relationship between the US military, PSO forces, and multilateral community had emerged rather organically in a kind of undeclared symbiosis, and what had happened was rather poorly understood. A number of European militaries, notably the British Army, embraced the new role in complex social settings and a multilateralized environment. British forces eventually wrote up a doctrine: *The Military Contribution to Peace Support Operations* (Joint Warfare Publication 3-50) and, later, *The Comprehensive Approach* (Joint Doctrine Note 4/05), which remains among the best articulations of the concept of peace support operations.[5] By the time *The Comprehensive Approach* was published, the US and British militaries were also expanding their concept of effects-based warfare beyond the original focus on kinetic actions and effects toward a broader mapping of the battlefield, requiring a move into the realm of political, economic, and social actions and effects.[6] The new effects map was much larger, although it was one potentially so large and complex that it might be difficult to use it to comprehend and plan optimum courses of action.

Although the US military had officers thinking about the management of complex social settings and PSO-type operations—most notably the cells working at the Combined Arms Center (and its Center for Army Lessons Learned) at Fort Leavenworth, Kansas, and the US Army War College at Carlisle Barracks, Pennsylvania—the US military as a whole was slower to embrace such missions as a core function and balked at the kind of organizational and cultural change appropriate to such circumstances. The American public and politicians also tended to recoil from the role of international social worker and nation-builder, and there was deep resistance in Washington to putting US forces at the service of multilateralized missions. What happened in Somalia in 1992–1993 ingrained this skepticism. Americans were inclined to put down the apparent increase in the utility of military power in the late 1990s to new military technologies rather than their deployment within the context of the new approaches to conflict management. US forces continued to focus on warfighting, especially the use of airpower, with peacekeeping and PSO capabilities remaining institutionally weak, largely confined to special operations and civil affairs units.[7] If solutions were needed to achieve dominance across the full spectrum of warfare, the material and technological ones held the attention of most US policymakers and commanders.

The new model of intervention also came with broader risks. The apparent rise in the utility of military power between Bosnia in 1995 and Afghanistan in 2001 may have encouraged some Western policymakers to be more inclined to use force to achieve political ends as well as to test the bounds of international law that restrained that. The war in Kosovo in 1999, for instance, was not backed by a consensus in the international community or formally authorized by a UN Security Council (UNSC) resolution. During the various debates in the UNSC, Russian and Chinese representatives denounced Western intervention and questioned its legality. In an article in *Foreign Affairs* in 1999, Michael Glennon perceived the potential magnitude of these events. Glennon was not sorry to see the world order defined by the original UN Charter of 1945 superseded, but he noted that

> as the 20th century fades away, so too does the international consensus on when to get involved in another state's affairs. The United States and NATO—with little discussion and less fanfare—have effectively abandoned the old UN Charter rules that strictly limit international intervention in local conflicts. They have done so in favour of a vague new system that is much more tolerant of military intervention but has few hard and fast rules. What rules do exist seem more the product of after-the-fact rationalization by the West than of deliberation and pre-agreement.[8]

Glennon recognized that such innovations might not represent the rule of law as it had been known but hoped that the building of multilateral coalitions would filter out the potential for abuses by large powers with self-interested motives.[9] Glennon's own view was that the contemporary makeup of the UN Security Council gave France, China, and Russia more weight than they justified and that the costs of gradually reforming the old anti-intervention order would be minimal.[10] It must be said, however, that vague mandates and poorly supported interventions were ultimately the recipe for real trouble. And what if it were Russia and China that one day took it upon themselves to reform the old anti-interventionist order rather than the responsible West?

The convergence of the US military, PSO and peacekeeping forces, and multilateral agencies in the new model of intervention embodied yet another danger. Working in war zones has always been dangerous for civilians, but the risks were set to mount as civilian agencies (international organizations and nongovernmental organizations [NGOs]) were drawn in, whether they liked it or not, to support what was really a new Western intervention machine. In particular, the UN's status as the international system's mediator and third party was in serious danger of being compromised. Thus, the UN and multilateral community were likely to face more resistance when operating in the RRA and governance zones. In Somalia and the former Yugoslavia, local combatants came to regard UN forces as quasi-participants in the conflict. When it came to Iraq in 2003, the multilateral intervention machine did not coalesce in good time, but when it finally did splutter to life it did so in an extremely problematic way. The multilateral community eventually found itself acting to support US objectives in Iraq rather than collective international ones. The multilateral community was identified as an instrument of the occupation by insurgents, and the UN, Red Cross, and other NGOs were largely bombed out of the country. It was only as the most ambitious US objectives fell by the wayside that the multilateral community assumed a more substantial role in Iraq, but by then it was too little, too late to stem the building resistance to the occupation. If the RRA activities of the civilian agencies were significantly curtailed by the threat of violence, intervening Western militaries might have little option but to do much more RRA work themselves. Notwithstanding some acceptance within Western military doctrine, however, the great body of regular forces did not have the money, manpower, and expertise to fill the gap left by civilian agencies. A dedicated stabilization corps did not exist.

Finally, the new intervention machine was far from providing an easy transit to final conflict resolution—involving reconciliation and assimilation, leading to stable long-term governance—as distinct from just conflict management and containment. Bosnia and Kosovo would remain UN-NATO protectorates for many years as the UN tried to work out how to transit through the RRA phase—that is, how to finally get the gun out of politics; how to foster economic growth and integration into the world economy; how to co-opt enemy camps into a long-term system of governance; how to build up the legitimacy and capacity of any new state apparatus; and how to deal with continuing resistance to any RRA and governance process from inside and outside. Lack of resources and political willpower inhibited the transition through RRA to long-term governance. Above all, few were keen to open the Pandora's box of redrawing borders, although the United States and some of its allies would eventually bite the bullet with respect to Kosovo, backing its unilateral declaration of independence in February 2008 (but not resolving the conflict and the need for international supervision). Thus, Western interventions were in danger of leaving multilateral organizations weighed down by an increasing number of indefinite stabilization and RRA jobs. Understanding exactly how war-torn societies could be normalized and returned to a viable system of long-term governance was the principal task in bringing the new model of multilateralized intervention to fruition.[11] The new Western intervention machine was still very much a work in progress.

The Impact of the Global War on Terror

The war on terror further changed the parameters for intervention. The wars in Afghanistan and Iraq were initiated unilaterally by the United States. With the international community's conferring lower levels of legitimacy and assistance, the United States would have to shoulder more of the risks and costs of the subsequent occupations, although it was scarcely equipped and minded to do this. Most important, with the United States (in reality) rather than the UN assuming stewardship over Afghanistan and Iraq, there would be much greater pressure from the outset for an early handover of long-term governance to locals regardless of what was happening in the RRA realm. Few people in Western countries and beyond wanted to see the United States and its allies hanging on to countries as imperial-type protectorates.

The problem, scarcely appreciated at the beginning, was that the actual sequencing of emphasis on force, RRA activities, and provision of governance was a critical dynamic; this sequencing could be tracked within the aforementioned trinity of policy emphasis (see Figure 3.3). In some cases—especially if the war objectives involved relatively limited political and economic reforms—it might be possible to expedite the move from the use of force (and achievement of security) to a system of long-term governance. By bypassing or only plotting a shallow curve into the RRA zone, the costs and commitment involved in the intervention might be much reduced (see Figure 3.3, Track A). In fact, this was initially what would happen following the war in Afghanistan in 2001–2002. However, if the end purpose of the intervention was to unify and significantly liberalize a society—that is, to install a system of consensual democratic governance as well as to introduce some measure of free market–type economic reform where there had been little or none before—the intervener would have to put much more effort into initiating reconstruction and economic development with a view to reconciling insurgents and hostile populations toward the desired end-state. Such was the problem of Iraq. In fact, the optimum course for the liberalizing intervention is likely to be Track B in most cases, although this implied a much longer and more costly transitional RRA process. In such cases, the use of force could be seen as largely a tactical instrument: Plotting a way through the RRA zone was the principal operational-level requirement, and the provision of a viable system of long-term governance (including economic practice) was the strategic goal.

What would also become clear in Afghanistan and Iraq was that the principal battlefield was the RRA zone—and it was in this realm that the contemporary insurgent was most capable of contesting Western forces. Apart from the lack of planning, preparedness, and capacity to begin society-wide RRA projects,

Western armed forces often poorly understood what they were doing in the RRA zone. In this respect, for instance, the use of the old British-popularized COIN catchphrase—winning hearts and minds—could be a problem because it was all too easy to be glib about what that was actually about. Some US and British officers regarded hearts-and-minds work largely as an adjunct to gathering intelligence in order to use force more efficiently. Finding and killing insurgents might well be useful in that it *might* help establish the necessary level of security to enable RRA activities to progress, but a focus on kinetic operations was apt to take the campaign in the wrong direction—that is, back up the Track B curve in Figure 3.3 toward the zone of force.

Other kinds of glibness were also put into practice. Simply delivering money, goods, and services to populations might look and feel like winning over hearts and minds, but the actual effects could be unpredictable. It might create an unwanted dependency among a population, even a sense of entitlement that was eventually bound to be disappointed.[12] Even worse, unless aid and reconstruction work were properly supervised, it might simply create a context for insurgents to do things. Soldiers in Afghanistan and Iraq, for instance,

Figure 3.3 Potential Tracks of Policy Emphasis in the Management of Conflict in Complex Social Settings (Idealized Possibilities)

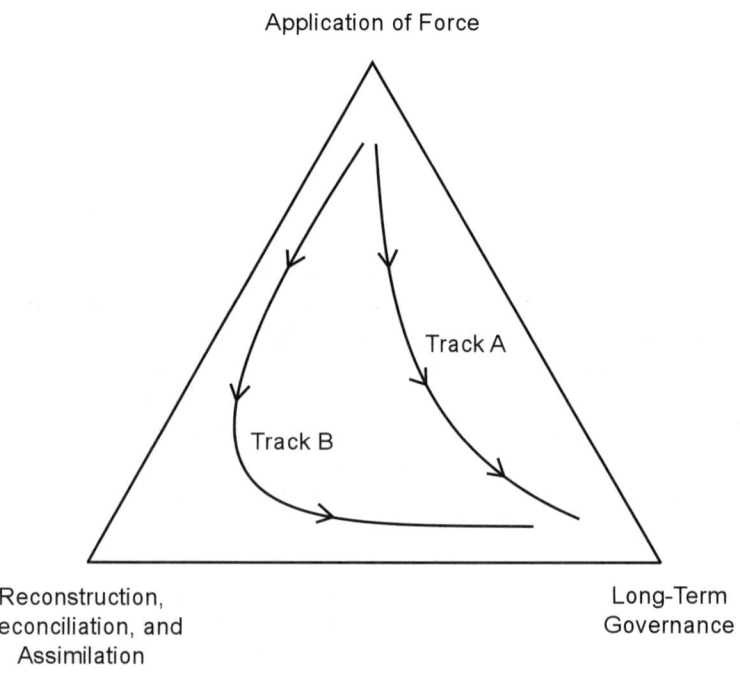

might build a village school (or deliver an electric generator or a water pump or something similar), but unless the facility was closely protected and supervised insurgents might simply burn down the school and kill the head teacher (thereby instilling terror) while propagating the claim that they had just saved the youth of the village from the corruption of an infidel education. It was all too easy for a relatively small group of insurgents to match RRA activities with destruction, discord, and dissimilation. Alternatively, in Iraq especially, insurgents were often able to successfully claim the credit for hearts-and-minds activities as their own, such as the provision of water or electricity services, by virtue of more effective information campaigning.

If the phrase "winning hearts and minds" was prone to glib interpretation and misfiring implementation, then "reconstruction, reconciliation, and assimilation" was probably a better use of language because it embodied a process of progress: Tie together a number of streams in the move from the provision of security to reconstruction to reconciliation to assimilation (perhaps) and, finally, to long-term governance (recall Track B, Figure 3.3).

The provision of security and reconstruction and economic incentives establishes a launching pad into the principal political contest of insurgent wars, that is, the ways in which and to what extent hostile populations and insurgents are reconciled and assimilated into the intended system of long-term governance. How that gap between providing security-economic incentives and the end state of long-term governance is bridged is likely to be a reflection of the balance of power that emerged through the zones of force and RRA—in short, who really prevailed in the conflict (see Figure 3.4). One important point is that reconciliation is not the same as assimilation. Indeed, while some degree of reconciliation must happen if discontented populations and insurgents are to stop fighting, it may be possible to proceed to a stable system of governance without a significant degree of assimilation. In the case of Malaya, for instance, the leader of the Malay Communist Party (MCP), Chin Peng, did hold negotiations with the mainstream Malay politicians from the Muslim-led Alliance Party in December 1954, but he failed to get their acceptance that the MCP be legalized; Chin Peng had little option but to return to the jungle.[13] The MCP was not assimilated as an organization in the system of governance being created, although many of its members were eventually reconciled (and some *individually* assimilated into other political factions and into the security forces) as they began to defect from the MCP. It was what a government victory in a nuanced COIN campaign looked like.

Conclusion

Waging warfare in complex social settings is not new. In the twentieth century, Western militaries repeatedly faced insurgent movements that had deep roots

Figure 3.4 Progressing Through the RRA Zone: Closing the Reconciliation and Assimilation Gap

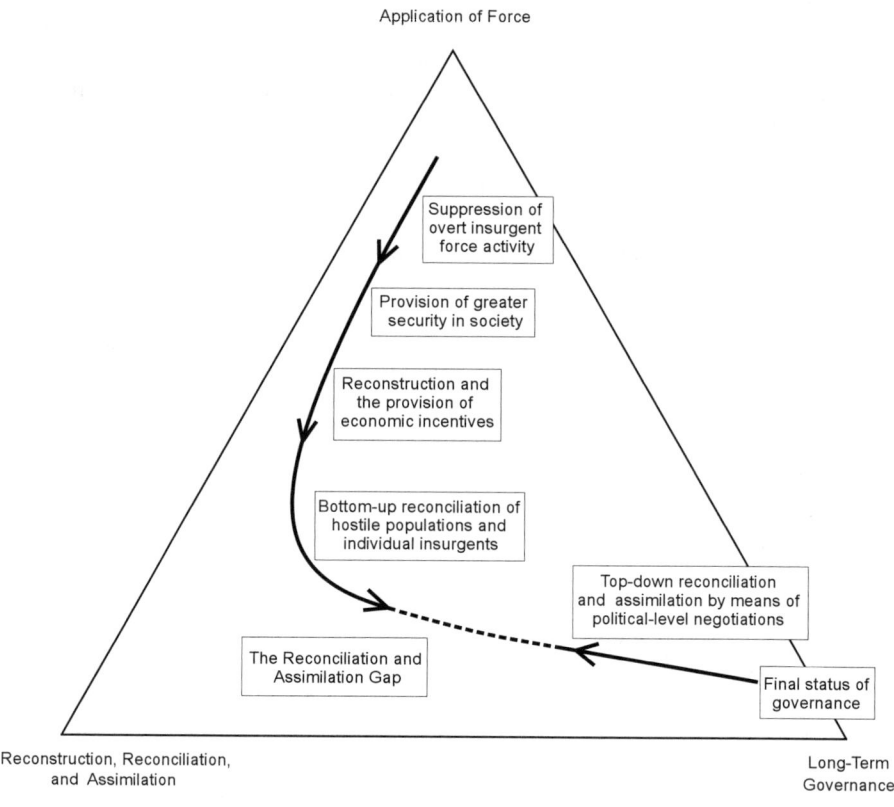

in their societies. The use of force to suppress insurgents had increasingly to be limited, with more nuanced political-social kinds of counterinsurgency needing to be developed. The Western occupier-intervener could no longer kill, destroy, and terrorize its way to victory. In the aftermath of the Cold War, as Western states became the principal managers of international security, further development took place. Following events in Bosnia in 1995, the United States and some of its allies deployed a new model of limited war that put together US airpower (used to coerce and persuade), more robust practices in peacekeeping and peace support operations, and a multilateralized follow-on of conflict stabilization and postwar management. For a time, these developments appeared to raise the utility of military power, but the model was not a magic bullet or universally applicable. In particular, while US airpower was a powerful and persuasive tool in the early stages of any intervention, the real challenges lay in the subsequent peace support and conflict resolution phases.

Notwithstanding the new practice and doctrine, most Western politicians and commanders were circumspect about taking ownership of complex social settings, as well as the difficulty and cost of managing them. The follow-on phases of Western interventions in the former Yugoslavia were subcontracted to international organizations and NGOs, but they lacked coherence and certain capacities, and their status as third-party interlocutors and providers of aid was also in grave danger of being compromised. If waging warfare in complex social settings required—as it always has—putting together a viable strategic aim, a coherent plan, an effective organization, and the means to implement on the ground, then the new multilateralized intervention machine was still very much a work in progress.

Amid the searing experience of waging the war on terror, especially the management of Iraq, it would become increasingly clear that Western militaries themselves had to be able to conceive, organize, and implement a myriad of political, social, and economic effects. It is the contention here that the key battlefield of warfare in complex social settings is the zone of reconstruction, reconciliation, and assimilation (modeled in Figures 3.1, 3.3, and 3.4). Succeeding in the RRA zone required marshaling society-wide project management that embodied both physical and cognitive elements; this was an inherently difficult thing for conventional militaries to accomplish.[14] It would be some years after 9/11 until US and British forces had a better understanding of how best to go about turning the provision of security into reconstruction, reconciliation, and assimilation. Even so, much of this project management effort—especially with respect to the development of long-term governance—remained beyond the influence and capacity of the militaries themselves. Looking back on it, US and British policymakers and commanders should have known better just how difficult the interventions of the war on terror would become. Whether they had pondered the British experience in Malaya, the US quagmire in Vietnam, or the international communities' missions in Bosnia and Kosovo, the lessons were that defeating insurgents, terminating conflicts, reconstituting fractured societies, and establishing viable systems of long-term governance were immensely difficult tasks.

Notes

1. See Sir John Kiszely (Lieutenant General, British Army), "Learning About Counter-Insurgency," *RUSI Journal* 151, no. 6 (December 2006): 16–21.

2. For an account of the British campaign in Malaya, see John Nagl, *Learning to Eat Soup with a Knife: Counterinsurgency Lessons from Malaya to Vietnam* (Chicago: University of Chicago Press, 2005), xvii, 59–111.

3. For an account of UN operations in Bosnia, see Rupert Smith, "Bosnia: Using Force Amongst the People," chapter 9, *The Utility of Force,* 332–370. General Rupert commanded UN forces [UN Protection Force—UNPROFOR] in Bosnia in 1995.

4. For an introduction to a discussion of the Kosovo campaign, see Stephen Biddle, "The New Way of War?" (review article), *Foreign Affairs* 81, no. 3 (May–June 2002). Available at the website of *Foreign Affairs,* www.foreignaffairs.org/20020501 faessay8063/stephen-biddle/the-new-way-of-war.html.

5. Contemporary British peacekeeping doctrine was first written up in the context of war in Bosnia by Colonels Charles Dobie and Philip Wilkinson at the Army Directorate-General of Doctrine and Development in Upavon. A more robust peacekeeping approach—the Peace Support Operation—emerged in Army Field Manual, *Wider Peacekeeping* (JWP 3-01), in 1997. The subsequent British doctrine booklet—*The Military Contribution to Peace Support Operations,* Joint Warfare Publication 3-50 (2nd ed.), Joint Doctrine and Concepts Center, Shrivenham, 2004—remains the leading account of its kind. It was followed by Joint Doctrine Note 4/05, *The Comprehensive Approach* (January 2006); Joint Doctrine Note 1/05, *The UK Military Effects-Based Approach;* Joint Doctrine Note 7/06, *Incorporating and Extending the UK Military Effects-Based Approach* (September 2006).

6. For information on the contemporary application of an "effects" methodology to warfare in more complex social settings, see Milan N. Vego, "Effects-Based Operations: A Critique," *Joint Forces Quarterly* 41 (2nd Quarter 2006): 51–57 (Milan N. Vego is professor of operations in the Joint Military Operations Department, Naval War College); Joint Warfare Center, "An Effects-Based Approach: Refining How We Think about Joint Operations," *Joint Forces Quarterly* 44 (1st Quarter 2007): 1–6. *Joint Forces Quarterly* is available online. Tim Bird, "UK Effects-Based Planning and Centre of Gravity Analysis: An Increasingly Dysfunctional Relationship?" *RUSI Journal* 153, no. 2 (April 2008): 46–49.

7. See Scott A. Cooper, "Air Power and the Coercive Use of Force," *Washington Quarterly* 24, no. 4 (Autumn 2001): 81–93.

8. Michael J. Glennon, "The New Interventionism: The Search for a Just International Law," *Foreign Affairs* 78, no. 3 (May–June 1999): 2–7, 2.

9. Ibid., 5.

10. Ibid., 4.

11. For an important discussion about some of the dilemmas involved in developing reconciliation and nation-building, see Francis Fukuyama, "Weak States and International Legitimacy," chapter 3 in his *State Building: Governance and World Order in the Twenty-First Century* (London: Profile Books, 2004), esp. 133–141.

12. See Greg Mills, "Calibrating Ink Spots: Filling Afghanistan's Ungoverned Spaces," *RUSI Journal* 151, no. 4 (August 2006): 16–25.

13. Nagl, *Learning to Eat Soup with a Knife,* 102.

14. For further discussion, see the important article on the project management of occupations and peace support operations by Marcus Fielding (Lieutenant General, Australian Army), "Regime Change: Planning and Managing Military-Led Interventions as Projects," *RUSI Journal* 151, no. 5 (October 2006): 20–29.

4

The Origins of the War on Terror, 1991–2001

It was a stunning moment, but the terrorist attacks that struck the United States on 11 September 2001 could not really be seen as bolts from the blue. What happened that day stemmed from international dynamics in the Middle East that had been in the making for more than a decade. The threat from the Middle East was forged with the merging of old and new conflicts, where the grievances produced by old-fashioned geopolitical conflicts were harnessed by the new cadre of glocal revolutionaries. Specifically, 9/11 was the culmination of the rise and fall of a US-sponsored security architecture in the Middle East that was put in place in the decade following the 1990–1991 Gulf War. This security architecture had promised a pax Americana in the region, but it was to be unfinished and unstable. With the United States routinely applying force throughout the 1990s to maintain its security system, the scene was set for 9/11, the war on terror, and the invasion of Iraq. Indeed, the war on terror itself would eventually become synonymous with an attempt by the United States to do an extreme makeover of its decayed security architecture in the Middle East. If the war in Afghanistan was antiterror intervention, the war in Iraq was really about the regional security architecture. The following chapter tells this story.

The Rise of the Pax Americana in the Middle East After 1991

The putative pax Americana grew out of the Gulf War and the coalition's 1991 invasion of Iraq. On the face of it, the Gulf War was a decisive victory. Most of the war objectives set out by President George H. W. Bush in National Security Directive (NSD) 54 were apparently achieved.[1] Saddam Hussein's regime was forced into a humbling retreat from Kuwait, the offensive power of Iraq's armed forces was broken, and Iraq's military-industrial capacity was denuded. Saddam's aspiration to become the principal Arab leader was dashed forever. The awesome display of military power also gave the United States new status worldwide. Indeed, the Gulf War seemed to vindicate the enthusiasts of the Revolution in Military Affairs, although from today's perspective, rather than its being the first of a new generation of warfare, it looks more like the last of an old. For US policymakers and commanders who had lived under the shadow of Vietnam, military force appeared to have regained its utility.

Yet from the very moment of triumph, it was clear that the Bush administration had not put sufficient thought into the end game of the war or even one of the primary aims of NSD 54: promoting the longer-term stability and security of the Persian Gulf. Although George Bush hoped for a change of leadership in Iraq and urged Iraqis to consider that possibility, too, his administration recoiled from the risks and responsibilities involved in undertaking a proactive policy of regime change. US policymakers perceived further intervention as a probable quagmire and were also conscious of the lack of support among the multinational Coalition that they had so assiduously cultivated during the conflict. A broader political-military strategy was not put into place. The Coalition-Iraqi disengagement talks conducted at Safwan by the commander of US Central Command, General Norman Schwarzkopf, went ahead with startlingly little preparation. Contacts with disaffected Iraqi officers were not fully pursued, and US forces stood back to watch Saddam Hussein's regime reconsolidate its grip on power by crushing a Shia revolt in southern Iraq and a Kurdish revolt in northern Iraq. Many thousands were killed. The disinclination of the Bush administration to become involved was altered only at urging from allies, the airing of video depicting Kurdish suffering, and a personal visit by US Secretary of State James Baker to northern Iraq. The United States agreed to create a safe haven for the Kurds and put together a NATO force to secure it. Shia in southern Iraq were left to their fate.

After the debacle of the end game of the Gulf War, however, the policymakers in the Bush and subsequent Clinton administrations came back strongly. The United States would foster a number of initiatives that together established a new security architecture in the Middle East with the United States as the principal arbiter. This architecture could be conceptualized in terms of three pillars, each supporting the other.

Pillar One: Dual Containment of Iraq and Iran

The first pillar stemmed directly from the first Gulf crisis. Following the Iraqi invasion of Kuwait on 2 August 1990, Iraq was subject to a raft of UNSC resolutions, including tough economic sanctions. Having decided not to go for regime change, US policymakers realized that a long-term containment policy was required to keep a recalcitrant Saddam Hussein under control. Events shaped what was to follow. Although the United States was initially reluctant to carve out a safe haven in Iraqi Kurdistan, once the safe haven was in place it gave the United States and the international community great leverage over the Iraqi regime. The protection of Iraqi minorities also led to the declaration of so-called no-fly zones. A UN-authorized US dominion was effectively created over Iraqi airspace north of the 36th parallel and, after August 1992, south of the 32nd (later 33rd) parallel. Iraqi aircraft and surface-to-air missiles entered these zones at their peril, and US and British bombing of Iraqi radars and air defense installations became routine for the remainder of the 1990s. Coalition airpower was also the instrument of coercive diplomacy. Iraqi targets were liable to be bombed if the Iraqi regime held back from cooperating with international monitoring or if it tried to pressure Kurds or Kuwaitis.[2]

An important element of Iraq containment came with the passage of UNSC Resolution 687 (3 April 1991), which established the framework for a comprehensive control regime.[3] UN Resolution 687 demanded that Iraq accept the Iraq-Kuwait border of October 1963; put Iraq's oil exporting industry under UN supervision; created a compensation fund to deal with claims made against Iraq; and defined limits on Iraq's military capabilities. The UN set a ceiling on Iraqi oil exports of US$1.6 billion in the first six months of the UN's Oil for Food program, of which 30 percent was immediately claimed by the UN for compensation claims and expenses, the rest being allocated to purchase food and medicine.[4] Iraq was required to unconditionally accept the destruction of all nuclear, chemical, and biological weapons capabilities as well as to dismantle all ballistic missiles possessing a range of more than 150 kilometers. The UN established the United Nations Special Commission (UNSCOM) to monitor Iraqi compliance. Alongside teams from the International Atomic Energy Agency (IAEA), UNSCOM would begin systematic investigation, on-site inspection, overflights, and dismantling activities.

Notwithstanding later claims to the contrary, the control regime that stemmed from UN Resolution 687 was successful. Iraq was substantially disarmed in the 1990s. UNSCOM and IAEA inspectors found far more of Iraq's WMD-related infrastructure than did Coalition bombers during the Gulf War. Inspections went on to uncover an enormous amount of information and set about destroying equipment, blowing up suspect sites, and bulldozing ballistic missiles into the ground. The brief defection to Jordan of Saddam Hussein's son-in-law, Hussein Kamel Hassan al-Majid—a former head of Iraq's military industries—provided the information to blow apart much of what remained secret, notably Iraq's biological weapons program. In addition, the Iraqi regime appears to have taken the initiative to rid itself of many of the banned weapons on its own accord, with chemical weapons stockpiles being disposed of as early as 1991, although much of this was done unilaterally and in defiance of UN rules. Later, the risk of getting caught also appears to have driven self-supervised disarmament, with bursts of activity in 1995–1996, 1998, and

2000–2001. Although Saddam Hussein balked at openly admitting capitulation on the WMD issue, by the late 1990s the military-industrial infrastructure related to the production of WMDs and medium-range ballistic missiles was largely gone.

For the remainder of the 1990s, the Iraqi regime had to balance giving up what remained of its strategic weapons and military secrets against the possibility of getting the UN sanctions lifted. Of course, in the end the calculation was a forlorn one. Although the United States wanted to see Iraqi disarmament, it did not want that disarmament validated; on both counts, the United States was successful. Indeed, under the Clinton administration the US policy of maintaining an indefinite containment and sanctions regime on Iraq was stiffened. The policy was articulated by two of Clinton's most senior national security staffers, Anthony Lake and Martin Indyk, in a series of speeches and articles in 1993 in which they enunciated the concept of dual containment. Lake and Indyk thought that in the post–Cold War world the United States had a special responsibility to stand up to "aggressive and defiant" countries that Lake called the "backlash states" and went on to argue that the United States was now so powerful in the Middle East that it was capable of isolating and containing the two problem cases of Iran and Iraq at the same time—the new policy of dual containment.[5]

Dual containment did not mean *duplicate* containment; it was possible to think about improvements in relations with the Islamic Republic of Iran as long as it gave up its extremism. The test for Iran was to give up its opposition to the Arab-Israeli peace process, stop its efforts to develop WMD, and cease to meddle in the affairs of its neighbors. But there could be no second chances for Iraq. Lake made it clear in a 1994 article in *Foreign Affairs* that Saddam Hussein's regime was irredeemably criminal and that the ultimate aspiration of US policy was that it should be overthrown.[6] Saddam was so evil and irresponsible that he could not be bargained with, much less rehabilitated. Thus, the Clinton administration had no interest in seeing the validation of Iraq's disarmament, much less the lifting of sanctions and the control regime. The reality was that sanctions were bound to last as long as Saddam was in power. The result was that by the mid-1990s Iraq was reduced to the condition of a wrecked third world country.

Pillar Two: The Arab-Israeli Peace Process

Shortly after the end of the Gulf War, the administration of George H. W. Bush began to develop an Arab-Israeli peace pillar. Bush had rejected the link between Kuwait and the Israeli Occupied Territories made by Saddam during the conflict but returned to the Arab-Israeli issue once the crisis was over. During October–November 1991, a joint US-Soviet initiative brought Israel and Arab states together at the so-called Madrid Conference in Spain. The conference eventually set off a series of bilateral and multilateral talks between Arabs and Israelis that produced much progress. Jordan went on to sign a full peace, and Syria also entered negotiations over the Golan Heights. Other Arab states engaged in contacts with Israel for the first time. Israeli delegations were invited to a number of regional meetings about economic development, and more followed. After the election of a Labor-led government under Yitzhak Rabin in 1993, the Madrid peace process was followed up by the Oslo peace process between Israel and the Palestinians. With the land-for-peace principle, as outlined in UN Security Council Resolutions 242 and 338, as the basis of a settlement, the Palestinian National Authority was established to which land and powers were to be progressively devolved.[7] The final status was not defined, but Palestinian self-rule, and even statehood, in most of the Occupied Territories by the year 2000 was on the agenda.

Madrid and Oslo were huge steps forward. Although Arab and Israeli rejectionists continued to threaten the process, Israel had crossed a barrier of acceptance vis-à-vis many Arab states. For a brief moment, a will for peace existed. US policymakers could also begin to dream that Israel might one day serve as a kind of conduit for overdue political and economic reforms in the Middle East. Up till this point, the wave of democratization that had swept the world since the end of the Cold War had bypassed the region. The senior Clinton administration staffer, Martin Indyk, later outlined the proposition that "our case was straightforward. There was a window of opportunity to negotiate a comprehensive peace in the Middle East. If the negotiations were successful, that outcome would have a profound effect on the region, as leaders would no longer be able to use the excuse of conflict with Israel to delay political and economic reforms at home. Once peace was established, moreover, resources previously devoted to war could be freed up for reform."[8]

More immediately, the Arab-Israeli peace process was vital to the emerging security architecture in the Middle East because it was the thing that made Arabs and Muslims want to cooperate with the United States as regional arbiter. Many Middle Easterners put up with US preeminence only reluctantly, but they did so because they expected the United States to deliver Israel to some final agreement with the Arab states and Palestinians.

Pillar Three: Consolidation of a Regional Alliance System

The Gulf War left the United States at the center of a much-strengthened regional alliance system that ultimately linked the Gulf States, Egypt, Israel, and Turkey. The inclusion of Israel meant that the alliance system would be informal and coordinated indirectly through Washington, but it still represented by far the most powerful configuration in the Middle East. The significance of this alliance system to the United States was also greatly enhanced by improved terms for the presence of US forces in the Gulf States following the Gulf War.

During the 1980s, the United States had built up an infrastructure of pre-positioned forces and bases across the Indian Ocean region, but the Gulf States had always sought to keep US forces at arm's length. Domestic opinion in the Arabian peninsula, especially in Saudi Arabia, was wary of allowing the United States too big a footprint. For instance, when the United States had intervened in the Iran-Iraq War during 1987–1988, protecting Kuwaiti oil shipments by re-flagging ships under the Stars and Stripes, Kuwait and Saudi Arabia had even declined to provide direct support and basing for US naval operations. The Gulf War changed all that. Kuwait was now a de facto protectorate of the United States, with the joint defense agreement of September 1991 formalizing access. US forces stored equipment in Kuwait that enabled rapid deployment and frequent exercising. A formal agreement with Saudi Arabia was not signed, but US combat forces would remain in the kingdom for the remainder of the decade. The United States also built up forces and facilities in Bahrain and Qatar. The garrisoning of the Gulf not only highlighted the security dependency of the Gulf States but also allowed the United States to cast the kind of military shadow across the region that had not been seen since the days of the British empire. US airpower in the Gulf States enforced the containment of Iraq.

The Decay of the Post-1991 Pax Americana

Initially, the post-1991 pax Americana in the Middle East worked brilliantly. Iraq was substantially disarmed of its offensive military capabilities and nullified as a regional power. The Arab-Israeli peace process delivered much. Most of the Arab states and the Palestinian leadership were co-opted, and life for many Palestinians improved greatly. At last, Israel seemed on the brink of a new level of acceptance and involvement in its region. The US alliance system was the dominant grouping in the Middle East, and the US garrisoning of the Gulf States cast a wide shadow. But the US security architecture was built upon unstable foundations, and US policymakers did not appreciate quite how time-limited it was. Between 1995 and 2000, pillar by pillar, the architecture began to crumble. It would all end in disaster.

The Failure of the Arab-Israel Peace Pillar

Things started to go wrong with the Arab-Israeli pillar. The problem was that the Israeli-Palestinian peace process was an interim deal that was always in danger of getting stuck in an endless confidence- and security-building stage. The terms of the final settlement—initially projected for 1999–2000—were never agreed, and there were fundamental differences over the division of territory, the degree of sovereignty to be allowed to the Palestinians, Jerusalem, and Jewish settlers in the West Bank. No Israeli government was ever sanguine about the idea of a fully independent Palestinian state throughout Gaza and the West Bank. Moreover, the longer the process dragged on, the more vulnerable it was to events as well as to attack by Arab and Israeli rejectionists. In fact, during 1995–1996 a series of events was to destroy it. The first major blow came on 5 November 1995, when Israel's Labor prime minister, Yitzhak Rabin, was assassinated by a Jewish militant. Rabin's assassination seriously weakened the peace platform in Israel. Then, in March and April 1996 a series of Hamas and Islamic Jihad suicide bombings in Jerusalem, Ashkelon, and Tel Aviv destroyed much Israeli good will. Shortly after, the Israelis went into Lebanon to get Hezbollah. Israel's Operation Grapes of Wrath killed many Lebanese civilians, including more than 100 in a single incident at Qana, and did much to destroy good will on the Arab side.

However, the real coup de grace for the Oslo peace process came with the election of the Likud-led government of Benjamin Netanyahu in May 1996. Netanyahu did not believe in land for peace—thus there could be no peace. The loss of momentum was decisive, and the situation drifted inexorably toward renewed violence. The subsequent Labor-led government of Ehud Barak briefly raised new hopes, but the moment of enthusiasm had passed. The failure of the Camp David peace talks in July and August 2000, conducted under the auspices of President Clinton, represented the last real chance for Oslo. Although Ehud Barak may have held out the promise of a Palestinian state, Palestinian leader Yasser Arafat could not accept the proposed borders or limits on sovereignty. Differences remained over East Jerusalem, Israeli settlers, and the right of return for Palestinian refugees. For the Palestinians, the objective was not only self-rule but also to escape Israeli domination. Holding out for so much would mean failure, and the return to protest and violence, with the visit of Likud's opposition leader, Ariel Sharon, to the al-Aqsa Mosque on 28 September 2000, sparking what was to become known as the second intifada. With the Israeli crackdown resulting in the deaths of hundreds of demonstrators, militia members, and ordinary people, Palestinian militants launched a sustained campaign of suicide bombings.

If what Ehud Barak offered was not enough, it was the best Palestinians were going to get. Oslo finally died with the election of the Likud-led government of Ariel Sharon in February 2001. Sharon was not interested in a negotiated peace on anything approaching the lines of Oslo and moved to effectively destroy the Palestinian National Authority and its security apparatus. Israel returned to the policy of colonizing a substantial part of the West Bank and waging a disproportionate battle of attrition in order to achieve that objective. Yasser Arafat was rejected as a negotiating partner and was virtually imprisoned inside his wrecked headquarters in Ramallah. Sharon set about making the occupation more effective and less costly, notably by building a security wall around the West Bank to reduce the numbers of suicide bombers getting into Israel.

In the Arab world, the United States had been expected to deliver Israel to a final peace. Yet amid the deteriorating situation, the United States was either impotent or disinclined to make the peace process work. If President Clinton had at least made one last effort to reconcile the parties at Camp David, President George W. Bush simply dropped any pretense that the United States was a genuine third-party mediator. Bush was instinctively sympathetic to Israel and actively hostile to Arafat. In the first year of the Bush administration, the United States stood back and essentially let Israel get on with its process of creating new facts on the ground.

The failure of Oslo represented a colossal blow to the stability of the US-managed security architecture in the Middle East. After the United States was unable to deliver, its ability to co-opt Arabs and Muslims into its regional system was diminished, and the decay of the peace process was to have meaningful consequences. Pillar by pillar, the US security system was about to crumble.

Decay of the Dual Containment Pillar: Iran and Iraq

In the late 1990s, the ability of the United States to contain both Iran and Iraq at the same time waned. In fact, Iran was never really contained in the first place. Although the United States had some success in limiting Iran's access to nuclear technology, US efforts to coordinate a broader sanctions regime, as well as to coerce the desired political posture from the Iranian regime, were always less successful. Amid the background of a bidding war to appear tough on Iran vis-à-vis the Republican-dominated US Congress, the Clinton administration introduced a series of new sanctions in 1995 and 1996. Imports from Iran were banned, and US exporters were prohibited from selling a broad range of goods to Iran, notably petroleum engineering equipment. Clinton went on to sign the Iran and Libya Sanctions Act of 1996, an extraordinary piece of extraterritorial legislation that also bound companies outside the United States. Foreign companies that did any appreciable business with Iran could be liable to US sanctions. However, without bilateral agreements or UN authorization, this sanctions regime found little support within the international community, and given the raft of Iran-related trade disputes looming with the European Union (EU), Russia, China, Turkey, Malaysia, and others, the Clinton administration would essentially back off from that aspect of the Iran and Libya Sanctions Act.[9]

The fact was that Iran had oil and dollars, and much of the world wanted to do business with it. The United States did not have a sufficiently persuasive case to mobilize international support at that time, and the US campaign was widely regarded to be self-serving scaremongering. The United States claimed that Iran remained one of the leading sponsors of international terrorism—to the point that the Clinton administration even appears to have toyed with the idea of major military action against it in 1996—but Iran was not the chaotic revolutionary state that it had been during the 1980s.[10] Notwithstanding interruptions over human rights controversies, European countries had resolved to pursue a strategy of critical dialogue and constructive engagement since the EU summit in Edinburgh in December 1992. The landslide election of the reformist cleric Mohammad Khatami as Iranian president in May 1997 effectively finished off any attempt to tighten containment. Indeed, by June 1998 even the Clinton administration began talking of a road map to better relations, although progress did not materialize.

The US-Iranian cold war was deeply entrenched in the strategic cultures of both countries, reinforced by domestic political forces that believed it was in their interest to perpetuate hostility. When the Iran and Libya Sanctions Act, which included provision for review and reconfirmation after five years, came up for renewal in August 2001, the legislation passed without significant changes. Despite the common view that Iran needed to deal with the United States, in fact Iran could live without the United States, and Iranian leaders appeared more than happy to do so. US policy toward Iran was at an impasse.

For its part, Iraq would also become a more difficult problem to manage during the late 1990s. Throughout that decade, Saddam tested the boundaries of the containment regime in a series of confrontations by testing the no-fly zones in 1992–1993, the security of Kuwait in 1994, and the independence of the Kurdish zone in mid-1996.[11] On all three occasions, the Iraqi regime was eventually deterred by coercive bombing or the deployment of additional US troops to the region. Saddam's purpose was doubtless related to bolstering his position in Iraq, but he also wanted to remind the world about setting a timetable for lifting the UN sanctions. Saddam achieved little with his coercive diplomacy in the first half of the 1990s. The containment and disarmament regime remained intact.

In the second half of the 1990s, the containment regime would come under more pressure. Sanctions were a blunt instrument. In Iraq itself, sanctions actually appear to have strengthened the regime by impoverishing ordinary people, making them more dependent on state rationing.[12] At the same time, sanctions contributed to a health crisis that led to the deaths of tens of thousands of Iraqis. A survey for the UN Children's Fund in 1999 estimated that changes in child mortality had led to the deaths of an extra 500,000 children under the age of five during the period 1991–1998.[13] The UN tried to alleviate the malnutrition and shortages of medicine with its Oil for Food program, but the Iraqi regime resisted until early 1996, objecting to the loss of sovereignty over its oil resources. US policymakers blamed Saddam Hussein and refused to accept any responsibility for Iraq's health calamity, but there were increasing misgivings in the international community. The French foreign minister, Hubert Vedrine, was reported to have described sanctions on Iraq as "cruel, ineffective and dangerous."[14] Arab and Muslim opinion was also becoming increasingly agitated.

Beside the humanitarian qualms, there was the practical economics of the situation. Sanctions on Iraq were the most enormous drag on the regional economy. Keeping Iraq poor made everyone poorer. By the late 1990s, neighboring countries were straining at the leash to do business again, as were former trading partners like Russia, China, and France.[15] The concurrent collapse of the Arab-Israeli peace process made Arabs less inclined to cooperate with US policy in general, and less willing to bear the costs of Iraqi containment in particular. By 1997–1998, Iraq's neighbors were facilitating the smuggling of larger quantities of oil outside UN control, especially through Syria, Jordan, and Turkey.[16] Syria was reported to be importing more than 100,000 barrels per day. A later British government dossier estimated that Iraq's income from smuggled oil went from US$0.8–1 billion in 1999, to US$1.5–2 billion in 2000, and to a projected US$3 billion in 2002.[17] Breaches in the UN Oil for Food program also netted the Iraq regime even more unregulated income. The UN Independent Inquiry Committee into the maladministration of the US$64 billion Oil for Food program, revealed in October 2005 that the Iraqi regime may have siphoned off US$228 million in oil surcharges and US$1.5 billion in contractual kickbacks and transport fees, mostly collected after mid-1999.[18] A later report by the Central Intelligence Agency (CIA) Iraq Survey Group estimated that the Iraqi regime made some US$11 billion from all its illicit revenue streams.[19] Iraq experienced big increases in gross domestic product in the latter 1990s, reportedly from US$8.3 billion in 1996, US$10.8 billion in 1997, US$13.7 billion in 1998, US$19.3 billion in 1999, and US$26.7 billion in 2000.[20] It was all a symptom of the fact that Iraq was beginning the break the containment leash.

The situation began ringing alarm bells in Washington and London. The assumption was that the money now flowing into Saddam's coffers would be used to restart Iraq's WMD and ballistic missile programs, although later information would cast much doubt on this. In the first instance, US policymakers tried to hold the sanctions regime together by making it more sensitive. Iraq's acceptance of UN Resolution 986 (14 April 1995) authorized the sale of US$1.8 billion of Iraq's oil every six months to purchase food and humanitarian goods.[21] By the end of the 1990s, the figure had been allowed to rise to US$5.2 billion every six months. The United States and Great Britain went on to propose further concessions: UN Resolution 1284 (17 December 1999) proposed the suspension of some sanctions in return for full cooperation with a newly constituted inspection organization, the United Nations Monitoring, Verification, and Inspection Mission (UNMOVIC).[22]

With the slow decay of the sanctions regime continuing, though, the Clinton administration had a number of potential options that it could ponder. The options were

1. Stay the course and attempt to bolster the containment regime by renewed diplomatic pressure and the application of tailored air strikes.

2. Come to terms and move to rehabilitate the Iraqi regime to some extent.
3. Commit to a covert action aimed at ousting Saddam Hussein.
4. Escalate the use of conventional military forces with a view toward overthrowing the Baathist state and transforming Iraq.

When US policymakers ran through the options in the late 1990s, it must have been obvious that none looked very good. The first option was more of the same. The second option was a view prevalent in the international community: Containment had run its course, and Iraq should be given a list of conditions linked to a timetable for the lifting of sanctions. But that idea was not acceptable to the Clinton administration, let alone to the Republican-dominated Congress. The kind of rehabilitation that would later be offered to the Libyan leader, Muammar Qaddafi, was never on offer to Saddam Hussein. The third option (removing Saddam) was not straightforward. Western intelligence agencies had limited assets in Iraq. Saddam was difficult to pin down, and even if he could be killed or captured he might simply be replaced by someone similar, such as one of his sons. The consequences for the Iraqis involved in any US-instigated coup would be dreadful, and so caution was the order of the day. If the fourth option (military action to overthrow the Baathist state) was being mulled over in the wider Washington policy community by the late 1990s, it was not a serious possibility for the Clinton administration. Political support at home and abroad simply wasn't there.

In the end, the Clinton administration went for a combination of the first and third options: Bolster sanctions and continue coercive bombing while beginning a covert action that ultimately aspired to overthrow the regime. Reports surrounding a failed plot in 1996 were chastening, but momentum to get rid of Saddam Hussein was gathering, with the US Congress pushing the Clinton administration along that road.[23] Under the terms of the Iraq Liberation Act of 1998, some US$97 million was made available to support covert action projects, especially the mobilization of Iraqi exiles and the development of contacts in Iraq.[24] In early 1999, Clinton also appointed Frank Ricciardone as the special coordinator for covert action.[25] The CIA and Iraqi opposition were not expected to deliver results anytime soon, but there was a ratcheting up of US covert activities, including a more systematic attempt to make use of the UNSCOM monitoring system. Information from UNSCOM inspectors rapidly found its way to the United States, and it also seems more than likely that the CIA and allied intelligence agencies had agents among UNSCOM staff in Iraq. Certainly, the Iraqis would come to believe that some UNSCOM staff were involved in spying related to tracking Saddam Hussein and other key figures. Not surprisingly, Saddam and his friends objected to this—thus the subsequent Iraqi sensitivity about the inspection of Saddam's presidential palaces.

The mounting conflict over the containment regime would come to a head in 1997 and 1998. With the Iraqi regime increasingly aware that regime change was on the US agenda, Saddam embarked on a policy of noncompliance aimed at forcing concessions. In December 1997, Iraq declared that eight presidential sites were now regarded as sovereign territory and no longer accessible for inspection. The Iraqis also wanted the suspension of U2 spyplane overflights and that US and British inspectors be removed from UNSCOM teams and replaced by more French and Russians inspectors.[26] The US responded with a buildup of forces, but UN Secretary-General Kofi Annan was able to broker a deal in February 1998 in which Iraq ended its obstruction in return for new restrictions on the inspection of presidential palaces and the appointment of a UN special representative to oversee the inspection of contentious sites. Visits to eight presidential palaces would require prior notification.

The February 1998 deal on inspections did not hold. By the autumn of that year, Iraq was again challenging inspections. UNSCOM inspectors were withdrawn on 16 December 1998, and hours later the United States and Great Britain launched a nationwide bombing campaign, Operation Desert Fox (16–19 December 1998). The stated purpose of Desert Fox was to target WMD-related and ballistic missile–related facilities with a view toward persuading Saddam to concede to UN demands on inspections, although by this stage there was little Iraqi WMD capacity left to bomb. But the subtext to Desert Fox was different in targeting members of the Iraqi security forces. In later written testimony to the National Commission on Terrorist Attacks upon the United States (the 9/11 Commission), former US secretary of defense William Cohen submitted that an estimated 1,400 members of the Special Republican Guard and Republican Guard had been killed and that the Special Republican Guard headquarters and other intelligence-related command-and-control facilities were destroyed.[27] Killing Republican Guard troops had little to do with enforcing UNSCOM inspections. Indeed, one of the consequences of Desert Fox was to cause the final collapse of UNSCOM monitoring. The actual effects of Desert Fox coincided with the objectives of covert action. Saddam's core security apparatus was weakened, and the bombing was a show of force and intent toward previously loyal Iraqi commanders and members of the Iraqi opposition.

Although Desert Fox may have conveyed a number of important messages, it was ultimately counterproductive. Few people sympathized with Saddam Hussein, but Desert Fox produced a wave of sympathy for the country. As mainstream Arab states sought to demonstrate solidarity with Iraqis, the isolation of Iraq was further reduced. Moreover, with any such bombing going well beyond the UN mandates, it fed into the ongoing debate about the legality of US and British actions. Indeed, following air strikes in February 2001, Russia, China, and France openly spoke of the attacks as being illegal. Saudi Arabia and Syria, too, signed a rare joint statement that condemned the bombing and demanded that it stop.[28] Saudi Arabia had long ceased to permit US forces on its soil to bomb targets in Iraq.

Thus, by the time of Desert Fox the politics of containment and coercive force against Iraq was increasingly difficult to sustain. The Iraqi situation was, as Robin Wright observed in 1998, an open-ended morass with no end in sight: "How had it come to this?"[29] In fact, following the counterproductive bombing offensive in February 2001, the United States and Great Britain would rein in their military action and instead seek to revive sanctions with the idea of so-called smart sanctions. The smart sanctions plan aimed to exclude civilian goods—in theory, lessening the suffering of ordinary Iraqi civilians—while tightening controls on goods with military applications, as well as oil smuggling. Seeing it as an attempt to breathe new life into sanctions, the Iraqis objected. So did other states, including Russia, which went on to block the passage of smart sanctions in the UN Security Council in summer 2001.[30] In short, the policy of containing Iraq, much less rolling it back, had hit a wall by summer 2001. The control regime on Iraq did not finish in an absolute sense, but it was in ongoing decay.

Growing Resistance to the US Alliance System

Before the Iraqi invasion of Kuwait in 1990, it was widely understood that to put US troops into the Arabian peninsula was to risk a backlash. The Gulf States were ultimately dependent on the United States for security, but the regimes had always sought to construct a Chinese wall to conceal that fact. The sensitivities were particularly acute in Saudi Arabia, where the idea of infidel troops acting as the protectors of the "land of the two holy mosques of Mecca and Medina" was regarded as outrageous among a body of Islamic-inspired opinion. The Gulf War broke the boundaries, and in its aftermath the United States maintained a postwar establishment of more than 20,000 personnel in the Gulf, including in Saudi Arabia. The line had been crossed and, sure enough, the backlash was on its way. The garrisoning of US troops in Saudi Arabia was important because it intersected with the preoccupations of a small but significant group of Islamic militants who had the money, ideas, and contacts do something different: They were to emerge under the banner of Al-Qaida.[31] In their refuges in Sudan and Afghanistan, Osama bin Laden and Ayman al-Zawahiri declared war not only on Saudi Arabia but also on its American backers.

As the global insurgency led by Al-Qaida and its allies emerged during the 1990s, it was marked by a series of bombings, including an attack on the World Trade Center in New York in 1993.[32] However, it was the bombings of US embassies in Dar-es-Salaam, Tanzania, and Nairobi, Kenya, on 7 August 1998 that really marked the first shots fired in the war. The bombings caused substantial destruction and killed more than 250 people, including nine Americans. They catapulted Al-Qaida onto the global stage and also contributed to a growing sense that Washington's ability to manage the security of the Middle East and Muslim world was drifting.

When the Clinton administration ran through the military options in the aftermath of the East Africa bombings, none promised a decisive effect. With full-scale regime change in Afghanistan ruled out as an option, US strategists came up with limited cruise missile strikes on Al-Qaida personnel and assets in Sudan and Afghanistan. The problem was that Al-Qaida had little in the way of fixed assets. Bin Laden and his deputies were also difficult to target because their security was good, they moved around frequently, and it could take more than six hours from incoming intelligence to missile strike. In the end, the United States launched Operation Infinite Reach, a wave of seventy-five cruise missiles at targets in Afghanistan and Sudan. Training camps were hit, but bin Laden and his colleagues escaped. The only substantial hit was on the Shifa pharmaceutical plant in Sudan—thought to be linked to bin Laden—but what effect it actually had (beyond destroying much of Sudan's production of modern medicine) was the subject of some debate.

Little was achieved through limited air strikes, and the subsequent feeling in Washington was that some expensive missiles had been sent to essentially "pound sand."[33] Thus, President Clinton's national security team began to develop a more sustained approach. Specifically, the CIA was authorized to develop a covert action plan in Pakistan and Afghanistan that included training sixty local paramilitaries to observe and track Al-Qaida leaders. The CIA station in Islamabad built up its infrastructure—something that would prove valuable later on—but the project had to be downshifted after General Pervez Musharraf's successful military coup in Pakistan.[34] Pakistan's army and its Directorate for Inter-Services Intelligence (ISI) were far too close to the Taliban for comfort. The CIA would continue to develop ideas, notably the use of Predator unmanned aerial vehicles to conduct surveillance and strike missions, but both the CIA and the US military exhibited some risk-averseness.

According to a later account by the White House's counterterrorism coordinator, Richard Clarke, during the last year of the Clinton administration the deputies committee of the National Security Council formulated a plan to contain and roll back Al-Qaida. If Clarke is to be believed, the plan was somehow lost in transition from President Bill Clinton to George W. Bush.[35] It took time for the Bush administration to get up and running, and time was wasted especially during August 2001. The new Bush administration also appeared to prioritize the bigger issues of missile defense and China over Al-Qaida.[36] Thus it was not until 4 September 2001 that the Principals Committee of the National Security Council met to discuss the plan, and it was not until 10 September 2001 that a National Security Presidential Directive was ready to go to the president.[37] Much had still to be done to implement any roll-back of Al-Qaida, notably relating to the requirement for new authorities and funding. In the subsequent 9/11 Commission hearings, a number of the key figures in the Bush administration retorted (against Clarke) that the plan was delayed because a more systematic strategy was being formulated.[38] President Bush was "tired of swatting flies," that was, he was waiting for an approach that did more than just respond one attack at a time. To develop a sustained approach, getting Pakistan on board was crucial, but this was frustratingly slow, with key members of Bush's team having to make representations throughout 2001. Whatever the truth, it all came too late. The intelligence was in, but it was missed. Al-Qaida was out there, and it was left with sufficient freedom to operate.

The Moment of Criticality: 9/11 and Its Aftermath

Around 2000–2001, the ability of the United States to shore up its decaying security architecture in the Middle East was diminishing. If President Clinton was stumped as to what to do about the situation, it was not for want of trying. George W. Bush was less inclined to even try, and his administration perceptibly stepped back from the ongoing difficulties of managing the failing Arab-Israeli peace process, the containment of Iraq, and the rollback of Al-Qaida (although this is disputed). Pillar by pillar, the US security architecture in the Middle East was faltering. The decaying system finally went critical in the most spectacular way on 11 September 2001. The sight of the two towers of the World Trade Center falling into dust became an iconic wakeup call; it was the sight of a dangerous new world in which America was being stalked.

Every calculus changed after 9/11. President Bush declared the US war on terror and, framing it in terms of a battle between good and evil, would unleash the most bellicose neoconservative elements in his administration.[39] Bush now proclaimed a doctrine of US primacy, preemption, and offensive defense.[40] The result was that the United States would not only set out to destroy Al-Qaida but also do something more fundamental about the problems in the Middle East. Shoring up the old security architecture would not suffice; the foundation had to be rebuilt. Thus, the agenda of the war on terror would soon sprawl and would become synonymous with an attempt to use military power to reconstruct the US security architecture in the Middle East.

Afghanistan was the first front in the new war, but this was not enough for the Bush administration. Thus, following the overthrow of the Taliban in Afghanistan in late 2001, US terror policy undertook a major shift in direction. In his State of the Union speech on 29 January 2002, President Bush identified new enemies and made it clear that something had to be done about their malign intentions. In a renowned passage, Bush proclaimed that

> States like these [Iraq, Iran, and North Korea], and their terrorist allies, constitute an axis of evil, arming to threaten the peace of the world. By seeking weapons of mass destruction, these regimes pose a grave and growing danger. They could provide these arms to terrorists, giving them the means to match their hatred. They could attack our allies or attempt to blackmail the United States. In any of these cases, the price of indifference would be catastrophic

... all nations should know: America will do what is necessary to ensure our nation's security. We'll be deliberate, yet time is not on our side. I will not wait on events, while dangers gather. I will not stand by, as peril draws closer and closer. The United States of America will not permit the world's most dangerous regimes to threaten us with the world's most destructive weapons.[41]

Bush's reference to the "axis of evil" gave the appearance of a new grand mission in world affairs, but first and foremost Bush's people were thinking about Iraq.[42] Although the theoretical possibility of WMD leakage could not be denied, in reality it was extremely unlikely that the Iraqi regime would ever pass WMDs to the likes of Al-Qaida. Apart from profound ideological differences, bin Laden's militants were hardly trustworthy surrogates, and plausible deniability was unlikely to be achieved on Saddam's part if he were, in fact, to transfer WMDs or WMD technology to a terrorist group. Nevertheless, the precautionary principle now served to justify a case for a US-led preemptive war against Iraq.

Beside the reality of US preparations for war (see Chapter 6), there was a distinct escalation of US rhetoric from mid-2002, with Vice President Dick Cheney's speech to an audience of veterans on 28 August 2002 seeming to be a point of no return. Cheney conjured up a dark future of a WMD-armed Iraq and a situation in which "Saddam Hussein could then be expected to seek domination of the entire Middle East, take control of a great portion of the world's energy supplies, directly threaten America's friends throughout the region, and subject the United States or any other nation to nuclear blackmail."[43]

The portrayal of such an all-powerful Iraq verged on the ridiculous, but it reflected the kind of worst-case thinking that the Bush administration was successfully able to sell to Americans. By the time of President Bush's speech to the UN General Assembly on 12 September 2002, the list of US demands that Saddam Hussein had to meet "if the Iraqi regime wanted peace" were so long, uncompromising, and humiliating that Saddam could not possibly accept them.[44] The reality was that the Bush administration was now intent on overthrowing the Iraqi regime, and the principal focus of US diplomacy thereafter was not to achieve a peaceful settlement but to execute a war plan.

So why was the Bush administration so intent on widening the war on terror? Although concerns about Saddam Hussein's irresponsibility and WMD leakage were real enough in the minds of Bush's national security team, the move to Iraq encompassed other goals, although it must be said that proving intent remains very difficult. Whether intended or not, invading Iraq was capable of fulfilling the longstanding desire among some of Bush's people for regime-change in Iraq; fulfilling what the neoconservatives viewed as America's exceptional role to make the world a better place; and rebuilding the failing US security architecture in the Middle East.[45] Regime change offered (again, whether intended or not) just so many potential benefits to the United States and its allies; indeed, it appeared to open the way to an entirely new geopolitics in the Middle East.⁴⁶ Taking down Saddam Hussein and occupying Iraq promised to

- Preempt a medium-term threat to US allies in the Middle East, especially Israel and Kuwait.
- Break up the recalcitrant bloc of anti-American states—Iran, Iraq, and Syria—and thereby make it easier to isolate and pressurize Iran and Syria. Subsequent military operations against these two powers were an option. In fact, Syria's position in Lebanon would become untenable.
- Enable the full withdrawal of US forces from Saudi Arabia and thereby undercut Islamist agitation about their presence in the Kingdom.
- Provide a demonstration of US power and bolster US authority among its Arab allies, especially Egypt and Saudi Arabia.
- Increase the flow of Iraqi oil into the world oil market and boost the Middle Eastern economy. Additionally, it would open new economic opportunities in Iraq for US businesses, especially Big Oil and contracting interests.
- Transform Iraq into an entry point for liberal political and economic reformism that might serve to encourage broader liberalization of the Middle East.

Thus, the Iraq option was not just about a war against terror. Indeed, there was little credible evidence that Saddam Hussein had meaningful contacts with Al-Qaida leaders, much less that he had formed an alliance.⁴⁷ Nor was the Iraq option principally about disarming Iraq of its residual WMD capacity. If the main aim had been to prevent the development of WMDs and keep Iraq under a tolerable degree of containment, any reasonable assessment of costs and benefits would surely have pointed to a strategy of UNMOVIC-plus inspection and reinforced coercive diplomacy. Although the Clinton-era containment regime had been in trouble, 9/11 breathed new life into it. Other members of the UN Security Council now accepted that the situation was different, and Iraq itself had also agreed to have UNMOVIC inspectors back; they returned to roaming widely across Iraq in search of weapons stockpiles and military-industrial facilities. However, for the Bush administration, settling for a UNMOVIC-supervised disarmament of Iraq would have been a lesser outcome. The administration did not trust the UN disarmament regime, and giving up the war option also meant forgoing the range of broader opportunities that lay ahead in the wake of regime change.⁴⁸ To the extent that WMDs figured in prewar diplomacy, it was not really as a genuine dispute capable of resolution but rather as a rationale to justify—for good or ill—the decision to go to war. The reality was that the Bush administration not only wanted to disarm Iraq; it wanted to subject Iraq to its will.

Notes

1. National Security Directive 54, 15 January 1991. Available at the website of the Presidential Library of George H. W. Bush, http://bushlibrary/tamu.edu/research/nsd/NSD/NSD%2054/0001.pdf.
2. See Daniel Byman, Kenneth Pollack, and Matthew Waxman, "Coercing Saddam Hussein: Lessons from the Past," *Survival* 40, no. 3 (Autumn 1998): 127–151.
3. UN Security Council Resolution 687 of 3 April 1991. Available at the website of the United Nations, www.un.org/scres/1991/scres91/htm.
4. See UN Security Council Resolution 706 of 15 August 1991. Available at the website of the United Nations, www.un.org/scres/1991/scres91/htm.
5. Anthony Lake was assistant to the president for national security. Anthony Lake, "Confronting the Backlash States," *Foreign Affairs* 73 no. 2 (March–April 1994): 45–55.
6. Ibid., 49–50.
7. UNSCR 242 of 22 November 1967, www.un.org/documents/sc/res/1967/scres67.htm; UNSCR 338 of 22 October 1973, www.un.org/documents/sc/res/1973/scres73.htm.
8. Martin Indyk, "Back to the Bazaar," *Foreign Affairs* 81, no. 1 (January–February 2002): 75–88.
9. James Petras and Morris Morley, "Contesting Hegemons: US-French Relations in the 'New World Order,'" *Review of International Studies* 26, no. 1 (January 2000): 65.
10. See Richard A. Clarke, "The Almost War," chapter 5 in Clarke, *Against All Enemies: Inside America's War on Terror* (New York: Simon and Schuster, 2004), xiii, 101–131. Clarke was the coordinator for counterterrorism, National Security Council.
11. Byman, Pollack, and Waxman, "Coercing Saddam Hussein," 127–151.
12. Toby Dodge, "Storming the Desert," *The World Today* 58, no. 4 (April 2002): 5–6; John Mueller and Karl Mueller, "Sanctions of Mass Destruction," *Foreign Affairs* 78, no. 3 (May–June 1999): 43–51; for a more substantial discussion of the impact of sanctions see Tim Niblock, *Pariah States and Sanctions in the Middle East: Iraq, Libya, Sudan* (Boulder: Lynne Rienner, 2002).
13. Report based on a survey carried out in Iraq between February and May 1999 by UNICEF and the World Health Organization. Report released by UNICEF on 12 August 1999. Eric Hoskins (MD), "The Impact of Sanctions: A Study of UNICEF's Perspective," www.unicef.org/newsline/ 99pr29.htm.
14. Comments made by the French foreign minister, Hubert Vedrine, on 2 August 2000. Reported in the *Middle East Economic Digest* (MEED), 11 August 2000, 3.
15. Judith S. Yaphe, "Iraq: The Exception to the Rule," *Washington Quarterly* 24, no. 1 (Winter 2001): 125–137, esp. 134–135; Robin Wright, "America's Iraq Policy: How Did It Come to This?" *Washington Quarterly* 21, no. 3 (Summer 1998): 53–70, esp. 62–63.
16. Iraq Survey Group, "Regime Finance and Procurement," *Comprehensive Report of the Special Advisor (Charles Duelfer) to the Director of Central Intelligence on Iraq's WMD* (findings of the Iraq Survey Group), 30 September 2004, www.cia.gov/reports/iraq_wmd_ 2004/index.html.
17. Chapter 3, "The Current Position: 1998–2002," *Iraq's Weapons of Mass Destruction: The Assessment of the British Government.* Available at www.number10.gov.uk/ Page271.asp.
18. UN News Center, "Annan Calls for States to Act, Pledges UN Reforms," 27 October 2005, www.un.org/apps/news/story.asp?newsID=16386&Cr=iraq&Cr1=oil.
19. Iraq Survey Group, "Regime Finance and Procurement," 2.

20. Economic Intelligence Unit, "Economic Structure," *Country Report: Iraq* (London: February 2001), 5–6.

21. UN Security Council Resolution 986 of 14 April 1995, www.un.org/Docs/scres/1995/scres95.htm.

22. UN Security Council Resolution 1284 of 17 December 1999, www.un.org/Docs/scres/1999/sc99.htm.

23. Wright, "America's Iraq Policy," 68.

24. Toby Ash, "In Search of a New Consensus on Iraq," *Middle East Economic Digest* 43, no. 4 (29 January 1999), 3.

25. F. Gregory Gause III, "Getting It Backward on Iraq," *Foreign Affairs* 78, no. 3 (May–June 1999): 54–65.

26. Byman, Pollack, and Waxman, "Coercing Saddam Hussein," 140.

27. From the *Written Statement of William S. Cohen to the National Commission on Terrorist Attacks upon the United States* (Eighth Hearing, 23–24 March 2004), 20. Available at the website of the National Commission on Terrorists Attacks upon the United States, http://govinfo.library.unt.edu/911/hearings/hearing8.htm, 20.

28. Brian Whitaker, "U.S. Urges Syria to Be Tougher on Iraq," *The Guardian*, 27 February 2001, 18.

29. Wright, "America's Iraq Policy," 53.

30. "Iraq Revels in 'Smart Sanctions' Debacle," *Middle East Economic Digest* 45 (13 July 2001): 2.

31. The issue of Zionist-Crusader occupation was prominent in the two key statements of bin Laden that declared the distant jihad: the "Declaration of War Against the Americans Occupying the Land of the Two Holy Places" of 23 August 1996, and the "Declaration of the World Islamic Front" of 22 February 1998. See Ahmed Hashim, "The World According to Usama Bin Laden," *Naval War College Review* 54, no. 4 (Autumn 2001): 12–35, esp. 22–29.

32. Steven Simon and Daniel Benjamin, "The Terror," *Survival* 43, no. 4 (Winter 2001): 5–18, 5.

33. Bob Woodward, *Bush at War* (New York: Simon and Schuster, 2002), chapter 8, 123.

34. Ibid., 5–6.

35. Clarke, "Before and After September 11," chapter 10 in *Against All Enemies*, 227–246.

36. Ibid., 196, 230–234.

37. Ibid., 26, 237; see also Woodward, *Bush at War*, 35–36.

38. Statement of the US Secretary of State, Colin Powell, to the 9/11 Commission, Eighth Hearing, 23 March 2004, http://govinfo.library.unt.edu/911/hearings/hearing8.htm; Statement of the US Secretary of Defense, Donald Rumsfeld, to the 9/11 Commission, Eighth Hearing, 23 March 2004, http://govinfo.library.unt.edu/911/hearings/hearing8.htm; Statement of the US National Security Advisor, Condoleezza Rice, to the 9/11 Commission, Ninth Hearing, 8 April 2004, http://govinfo.library.unt.edu/911/hearings/hearing9.htm.

39. The administration of George W. Bush was composed of a spectrum of American conservatives: traditional conservatives, social conservatives, and the Christian right, but the most dynamic force in foreign and defense policymaking was a distinctive group of so-called neoconservatives and allied traditional conservatives. Dick Cheney was the vice president; Donald Rumsfeld, Paul Wolfowitz, and Douglas Feith dominated the Department of Defense; John Bolton was undersecretary of state for arms control and international affairs; Richard Pearle, William Kristol, Louis Libby, J. D. Crouch, Francis Fukuyama, and Zalmay Khalilzad served in various executive, advisory, or inspirational capacities. The neoconservatives thought on a global and historic scale.

Originating from an intellectual cadre at the University of Chicago in the 1960s, the neoconservatives argued that liberal democracy must have a moral mission and that that mission should encompass America's "exceptional" role in world history to lead humanity toward democracy and free markets. During the Clinton years, the neoconservatives had refined a portfolio of policies within the context of a number of conservative publications and think tanks, most notably the American Enterprise Institute and its Project for the New American Century. They believed in American leadership of the world and were skeptical about the usefulness of international organizations if that involved multilateralizing decisionmaking and limiting the ability of the United States to act decisively. US leadership required moral clarity. The was on terror was seen as an historic opportunity to demonstrate this moral clarity. For further insight into neoconservatives, see the website of the Project for the New American Century, www.newamericancentury.org/; see also Stefan Halper and Jonathan Clarke, *America Alone: The Neoconservatives and the Global Order* (Cambridge: Cambridge University Press, 2004).

40. See Colin Dueck, "Ideas and Alternatives in American Grand Strategy," *Review of International Studies* 30, no. 4 (October 2004): 511–535, esp. 527.

41. George W. Bush, State of the Union address, 29 January 2002, American Rhetoric Online Speech Bank, www.americanrhetoric.com/speeches/stateoftheunion2002.htm.

42. According to Bob Woodward, citing US National Security Adviser Condoleezza Rice, the generalizing concept of the "axis of evil" was partly promoted by the Bush administration because it avoided singling out Iraq at a time when secret war planning (Polo Step) against it was already under way. Bob Woodward, *Plan of Attack* (London: Simon and Schuster UK, 2004), 87.

43. Comments made by US Vice President Dick Cheney to the 103rd National Convention of Veterans, 26 August 2002, American Rhetoric Online Speech Bank, www.americanrhetoric.com/speeches/dickcheney103rdvfw.htm.

44. In his speech to the UN General Assembly on 12 September 2002, President Bush made it clear that "if the Iraqi regime wishes peace, it will immediately and unconditionally forswear, disclose, and remove or destroy all weapons of mass destruction, long-range missiles, and all related material. If the Iraqi regime wishes peace, it will immediately end all support for terrorism and act to suppress it, as all states are required to do by U.N. Security Council resolutions. If the Iraqi regime wishes peace, it will cease persecution of its civilian population, including Shi'a, Sunnis, Kurds, Turkomans, and others, again as required by Security Council resolutions. If the Iraqi regime wishes peace, it will release or account for all Gulf War personnel whose fate is still unknown. It will return the remains of any who are deceased, return stolen property, accept liability for losses resulting from the invasion of Kuwait, and fully cooperate with international efforts to resolve these issues, as required by Security Council resolutions. If the Iraqi regime wishes peace, it will immediately end all illicit trade outside the oil-for-food program. It will accept U.N. administration of funds from that program, to ensure that the money is used fairly and promptly for the benefit of the Iraqi people. If all these steps are taken, it will signal a new openness and accountability in Iraq. And it could open the prospect of the United Nations helping to build a government that represents all Iraqis—a government based on respect for human rights, economic liberty, and internationally supervised elections." President George W. Bush, speech to the UN General Assembly, 12 September 2002, www.un.org.webcast/ga/57/statements/020912usaE.htm.

45. Many of Bush's national security team had a longstanding desire to see the overthrow of Saddam Hussein. Many of its key figures had used the platform of the Project for the New American Century to sign an open letter to President Bill Clinton on 26 January 1998 arguing that the policy of containment and inspections had failed

and that "The only acceptable strategy is one that eliminates the possibility that Iraq will be able to use or threaten to use weapons of mass destruction. In the near term, this means a willingness to undertake military action as diplomacy is clearly failing. In the long term, it means removing Saddam Hussein and his regime from power. That now needs to become the aim of American foreign policy. . . . We believe that the US has the authority under existing UN resolutions to take the necessary steps, including military steps, to protect our vital interest in the Gulf. In any case, American policy cannot continue to be crippled by a misguided insistence on unanimity in the UN Security Council. We urge you to act decisively. If you act now to end the threat of WMD against the US or its allies, you will be acting in the most fundamental national security interests of the country. If we accept a course of weakness and drift, we put our interests and our future at risk." Those signing the letter included Richard Armitage, John Bolton, Francis Fukuyama, Robert Kagan, William Kristol, Richard Perle, Donald Rumsfeld, Peter W. Rodman, Paul Wolfowitz, and Zalmay Khalilzad. The letter is available online at www.newamericancentury.org/iraqclintonletter.htm; see also Tom Quiggin, "Marching to War: The Invasion of Iraq—A Plan Fourteen Years in the Making," *RUSI Journal* 148, no. 5 (October 2003): 60–65.

46. See also the reasons cited by Richard Clarke (coordinator for counterterrorism, National Security Council): Clean up the mess left by first Bush administration; improve Israel's strategic position by eliminating a large hostile enemy; create an Arab democracy to serve as a model; permit the withdrawal of US forces from Saudi Arabia; and create another friendly source of oil for US market and reduce dependency on Saudi Arabia. Clarke, "Right War, Wrong War," chapter 11 in *Against All Enemies,* 247–287, esp. 265.

47. Clarke, *Against All Enemies,* 33, 268–270.

48. The Bush administration was not really interested in, or trusted, UN monitoring and disarmament. On 19 September 2002, Donald Rumsfeld told the US Senate Armed Services Committee that "even the most intrusive inspection regime would have difficulty getting at all of his weapons of mass destruction. Many of his WMD capabilities are mobile. They can be hidden from inspectors no matter how intrusive. He has vast underground networks and facilities and sophisticated denial and deception techniques. . . . There is a place in this world for inspections. . . . They tend not to be as effective in uncovering deceptions and violations when the target is determined not to disarm and to try to deceive. And Iraq's record of the past decade shows that they want weapons of mass destruction and are determined to continue developing them." Written Testimony by the US Secretary of State for Defense, Donald Rumsfeld, 19 September 2002, http://armed-services.senate.gov/testimony.cfm?wit_id=187&id=442.

5
The War in Afghanistan

Bringing those responsible for 9/11 to account meant going to Afghanistan. Although in some accounts there was a degree of reticence among President Bush's national security team about a campaign in Afghanistan—with some at the Pentagon led by Donald Rumsfeld already thinking about Iraq and worried about getting bogged down in central Asia—Bush realized that the Global War on Terror really had to start by striking at those most culpable.[1] The political context was permissive for a war in Afghanistan. By any stretch of the imagination, military action was justified under the right to self-defense outlined in article 51 of the United Nations Charter, and this right was affirmed by the passage of UN Security Council Resolutions 1368 and 1373.[2] The United States did not need to press for specific authorization for the use of force. The overwhelming consensus across the international community was that something had to be done about the Taliban regime and its Qaida allies in Afghanistan.

For US military planners, however, Afghanistan was a challenging proposition. A developed war plan did not exist, and military planners were under intense pressure to get on with it. The geography was difficult. Afghanistan is isolated and mountainous. The country is 300 miles from the Indian Ocean and 700 miles from the nearest major base in Oman. B-1 and B-52 bombers could fly long-haul missions from the Indian Ocean base of Diego Garcia as well as from further afield, and US aircraft carrier forces could reach it. The carrier *Kitty Hawk* was also pressed into service as an amphibious base. But none of this was ideal. Pakistan was the obvious place to base operations, but although President Pervez Musharraf was induced to go along with the war on terror, the Bush administration was aware that his political situation was finely balanced.[3] If anti-Qaida operations were to be sustained in the medium to long terms, Musharraf had to be shielded from too obvious an involvement at the outset. A light footprint in Pakistan was deemed sensible. Thus, it was vital to gain access to the central Asian states of Uzbekistan and Tajikistan. Russia acquiesced. Getting the relevant permissions from Uzbekistan took some time—it wanted to talk about various aid and security commitments—and it would take a visit by Donald Rumsfeld himself on 4 October 2001 to get things cleared for US humanitarian and search-and-rescue operations.

With access to Afghanistan being such a problem, US military planners were encouraged to think about going light and being innovative. Even so, according to Bob Woodward's account of administration politics during the war, *Bush at War,* the US military was slow to present a plan, notably in the key weekend meetings at Camp David on 15 September 2001, with the result that the CIA stepped into the breach.[4] Director of Central Intelligence George Tenet, in association with deputy director John McLaughlin, as well as the director of the Counterterrorism Center, Cofer Black, came forward with an alternative to a conventional military campaign, partly stemming from the ongoing covert action planning since the East Africa bombings in 1998. The CIA had an existing presence orchestrated from its station in Islamabad, and the agency had already developed a network analysis and target list. CIA agents and paramilitaries were familiar with the landscape in a way that the US military was not.

Getting among Afghan tribal politics and tipping the balance was the key operational-level concept of the CIA plan. The plan embodied three elements. First, advice, money, and equipment were to be channeled into Afghanistan to harness local forces that could be turned against Al-Qaida and the Taliban; this involved mobilizing the armed opposition of the Northern Alliance, mostly composed of Uzbek and Tajik minorities in the north. Second, the CIA argued that Arab and other foreign fighters represented the backbone of the Taliban military—it was the force that cast a disciplining shadow over Taliban conscripts—and so should receive particular attention in targeting. Third, the Taliban was an alliance of Pushtun tribal forces in southern and eastern Afghanistan, and the United States needed to develop a southern strategy to get among that alliance and break it up. A mixture of carrots and sticks might be used to detach Pushtun groups from the Taliban, although even as the United States began military operations in October 2001 it was very unclear what the southern strategy was in practice.

The centrality of the Northern Alliance to CIA strategy was not without problems. Relying so heavily on the Northern Alliance was bound to sacrifice a degree of control. The Northern Alliance was known for divisions, and its leading personality, Ahmad Shah Masoud, was assassinated by Arab jihadists two days prior to 9/11. The warlords who made up the Northern Alliance also had a record of criminality and human rights abuses, as well as of being variously allied with regional powers like Russia, India, and Iran. Moreover, a strategy that promoted ethnic Tajiks and Uzbeks would struggle to appeal to the dominant tribal grouping, the Pushtuns in the south and east. Nevertheless, with the US military slow to come up with a plan in the time frame envisaged, the CIA promised quick and cost-effective action.

Beyond the inevitable turf war between the Pentagon and CIA about who was running the Afghan campaign, there was also initially some debate at the highest levels about strategic purpose. Two potential options presented themselves. If the principal aim was to disrupt and destroy Al-Qaida, then it might be possible to do so without going to the extra trouble of actually overthrowing the Taliban regime; Colin Powell and Donald Rumsfeld appear to have been willing to think about this possibility.[5] If a distinction was made between Al-Qaida and the Taliban, the campaign might be conducted more persuasively, with the application of force less about decisively destroying the Taliban than about inducing them to give up Al-Qaida. By contrast, the CIA's analysis was that no distinction could be made. Al-Qaida and the Taliban were too intertwined, and notwithstanding the reservations of Taliban leader Mullah Muhammad Omar about some of Al-Qaida's activities, he would never give up his Islamic compatriots to the United States. The CIA believed that Omar would accept developments with fatalism. In this analysis, persuasive war techniques were irrelevant, with the only option being to deploy decisive force in order to completely overthrow the Taliban regime and then mop up the remnants.

Although the CIA's analysis ultimately prevailed, and the aim of overthrowing the Taliban was more or less agreed to by early October 2001, a persuasive-war approach may have retained some inertia in the opening phase of the campaign. President Bush was still issuing demands to the Taliban to give up bin Laden even after US air attacks were initiated on 7 October 2001. Donald Rumsfeld would also articulate the purpose of the campaign in restrained terms. At a press conference on 7 October, Rumsfeld set out six aims designed to ratchet up the pressure and gradually change the balance of power in Afghanistan: send a message to the Taliban; acquire intelligence; develop relations with anti-Taliban groups; strike at terrorist groups; alter the military balance over time; and provide humanitarian relief.[6] US airpower was also to initially focus on Taliban air defense and infrastructure targets that were largely symbolic and seemingly more appropriate to a persuasive campaign than supporting the CIA's effort to marshal decisive force by means of supporting Northern Alliance forces. In fact, US bombing to support the decisive option would not be properly focused until much later in October.

The Conduct of the Afghan Campaign

The CIA was first into action. The first CIA team, Jawbreaker, made up of ten men (case officers, communication specialists, a Navy SEAL, and a medic) flew into the Panjshir Valley about seventy miles north of Kabul on 26 September and quickly began to liaise with the forces of the Northern Alliance commander, Mohammad Fahim.[7] Jawbreaker was followed by a number of other teams (see Figure 5.1) that set about liaising with other local leaders and preparing follow-on operations. Jawbreaker got on with preparing air strips, arranging the delivery

Figure 5.1 Map of the War in Afghanistan, 2001–2002

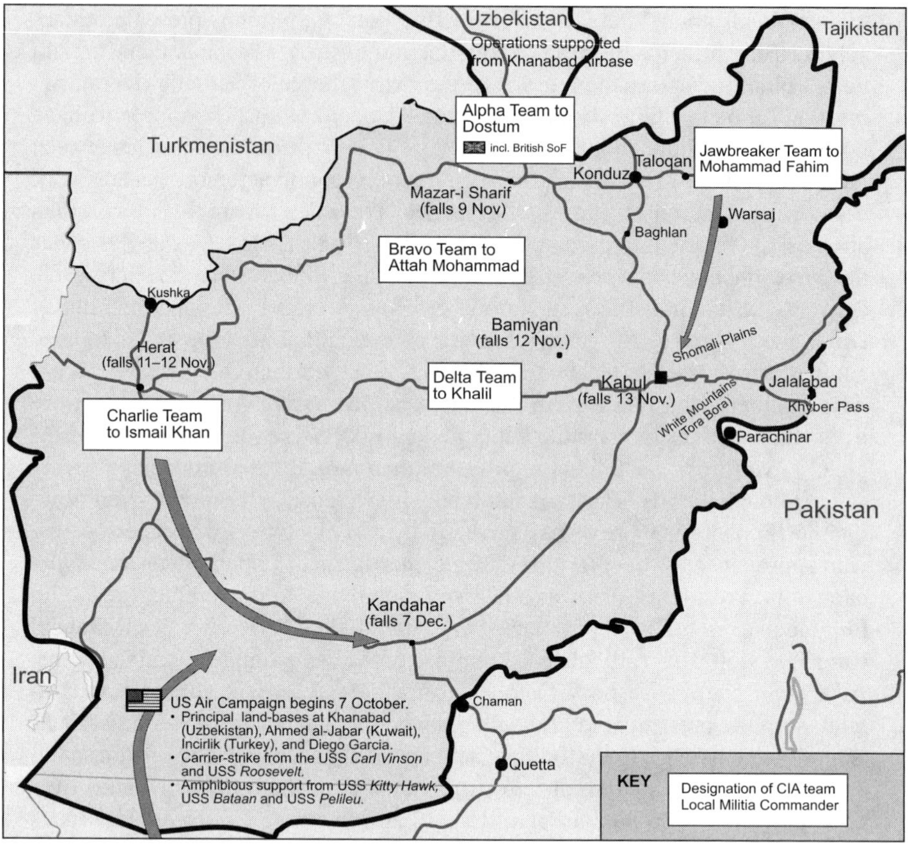

of aid and war materials, paving the way for the arrival of US Special Operations Forces teams, gathering intelligence for future military operations, and beginning to tip the balance of tribal politics. The CIA moved lightly. Its principal weapons were satellite phones and suitcases of money, and with little more than $70 million in direct cash outlays the CIA established the infrastructure for the coming intervention.[8] In contrast, the US military took another three weeks to get on the ground.[9] Notwithstanding a demonstrative airdrop by US Army Rangers on a deserted airfield near Kandahar on 19 October, it was not until 20 October that US special forces (A-Team 555, "Triple Nickel") came to support Jawbreaker. Tensions between the Pentagon and the CIA persisted, with Donald Rumsfeld reportedly frustrated by the pace and risk-averseness of his military planners and irritated at the way the CIA had hijacked the campaign.[10]

On the ground, the initial focus of the CIA and special forces was to push the Taliban back from Mazar-i-Sharif (a hub of the roads system in northern Afghanistan) as a way of opening a supply bridge from Uzbekistan. Ammunition, uniforms, and other materials were already being assembled in Uzbekistan. It was not long, however, before CIA teams on the ground identified the Shomali Plains, just north of Kabul, as the enemy's center of gravity.[11] The analysis was that once Taliban forces on the Shomali Plains were defeated, everyone would know that the Taliban could no longer defend Kabul—with the effect that the alliance of Pushtun forces behind it would likely begin to disintegrate. Such an analysis was to be vindicated by events on the ground.

Meanwhile, the US bombing campaign that began on 7 October—Operation Enduring Freedom—was initially focused on the Taliban's air defense system, communications system, and logistics infrastructure, as well as on a long list of underground systems (read: caves) along the Afghanistan-Pakistan border that may or may not have been occupied by Al-Qaida fighters. In retrospect, US air planners were not entirely on top of things. The air campaign quickly ran out of strategic-type targets, and the bombing of caves was a hit-or-miss affair. In fact, it was not long before the air campaign had hit something of a plateau, with corresponding grumblings in the US and Western media. Matters were not helped by the bombing of a Red Cross/Red Crescent food distribution warehouse, not to mention a number of other incidents in which significant numbers of civilians were killed.[12] With the Taliban largely intact, few local leaders outside the north were prepared to come over. Meanwhile, the Northern Alliance was becoming disillusioned, refusing to take the offensive without more direct air support. The Northern Alliance's military commander in the Panshjir Valley, Mohammad Fahim, reportedly even went back to Tajikistan in protest, prompting brief consideration in the Pentagon about an outright Americanization of the war.[13]

What was required to fulfill the potential of the CIA's plan was more focused bombing on the Taliban front lines opposing Northern Alliance forces in the north and, then, on the Shomali Plains. However, it would appear that it was not until the arrival of increasing numbers of US special forces later in October that the message eventually got through to US Central Command and the Pentagon. US airpower was accordingly redirected. In the first week of November, the focus on Taliban front lines was decisive.[14] By 10 November, Taliban positions around Mazar-i-Sharif had fallen, allowing the opening of an air and road bridge. The major tipping point came around 12 November, with Northern Alliance forces going on the offensive across the front. The Taliban soon lost its control of Bamiyan, Kunduz, and Herat. With fearsome air strikes around the Bagram air base thirty miles north of Kabul breaking the will and ability of Taliban forces to defend the capital, Northern Alliance forces moved across the Shomali Plains.

CIA money again came into play. Tribal leaders sympathetic or allied to the Taliban now began to switch sides.[15] In the south, one of the few Pushtun leaders who had actively supported the US operation from the outset, Hamid Karzai, at last began to make inroads. Taliban field units began to dissolve and go home. The Northern Alliance and anti-Taliban Pushtuns prepared to move on Jalalabad, Kandahar, and Kabul.

However, the inherent problems with the CIA's approach would now become clear. Having gone down the road of contracting local warlords to occupy the ground, controlling the direction of events during the end game was bound to be more difficult. For fear of a sectarian bloodbath as well as to pacify Pakistani concerns, the United States had indicated that Kabul should be internationalized rather than taken by the Northern Alliance. But US assurances to Pakistan would be short-circuited by events on the ground. At first, Northern Alliance commanders agreed not to enter Kabul, holding their forces on its outskirts, but when the anti-Taliban Pushtun forces of Abdurrab Rasul Sayyaf began to enter Kabul on 13 November, the Northern Alliance would no longer be held back.[16] Northern Alliance forces took the city. Fortunately, while there was some settling of scores, a bloodbath did not materialize. But some in Pakistan felt betrayed. The campaign quickly progressed to its conclusion. The Taliban's evacuation of Kandahar on 7 December marked the final crumbling of the regime.

The control problem during the end game would also manifest itself in the mopping-up operations against Taliban and Qaida forces on the Afghanistan-Pakistan border. Although US Marines established a forward operating base southwest of Kandahar beginning on 26 November, US forces remained sparse on the ground. And while a handful of US and British special forces units dogged the escape of Taliban and jihadist fighters by calling in air strikes, significant numbers were able to stream through the mountain passes to Pakistan. When Osama bin Laden himself was tracked to the caves of Tora Bora in the White Mountains in December, US airpower pounded the area, but contracted tribal forces were unable to pin him down. Bin Laden probably walked out to Pakistan. By the time larger US and British units arrived to conduct a more systematic search, the enemy had gone to Pakistan or had merged back into the landscape. During Operation Anaconda in Paktia Province in March 2002, US forces briefly encountered a few hundred Islamist fighters, especially in the area of the Shah-i-Khot Valley, and heavy fighting ensued.[17] But a following force of British Royal Marines found nothing apart from "old arms caches and truculent shepherds."[18] The inertias of mopping up had not been sufficiently anticipated, and regular forces could not be moved into place in time. It was mostly a case of chasing shadows. By May 2002, US and British commanders were talking less about engaging and destroying and more about denying territory to the enemy—although in the longer run that, too, seemed likely to be a forlorn hope.[19]

Yet the 2001–2002 war in Afghanistan was a triumph. The master aims of the campaign—overthrowing the Taliban and routing Al-Qaida—were achieved more quickly than anyone had expected. Al-Qaida no longer had a safe haven in Afghanistan and could no longer network across the Islamist training camps that had been there. To the extent that Al-Qaida had lost its pivotal position amid the interlocking circles of the Islamist movement (recall Figure 2.2), the war could be counted as an operational-level success (verging on the strategic) for the United States. Many of the contingent relationships that had made Al-Qaida what it was were broken.

The context for ongoing operations against Al-Qaida in Afghanistan and Pakistan also looked positive. With a nominally pro-Western government now in Kabul, supported by revived local warlords who despised the Taliban and its foreign fighters, Al-Qaida had little room to return to Afghanistan. Even in Pushtun areas, Al-Qaida was hardly safe from informers, and some Taliban elements had become hostile to them; Al-Qaida attracted too much fire. Although the enemy leadership itself—bin Laden, al-Zawahiri, and Muhammad Omar—had escaped, they inhabited a twilight world in which they could only rarely raise their heads.[20] They remained leadership symbols but were no longer real managers in the global jihad. Many other top figures in Al-Qaida were killed in the war, notably Muhammad Atef, or would be killed or captured within the next few years. In the process, enormous amounts of intelligence would be retrieved. By early 2004, the United States had caught up with two-thirds of Al-Qaida's leadership, including 9/11 mastermind Khalid Shaikh Muhammad and key plotters like Ramzi bin al-Shibh and Abu Zubaydah.[21]

US policymakers and commanders must have been struck by the efficiency of force in Afghanistan. The overthrow of the Taliban was largely orchestrated by little more than 100 CIA agents and 300 special forces troops. Their effect had been multiplied by the intelligence-gathering and precision-strike capabilities of US airpower; some 60 percent of the bombs dropped were precision-guided munitions, including 5,000 satellite-guided weapons.[22] Although the number of civilians killed ran into the thousands, the war could be still presented as a humanitarian as well as military success. By early January 2002, only two members of US forces had been killed. In a place where the Soviet war machine had been tied down for many years, the United States was apparently victorious in little more than two months. The agenda of transformation that Donald Rumsfeld had been promoting at the Pentagon appeared to be vindicated. With local allies on the ground and the international community also signing up for peace support work, the United States seemed to have the follow-on phases covered, too. No one had dared hope for so much. The Bush administration could almost be forgiven for believing that the United States had happened upon a magic bullet.

Follow-Up Events in Afghanistan

Following the overthrow of the Taliban, the Bush administration was reticent about expending too much time and effort on Afghanistan; its attentions were already turning toward Iraq. The US forces committed to follow-on operations in Afghanistan were largely guided by a counterterrorist concept in which the killing or capture of terrorists was the principal concern. Later, a slightly more nuanced counterinsurgency concept emerged in which lip service was paid to winning hearts and minds as well as to persuading some Taliban elements to come to terms.[23] Thus, US policymakers were happy to expedite the move to a system of long-term governance under the rather light supervision outlined in an international agreement in Bonn, Germany, in December 2001.

The Expedited Move to Long-Term Governance

If postwar operations in Afghanistan are modeled in terms of the trinity of waging warfare in a complex social setting (see Chapter 3)—that is, as a balance between the application of force, RRA activities aimed at the population and enemy forces, and the creation of a system of longer-term governance—then the United States and its allies expedited the move to governance on a rather shallow curve (see Figure 5.2). The decision to merely skirt the RRA zone was a much less time- and resource-consuming option.

The expedited move to governance went about as smoothly as anyone could have imagined. Although the United States had not developed much of a southern strategy to co-opt Pushtun tribal groupings during the war itself, the emergence of the Pushtun leader, Hamid Karzai, during its latter stages was a fortunate windfall. Karzai was Western-inclined and progressive, and US patronage bestowed tremendous advantages upon him. As Karzai emerged as the leading political figure in postwar Afghanistan, he was able to convey the impression that what had happened was not simply a Northern Alliance takeover. Karzai's position was confirmed by the international conference involving Afghan factions in Bonn during late November and early December, and he was inaugurated as the new leader of Afghanistan on 22 December 2001. At a subsequent meeting of tribal representatives (*loya jirgah*) in June 2002, Karzai was appointed as interim president for the following two years, receiving the backing of more than 80 percent of the votes cast.[24] Karzai's position was a frustrating and dangerous one, but with US backing he was able to consolidate a position in Kabul and very slowly begin to extend his authority.

The meeting in Bonn initiated a political process that set up interim institutions and outlined a transitional timetable (see Figure 5.3). The interim government was constituted in the form of a thirty-member power-sharing council. For the time being, the Northern Alliance was the power behind the scenes, with some of its principal figures due to take the most important ministries:

Figure 5.2 The Expedited Move to Governance in Afghanistan as Embodied in the Bonn Process

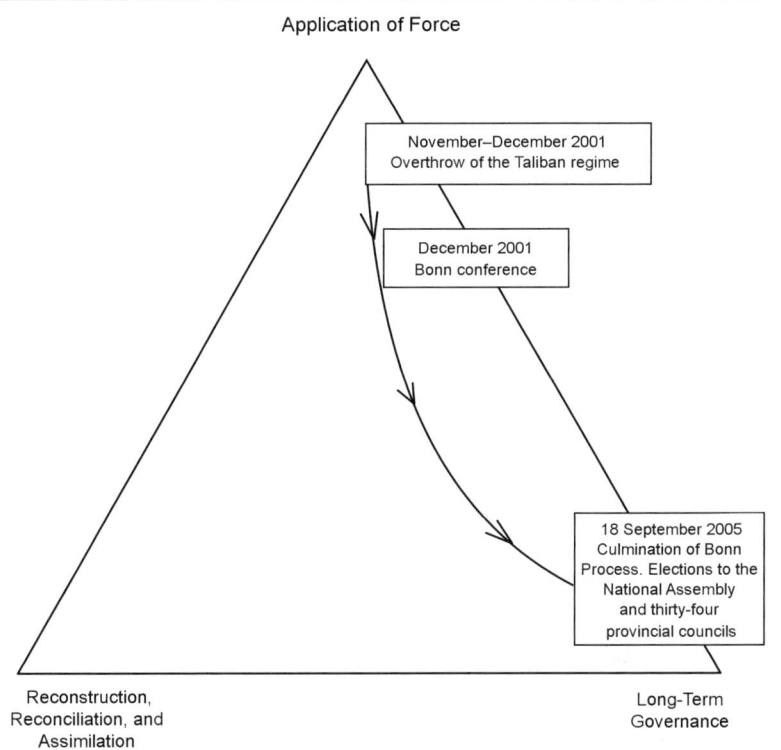

Yunis Qanooni as interior minister, Muhammad Fahim as defense minister, and Abdullah Abdullah as foreign minister.[25] The interim council was due to run for six months until a *loya jirgah* would elect a transitional government for two years until a permanent constitution could be drawn up by another *loya jirgah* in December 2003 or January 2004. Finally, the Bonn process would come to fruition with elections to install a president and members of national and provincial assemblies. Although tribal headsmen and local warlords were an integral part of the process, the kind of reform process primed by Bonn was—in principle—radical. The constitution that was approved by the *loya jirgah* in January 2004, for instance, included guarantees about the freedom of religion as well as equality between men and women. Women were reserved some 68 of the 249 seats in the lower house of the national assembly. To support the political process, the international community embarked on a civic education program that included an effort to register women as voters, and in the presidential elections of October 2004, 41 percent of registered voters were women.

Figure 5.3 The Bonn Political Process in Post-2001 Afghanistan

December 2001
An international conference in Bonn agrees on a framework for political reconstruction and the appointment of a power-sharing council for six months, headed by Hamid Karzai

June 2002
A tribal *loya jirgah* inaugurates a representative government headed by President Hamid Karzai

January 2004
Another *loya jirgah* approves a constitution, including a president, two vice presidents, and a parliament composed of a directly elected lower house (the 249-seat Wolasi Jirgah) and an indirectly elected house of elders (the 102-seat Meshrano Jirga)

October 2004
National elections for president won by Hamid Karzai

18 September 2005
Culmination of Bonn Process
Elections to the lower house of the National Assembly as well as to seats on the thirty-four provincial councils

Fears that the elections would be badly disrupted by violence and electoral rigging did not materialize. In the election for president in September 2004, Hamid Karzai won 55.4 percent of the vote, with particular support from Pushtun and city districts, bestowing a national mandate that significantly enhanced his authority.[26] National parliamentary and provincial elections were also successfully conducted in September and October 2005.[27] It could scarcely have gone better.

Flaws in the Bonn Process

Bonn was a great success as a process, but the move to liberal and democratic principles of governance marked a radical departure for Afghanistan, and expediting the move on such a shallow RRA curve while involving all sorts of traditional-type headsmen was always going to embody a certain incongruence. In retrospect, far more time and preparation were needed to make the new system of governance work in the way actually desired by the United States and its Western allies, if not by many of its Afghan clients. Above all, expediting the move to governance would lock in two big flaws.

First, the new system of democratic institutions was a façade that masked the continuance of older and deeper governance structures. The ghost in the machine was warlordism. A feudal system of local and regional fiefdoms persisted; this social system was premised on a weak government in Kabul, which scarcely taxed or policed most of the country, as well as the existence of deviant local economies. Local warlords did most of the taxing and policing in Afghanistan and were involved in such things as the opium trade. The patterns of overlapping conflict and cooperation among warlords and their minions could be bewildering to the outsider. Warlord politics was going on within Kabul, between Kabul and the provinces, and among the provinces and local areas. The government in Kabul itself was a forum for countrywide warlord politics as well as being a warlord-type actor in its own right.

Second, the expedited move to governance on a shallow RRA curve inevitably meant that there was a security, development, and expectations vacuum in most of the country; this vacuum was a context in which warlords, bandits, drug smugglers, and returning Taliban fighters might prosper. In the short to medium terms, the new Kabul government was utterly reliant on the United States and the international community to prime the required RRA activities. The passage of UN Resolution 1386 (20 December 2001) established the International Security Assistance Force, but with force numbers rising from 4,500 in June 2002 to only 6,500 by August 2003, its writ of authority did not run very far beyond Kabul.[28] An enormous amount of postconflict work was there for the doing throughout Afghanistan: Millions of refugees had to be resettled; a national system of law and order instituted; the road and communications systems rebuilt and extended; a health and education crisis reversed; the agricultural sector developed to provide a sustainable alternative to opium poppy; a legal and institutional framework created to secure the activities of private interests and foreign companies and agencies; and a national economy and system of taxation restored.

It would be wrong to say that the US and international aid efforts did not achieve things. Millions of refugees did return. Hundreds of schools and clinics were restored or constructed.[29] By early 2003, 3 million Afghan children were able to go back to school, including 1 million girls.[30] The road system linking Kabul, Kandahar, and Herat was upgraded in a joint US-Japanese-Saudi venture. When the Kabul-to-Kandahar road reopened, it reduced a journey of thirty hours to five or six hours. New roads and the introduction of a new currency also primed the potential for a national economy. Observers on the ground could witness a significant increase in economic activity, especially around Kabul, which experienced a construction boom and rapid population growth. But beyond Kabul, just as often it was warlords and drug smugglers who were at the heart of economic and social development. The opium trade drove a shadow and deviant RRA process that was hardly in accord with the intentions of the international community, although the economic growth that it did generate was not completely unwelcome.

The reality was that even though the United States and the international community provided enough assistance to bolster Hamid Karzai's position in Kabul, there were simply not enough outside money and personnel to begin national reconstruction and reconciliation. Foreign aid was modest in scale and apt not to arrive at all, and significant amounts of what did turn up were not properly supervised and thus lost to bureaucracy, corruption, and crime. Between 2001 and the beginning of 2004, the United States provided only US$3.7 billion in aid—and much of that went to security assistance.[31] The international community was similarly measured. At a donor's conference in Berlin in March 2004, the UN and the Afghan government estimated that US$27.5 billion was required over the next seven years.[32] Less than half that was pledged over the next three years. Afghanistan would also have to compete for resources against all the other postconflict jobs, especially in Iraq, as well as natural disasters and other worthy causes in the coming years. In fact, when compared to other postconflict situations, the aid to Afghanistan was relatively low.

The performance of some Western states in fulfilling their peace support tasks was also disappointing. At a conference in Berlin in 2002, a number of key tasks were allotted: the United States was to focus on counterinsurgency; the United Kingdom was to lead the counternarcotics effort; Germany was tasked with building up the Afghan national police and security forces; and Italy was to reform the judicial system. France came in to help the United States with training the Afghan National Army (ANA). But the buildup of the national police force and ANA was to be slow and problematic. The pool of educated recruits was small, and the disarmament, demobilization, and reintegration of local militias into the ANA meant taking on board all sorts of baggage. By mid-2004, there were only some 10,000–15,000 in the ANA and 30,000 in the national police force.[33] The program was significantly accelerated in 2004 with the target of constituting a force of some 70,000 by October 2007.[34] In order to operate more effectively across Afghanistan, the ANA also needed to construct a national system of barracks and bases, including village and mountaintop posts, and it needed armored vehicles and helicopters to support them. It was all bound to take a long time. The buildup of an effective national police force was even further behind the curve, and the realization, as early as 2005, that such an objective was many years away was the cause of some irritation in Washington about the performance of Germany as the lead nation, although the efficiency of the principal US-based training provider, DynCorp (a Virginia company), would not go unquestioned either.[35]

More serious than just the numbers problem, the security forces were developed without a sufficient degree of supervision. The slowly developing ANA was the best-trained and -controlled force, imbued with a culture that was relatively national as distinct from subnational. The police forces were a different matter. The Interior Ministry, local and national police forces, and the judiciary were thoroughly penetrated by partisan interests and were soon immersed in all manner of corrupt practices. Corruption went from the endemic extortion of goods or money from motorists at police checkpoints to the trading of valuable police stations among elite factions for the purposes of tax farming. In many parts of the country, the average Afghan could expect little from the law without the payment of bribes. Quite predictably, the police and judiciary also became entangled in opium production and smuggling, expropriating property, and skimming foreign aid and reconstruction assistance.

As Afghanistan hurtled toward its problematic system of governance, as outlined in the Bonn process, it was increasingly clear that a deeper RRA process was required: The RRA vacuum in the provinces had to be addressed, and when Kabul's writ was expanded, its men had to be properly supervised. In fact, US forces were to pioneer an important new approach by constituting multiagency provincial reconstruction teams (PRTs) to act as conduits for local RRA-type activities. Each PRT typically had a permanent military staff of approximately seventy, incorporating protection forces, civil affairs, engineering, and logistics personnel, and included input from the US State Department, US Agency for International Development, and US Department of Agriculture.[36] The teams also co-opted personnel from the United Nations Assistance Mission to Afghanistan (UNAMA) and NGOs operating in local areas as well as Afghan local and national governments. Following their conception in late 2002, PRTs were set up in the provincial centers of Gardez, Bamiyan, Kunduz, Kandahar, Herat, Mazar-i-Sharif, Jalalabad, and Parwan in 2003, with more established in 2004. The United States did most of the initial setup work using a model that others could follow. The PRT in Mazar-i-Sharif was taken up by the forces of Great Britain, Bamiyan by New Zealand, and Kunduz by Germany. More followed, and by 2004 nearly twenty PRTs would be in place in the provinces.

In the first instance, PRTs were intelligence gatherers and an adjunct to COIN operations. The US military was apt to use the PRTs to incentivize local people before and after military operations, although this sometimes meant providing reward and compensation (at some risk to the recipients) rather than a deeper and better-supervised RRA process. Nevertheless, PRTs primed hundreds of small-scale projects, providing drinking water, medical care, and improvements in transportation and agriculture. Beyond COIN, and once a degree of security was established, the PRTs could be used for ongoing operations through the RRA zone, especially for "planting a flag for the Kabul government" under a degree of close supervision by the US and Western forces.[37] The aspiration was to hand as many PRTs over to NATO forces as possible by the end of 2006. The PRT infrastructure might then serve as a platform for Kabul to extend its jurisdiction and services into difficult-to-reach localities.

For all the good work done by PRTs, a number of criticisms can still be leveled. First, PRTs were underresourced. Of the US$1.4 billion in nonsecurity funds allocated to Afghanistan in 2004, for instance, only US$100 million went to PRTs.[38] Most aid money continued to go to large-scale prestige projects, especially around Kabul and Kandahar, which often employed foreign contractors and did little to help ordinary villagers.

Second, aid and development work required physical protection, but the way in which RRA activities were so obviously being used by Western forces put the entire aid and development community at greater risk. Old dividing lines were being blurred. The level of violence directed at those working on RRA activities increased appreciably from 2003 to 2005. By the time five staff members of Médecins sans Frontières were murdered in an incident in June 2004, more than thirty aid workers had been killed since the first death of a foreigner in March 2003.[39] The Medicins sans Frontieres murders led to a significant curtailing of foreign aid activity, including that group's own departure after more than two decades of heroic service in-country. Another thirty aid workers would be killed in 2005.[40] Taliban remnants also went on to attack reconstruction projects themselves, most notably by burning down new and refurbished schools as well as killing school staff. The education of girls often led to and focused their violence.

Third, as NATO and other forces took over PRTs, significant differences in approach as well as separate chains of command were institutionalized across Afghanistan. Writing in the *RUSI Journal* in October 2008, Colonel Ian Westerman (British Army) observed that although the multinational nature of the operation required some flexibility in implementation, notably an acceptance of differing national restrictions and caveats on the use of national assets (or else, some participants might take away their people and money), "now the situation is such that it would seem that almost anything goes, and a virtual free-for-all in terms of what constitutes a PRT has ensued."[41] ISAF Regional Commands and HQ ISAF in Kabul could not order but only suggest and loosely coordinate local PRTs. Recalling the lessons of the Civil Operations and Revolutionary Development Support program during the Vietnam War, Westerman argued that the absence of a single chain of command and a common integrated approach had hampered the civil element of the campaign. The outcome was that some PRTs were driven as much by national predilictions, internal bureaucratic machinations, and alliance politics as by their role in actually trying to win the war. Afghans had become confused and skeptical about the PRTs, with few developing anything more than token Afghan participation.[42] Westerman believed that it was likely to be difficult to improve matters until the unity of command issue was addressed, a consistent approach to PRT operations was adopted (advocating a common PRT handbook), and a refocusing of effort away from humanitarian aid to good governance was undertaken. The most important thing was for PRTs to concentrate on building up the personnel, capacity, and legitimacy of the Afghan government. Westerman was left wondering whether a coalition organization like NATO could ever run an effective counterinsurgency campaign.[43] In truth, the kinds of inputs required to rebuild a country as poor, ruined, and lawless as Afghanistan were never on offer. Afghanistan was a black hole for resources that neither the United States nor its NATO partners were really prepared to fill.[44] The result was that the provision of security and RRA activities in the countryside was limited. Moreover, whatever security and reconstruction that were being provided were not translated into much reconciliation and assimilation. In fact, by 2004–2005 the postwar mission in Afghanistan was in serious trouble, as it became increasingly clear that two related security problems threatened the success of the entire mission: the insidious effect of the flourishing narcotics trade, and the resurgence of the Taliban in southern and eastern Afghanistan. The growing security crisis would soon lead to the outbreak of a major insurgency in the south, and by 2006–2007 many other parts of Afghanistan would experience renewed insecurity as well.

The Narcotics Problem

Although the Taliban did not have a consistent record on suppressing the opium trade, following a number of deals with international donors, notably the British government, in 1999, the regime acted to ban the cultivation of opium poppies. Indeed, in retrospect the way in which the Taliban clamped down on the opium trade may have seriously weakened its support base in the country and thus made it more vulnerable to the US onslaught in 2001. With the Taliban defeated, the logics of Afghanistan's geography and society resurfaced. With irrigation and transport systems smashed, and the country experiencing a prolonged drought, the economics of opium was irresistible. Even if fields could be irrigated for legitimate crops, perishables could not be gotten to market. Opium was durable (raw opium can last years), is easily transportable, and might yield as much as ten times the value of crops like wheat. But it was not merely the logic of the landscape. Traditional patterns of society and economic practice continued to foster the narcotics trade. Many poor and indebted farmers had little option about crop choice because of demands for payment or tribute from moneylenders and local warlords. The consequences of not paying debts could be dire. Narcotics might run counter to Islamic norms and laws, but Afghan farmers often justified opium production to themselves as long as Muslims did not consume it—some local mullahs agreed that what infidels did with their souls was not their concern!

As something of a gold rush swept many parts of Afghanistan, opium production soared, from an estimated low of 185 tons in 2001, to 3,400 tons in 2002, 3,600 tons in 2003, and 4,200 tons in 2004.[45] The patterns of production would change over the years, with the north fading as a producing area and the south increasing in importance, but Afghanistan would consolidate its status as the world's principal provider of opium and heroin, producing more than 90 percent of the world's supply. The 2007 annual report on Afghanistan by the UN's Office on Drugs and Crime noted that 3.3 million people were involved in the trade; 193,000 hectares were under poppy cultivation; and opium production was 8,200 tons, a rise of 34 percent on the previous year. By 2007 more than half of Afghanistan's opium production came from the single southern province of Helmand.

Opium was a complex problem that demanded a response beyond simple eradication. For poor farmers, it was the only alternative to debt, hunger, and expropriation. The opium trade was also behind much of the post-2001 economic bounce in Afghanistan, evidenced by the construction and retail boom in Kabul, Mazar-i-Sharif, and other provincial centers.[46] Many of the coalition allies either directly or indirectly profited. However, the urgent problem was that the Taliban began to tap into the opium trade in the south. Opium producers were liable for an Islamic tax of some 10 percent of earnings, and the Taliban also drew income from the smuggling routes. With the trade in the south worth hundreds of millions of US dollars per year, it seems likely that Taliban earnings were soon amounting to tens of millions of US dollars annually.

The British leaders of the counternarcotics efforts were sensitive to the complexity of the problem. In the first instance, with too few reliable forces on the ground and not wishing to alienate Afghan warlords and villagers, the British opted for a strategy that embodied a lot more carrot than stick. The initial focus of the program was on public affairs and alternative livelihood schemes.[47] Incentives were offered to Afghan farmers to give up planting poppies. It did not work. In the absence of adequate scrutiny and policing, Afghan farmers were presented with a no-lose situation: They could plant opium in order to get paid not to plant it, and if the payments did not appear, they could simply sell the opium crop.

A better balance of carrot and stick was needed. In the last analysis, building up the will and capacity of the Kabul government to police the opium trade, including policing warlords, was the only viable strategy in the long term. President Karzai was apparently on board with the antinarcotics effort, declaring a jihad against the poppy in April 2004, but his capacity to act was limited. Narcotics interests were embedded at all levels of government, with the twenty-five or thirty top opium traffickers working with associates in the national government.[48] Karzai was also aware of the economic significance of narcotics, as well as the likely backlash in the provinces if Kabul approved a sudden and widespread clampdown. Karzai emphasized the need for alternative livelihoods first.

The Kabul government did begin to send out centrally organized eradication teams, although this soon demonstrated the complex bargaining over narcotics between central-central and central-local interests. Eradication was limited in extent and was often carried out in a rather symbolic way. In 2007, for instance, of the 193,000 hectares reportedly under poppy cultivation, only 19,047 hectares were eradicated.[49] Moreover, with local police chiefs and judges beholden to warlord and drugs interests, local officials were apt to delay the work of national eradication teams, and it was difficult to get arrests and convictions of drug traffickers. With the help of satellite intelligence, it was possible to imagine aerial eradication, but the UN and the British balked at going over the head of the central-local bargaining understandings. The backlash from warlords and locals would likely take a violent turn.

As it became increasing clear that the Taliban were tapping into the opium trade in a significant way, the United States became more attuned to the problem, pressing the Karzai government, the United Nations, and Great Britain to do more. US courts also began to indict major drug traffickers. In October 2005, Baz Muhammad, a captured trafficker accused of controlling fields in Nangahar Province and smuggling heroin to the United States, was the first to be extradited.[50] By 2005–2006, the US State Department was more active in marshalling the antinarcotics effort in Afghanistan itself. The US program embodied less carrot and more stick, focusing on building up the capacity of Afghan law enforcement and speeding up eradication. The US inclination was to edge Karzai and coalition partners toward aerial eradication as well as "stripping the mask of legitimacy" from some of the government officials and warlords involved in the opium trade.[51]

The bottom line was that more coalition troops and resources were needed on the ground to provide security, supervise alternative livelihood schemes, and build up the capacity and reliability of Afghan counternarcotics forces. Partly in response to the building pressure, the British responded by leading a major NATO reinforcement in southern Afghanistan from April to May 2006, including sending some 3,500 troops to what had become the principal producing area, Helmand Province. But again, the experience was not a straightforward one. Reports were already circulating in late 2005 that narcotics interests were looking into moving production to isolated Nimruz Province in anticipation of more eradication in Helmand.[52] When British forces did arrive in Helmand they were immediately involved in heavy fighting with the Taliban and local people; to avoid exacerbating the situation, the British quickly distanced themselves from the idea of an immediate eradication offensive in Helmand.

The British-led counternarcotics effort would continue to be characterized more by alternative livelihood schemes and governance capacity-building than by direct large-scale eradication.[53] The introduction of a number of new counternarcotics agencies—including counternarcotics police, a commando force, detention facilities, and courts—that were closely mentored by British police and soldiers may have had some effect on the trade by the time the 2008 crop was being harvested. While the Interior Ministry was going district to district sacking corrupt officers (in response to US and British pressure in Kabul), the possibility of getting caught by counternarcotics police may have given pause to some corrupt police officers among the regular national and local forces. Patterns of bribery were disrupted, with police and judicial favors costing more, although the result may have been to begin consolidating control of the opium trade among the largest producers and smugglers, who had the money and contacts to overcome the new risks.[54] The British would also start planning smart eradication, using aerial and satellite survey information to begin eradicating in areas in which alternative livelihood schemes were viable, as well as trying to get a fairer balance between small farmers and the largest producers and smugglers.

The significant declines in total opium production (partly weather-related) and the number of provinces under cultivation in 2008 were the cause of some optimism among officials, but in reality any progress was unlikely to be in a single direction. Thousands of tons of opium were already in storage. Eradicating crops and making smuggling more difficult were also likely to raise prices, thereby incentivizing new cultivation. The torrid economic times of 2007–2008—which saw huge increases in the price of food and fuel, followed by a global economic recession—may have increased the pressure on poorer Afghans to again take a risk. It was easy to imagine that other parts of Afghanistan—especially in the north and east—might once again become large production areas. Conquering the trade in opium and the dysfunctional social systems it supported was going to be an extremely long haul.

Taliban Resurgence

The return of the Taliban was always the principal threat to the success of the follow-on mission in Afghanistan. In the first instance, US forces sought to decisively defeat the threat largely through the application of force. It was not long, however, before US strategy was evolving to accept that winning hearts and minds and bargaining were required. US forces would try to win over some Taliban by offering a deal, and they provided incentives to other Pushtun tribesmen for the right sort of behavior. In late 2004, the US and Kabul governments initiated the Allegiance Program, aimed at detaching lower echelons of the Taliban from the leadership. It offered reconciliation and assimilation for individuals. If Taliban fighters came forward to give up their weapons and pledge support to the Karzai government, then they might qualify for amnesty and financial assistance. A program of releasing cooperative Taliban fighters from detention—up to eighty per month—was also begun.[55] Some former Taliban allies even assumed positions in the Karzai government, especially in provincial administrations.

The war had left the Taliban shattered and unpopular. The hardcore elements escaped to Pakistan or went underground; allied Pushtun militia leaders and elders abandoned the movement and looked elsewhere for allies. The effect on Al-Qaida and other foreign Islamists was even more severe. Afghanistan was now dominated by US forces and the warlords who hunted them. No ordinary Afghan in his right mind could think that sheltering Al-Qaida fighters was a good idea. And most ordinary Afghans, even in the Pushtun south, also did not want to see a return to Taliban austerity. Yet by 2005 a number of internal and external factors were coming together to enable a resurgence by the Taliban.

First, the way in which US and Afghan national forces initially conducted COIN operations alienated villagers in the Pushtun south. US forces were apt to try to exert too much control without the resources and presence to sustain it, and they sometimes showed a dramatic lack of cultural knowledge and sensitivity when sweeping through villages. When US troops and their Afghan allies kicked in villager's doors; humiliated men in front of women; rifled through personal possessions; seized guns, opium, and other valuables; and took men away to detention and who-knows-what, they primed support for resistance. US bombings killed too many villagers. Even though few Pushtuns really wanted to take on US forces, sometimes fighting back was simply a matter of personal honor. In fact, the Karzai government would eventually intercede to try to mitigate the effect of US heavy-handedness. In 2005, an agreement limited what US forces could do: They could no longer conduct nighttime raids on Afghan homes, and any nighttime operation was to be led by the ANA.[56]

Second, even though the ANA was probably the least corrupt of all the Afghan security forces, when Western and ANA troops consolidated control in particular areas they paved the way for Kabul's governors, bureaucrats, and policemen. Few Afghan provincials ever wanted Kabul's writ to run across the country, and many Pushtuns certainly did not want Hamid Karzai's Kabul—under the sway of the Northern Alliance and its foreign friends—to extend to the south. For many in the provinces, Kabul was just another warlord or mafia network, which simply competed with local and regional warlords to extort yet more money from the country and its people. Where Kabul was more racket than rule of law, local Pushtuns might expect more help and justice by appealing to the Taliban than to the government. In fact, the Taliban's rule of law had been instrumental in its rise during the mid-1990s.

Third, the Taliban had always been a cross-border phenomenon—sharing tribal affiliations and associated with the Wahhabist-inclined Deobandi movement of India and Pakistan—and Pakistan was the place where the organization would begin to recover between 2002 and 2005.[57] The madrassas of Quetta and elsewhere were trawled for new recruits. By 2005, coalition forces were detecting larger groups of Taliban fighters making forays across the Afghanistan-Pakistan border. Fortified camps and outposts occupied by US and Afghan forces were initially a favorite target for attacks. Rocket and mortar attacks were reported as widely as the provinces of Nangahar, Paktia, Khost, Paktika, Kandahar, and Urugan. Later, the fortified outposts would face the risk of being overrun altogether in assaults involving scores of Taliban fighters. Mines and ambushes along coalition supply routes also became more frequent.

During 2005–2007, other events in Pakistan were also increasing the potential for an insurgency in Afghanistan. President Pervez Musharraf's alliance with the United States was unpopular in Pakistan, and his determination to hang on to power primed a broader political crisis. One of the manifestations was growing restlessness in the tribal zones of the North-West Frontier Province, where resistance to Islamabad's writ was becoming more organized and militant, especially following the storming by security forces of the militant-held Red Mosque in Islamabad in July 2007, which killed more than 100 and precipitated a new level of hostility between the Musharraf regime and Islamic militants.[58] In fact, in the Pushtun tribal area there was about to emerge, as Jason Burke described, a chaotic and borderless "entity" presided over by a "ragtag network of mullahs, militia leaders, and 'merchants'" (notably smugglers of drugs, guns, and timber).[59] The eastern portion of South Waziristan was the base of Baitullah Mehsud, who was to become the leading figure of the so-called Pakistani Taliban (Tehrik-e Taliban Pakistan), an umbrella organization for tribal Islamists that was formed after the storming of the Red Mosque. Mehsud was to launch a sustained campaign of violence against Pakistani authorities, including suicide bombings in Pakistan's major cities. In North Waziristan, Jalaluddin Haqqani and his son Sirajuddin Haqqani led Afghan Taliban forces and foreign jihadists around mountain border towns like Miram Shah and Mir Ali.[60] Other armed bands operated farther north in Mohmand, Bajaur, and the Swat valley. Together these forces created governance blackspots along the Afghanistan-Pakistan border. The border fiefdoms constituted a realm that not only provided refuge and logistics for the insurgency in Afghanistan but also personnel to directly participate in cross-border attacks.

The ability of Pakistan's security forces to police the border areas was not clear cut. Rumors continually circulated that elements in the army and the ISI continued to be directly involved in supporting the Afghan Taliban, partly due to burgeoning contacts between the Karzai government and India.[61] The bombing of the Indian embassy in Kabul in July 2008, which killed fifty-four people, prompted open accusations about Pakistan-Taliban collusion from the US and Karzai governments.[62] Certainly, the army rarely exerted physical pressure on the Afghan Taliban in Baluchistan or North Waziristan, and the Taliban thereby retained significant freedom to operate from those areas.

The army's effort against Pakistani tribal militants and foreign jihadists was far more committed. It garrisoned more than 100,000 troops in the tribal areas and faced an insurgency that killed hundreds of troops and occasionally led to pitched battles. For the most part, however, Pakistani forces were engaged in a bargaining war in the tribal zones. The political echelons of the army had ties with mainstream Islamist groups such as Jamiat Ulema-i-Islami, and according to Ahmed Rashid, an expert on Afghanistan and Pakistan, Musharraf's years in office were always marked by a deep confusion as he had tried to "run with the hares and hunt with the hounds."[63] Between 2005 and 2008, various deals with tribal elders in North and South Waziristan would see the army pull back its forces in return for promises to expel foreign fighters. Tribal leaders would put some pressure on foreign jihadists—notably resulting in two full-scale battles fought between Waziris and Uzbeki militants in 2007—but such pressure would be sporadic.[64] In the end, none of the deals were really honored. Moreover, following the various cease-fires, cross-border attacks into Afghanistan rose markedly.

The resignation of General Musharraf as president in August 2008 and the resulting resumption of civilian rule would further sharpen the conflict between Islamabad and tribal militants. The new government, led by President Asif Zardari (husband of Benazir Bhutto, the leader of the Pakistan People's Party who was assassinated in December 2007), was actively hostile to militants, and following the suicide bombing of the Marriott hotel in Islamabad on 20 September 2008, which killed more than fifty, political and military leadership alike drove home a major offensive in the tribal areas that undoubtedly hurt the militants. But it seemed unlikely that the army had the will or ability to fully subjugate tribal areas. What seemed likely to continue was a sporadic and indecisive bargaining war. The strategy in the tribal areas was ultimately one of "divide and rule," and this often meant making concessions to some militants, often with unpredictable consequences. Moreover, following the government offensives after the Marriot Hotel bombing, it was clear that while the army could sweep through an area, it could rarely stop the militants from seeping back. Having put so much effort into suppressing the insurgency in the Swat valley in 2008, for instance, Pakistani authorities negotiated a deal with Islamists in February 2009 that promised to concede to many of their grievances with the implementation of sharia law in the Malakand division of the North-West Frontier Province. The proposed deal would permit Islamists associated with the Pakistan Taliban to control much of the Swat valley. Of course, it was difficult to know whether such compromise would divide and deactivate the insurgent movement or whether it would consolidate the conditions in Pakistan that supported the insurgency in Afghanistan. Finally, the Taliban would also make a significant alliance with the Afghanistan-Pakistan Islamist group Hizb-i-Islami, led by Gulbuddin Hekmatyar. The alliance was important because Hekmatyar added another dimension to the connections in Pakistan, and had a stronger presence in Afghanistan among Ghilzai Pushtuns in the northern provinces of Kunar, Laghman, Nangahar, Logar, Paktia, and Khost.[65]

Thus, by 2005 there were reportedly an estimated 2,000 Taliban and several hundred Hizb-i-Islami fighters active in Afghanistan. Cross-border fighting between US and Taliban elements from Pakistan also escalated, with sixty-six US troops being killed that year.[66] Things became a lot worse in 2006. The number of reported attacks tripled from 1,632 in 2005 to 5,388 in 2006, resulting in the death of 191 coalition troops and more than 4,000 Afghans.[67] The tactics being used were also changing. Taliban forces began massing fighters (in groups of 50 to 100) for assaults on fixed positions in the hope of completely overrunning outposts. Insurgency techniques deployed elsewhere were also introduced. The number of suicide bombings and improvised explosive device (IED) detonations rose significantly (including a fourfold increase in the number of suicide bombings between 2005 and 2006, with a rise to more than 120 in 2006).[68]

During 2005–2006, the Taliban was casting a more sustained shadow over Pushtun rural areas, especially as some Taliban main-force elements were no longer returning to Pakistan for the winter.[69] Villagers who talked to coalition forces, much less became involved in RRA activities, did so at extreme peril. Thus, even though the Taliban represented a limited insurgent threat, and its forces sometimes struggled to keep up the fight in eastern Afghanistan against the US military, it was difficult to write off the movement entirely. Its core supporters were ruthless and determined men, it continued to draw on support from Pakistan, and the Western presence inspired support for the resistance.

Making the Afghan Intervention Work: NATO Deployment in the South

By 2005, the mission in Afghanistan was at a crossroad. The political process outlined at Bonn had come to fruition, but it also locked in some serious problems. The United States and its allies were lucky to have Hamid Karzai, but he was supported by too few of his kind. Kabul was utterly penetrated by selfish insider interests. Beyond Kabul, there was a growing sense that things were beginning to slip. The provinces were the realm of warlords and drug smugglers, and either Kabul was too weak to be effective, or its agents were apt to act as warlords themselves. In southern and eastern Afghanistan, Kabul's writ was scarcely welcome, and Taliban and Islamist insurgents increasingly cast a shadow over Pushtun areas. Taliban activity was to increase again in the summer of 2006.

Responding to the developing situation meant going back to RRA in a much more concerted way. A model for action already existed by 2006: establish security in local areas; expand the geographical and functional scope of PRTs to extend the reach of reconstruction and reconciliation; persuade tribal elements among the Taliban to give up resistance and sign up for the Allegiance Program; supervise training and deployment of Afghan security forces and expand Kabul's writ; and gradually address the longer-term threats to security, especially the narcotics trade and the power of the warlords vis-à-vis Kabul.[70] Clear enough—but how were the coalition forces supposed to go about doing it? Amid the background of the Taliban resurgence, it was difficult to imagine getting past the first stage of establishing security across great swathes of the south and east. Thus, in areas where the Taliban menaced the establishment of security, a significant escalation in the use of force might be necessary to re-create the appropriate conditions for follow-on RRA.

Having taken over stewardship of the International Security Assistance Force's mission, NATO forces would lead the offensive back into RRA. The expansion of the NATO mission was already under way in a geographical sense. Stage-one expansion, to the relatively benign areas of northern Afghanistan, was led by German troops and completed by October 2004 (see Figure 5.4). Stage-two expansion, led by Italian forces, took over the eastern provinces around Herat by September 2005. However, it was the stage-three deployment, into the lawless Pushtun south, that was by far the most important, representing a qualitative change in NATO's mission. In spring and summer of 2006, NATO deployed 8,000 British, Canadian, Dutch, and other troops to the southern provinces of Nimruz, Helmand, Kandahar, Uruzgan, and Zabul. Thus, between 2006 and 2007, the number of US and NATO troops in Afghanistan would double to more than 31,000.[71]

Once the stage-three deployment was under way and PRTs had begun priming the RRA zones locally, it was hoped that "ink spots" of security and governance could be dropped in, eventually grow, and be joined up. At an operational level, the deployment was to work hand in glove with a new national coordinating body, the Policy Action Group, which consisted of key Afghan ministries (Interior, Defense, Finance, and Rural Rehabilitation) and co-opted members of the international community, including the commanding general of the Combined Forces Command–Afghanistan. An implementation team was put into place for follow-up action in key areas. It all seemed comparable to best practices in previous British and US COIN campaigns.

At the outset, NATO deployment in the south promised to reduce frictions caused by the US military on the ground, as well as to breathe new life into RRA activities. It would not go as planned, for two reasons. First, the United

Figure 5.4 Expansion of NATO (ISAF) in Afghanistan, 2004

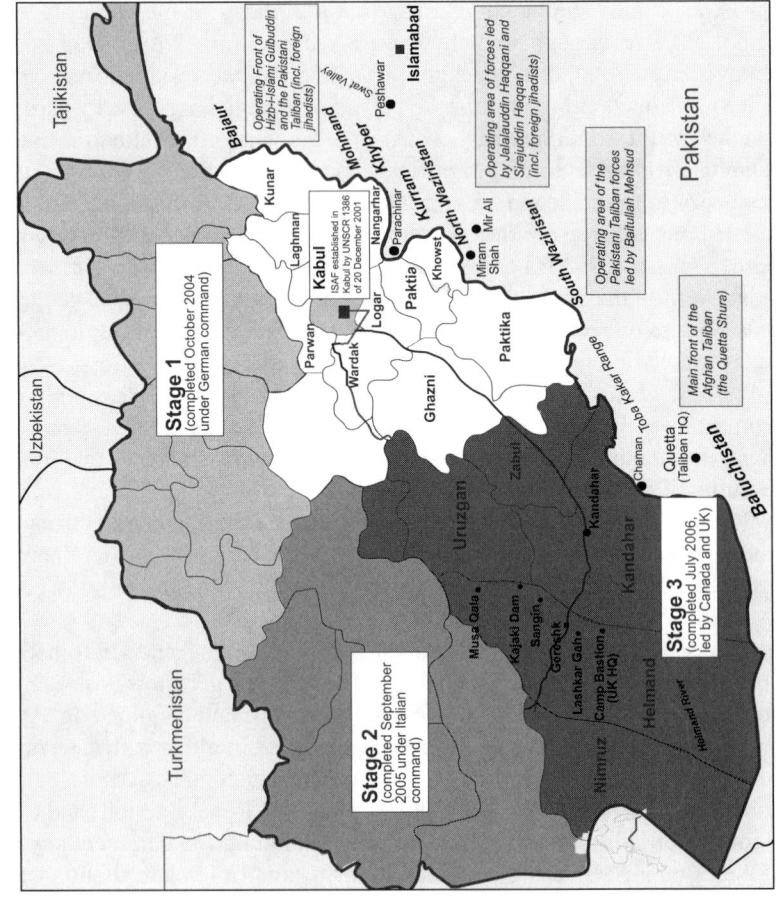

States had its own perspective about how things should be rolled out. Just as European troops were about to go in, US forces launched an offensive across the south. In fact, US commanders tended to see the supply of new NATO troops as a means of escalating the force element in COIN operations (as they now had the resources to conduct simultaneous attacks on multiple Taliban strongholds) as much as doing anything new. The new NATO commander, General David Richards of the British Army, fell into line with this strategy because of his assessment that locals would support whomever seemed strongest. As NATO deployed, US and Canadian forces set the tone by launching Operation Medusa, a major effort to clear the Panjwayi Valley in Kandahar Province through destructive force against Taliban elements in Pushtun villages.

Second, the British deployment to Helmand Province was marked by particular problems at the start. Relations with the local governor were poor following an incident in April 2006 when British pathfinders killed a group of Afghan police. The full-scale deployment of British troops was also problematic. A disillusioned British officer, Captain Leo Docherty of the Scots Guards, later told *The Sunday Times* what he believed the mistakes had been in the period from May to July 2006.[72] At the request of the Kabul government, British troops had been sent to occupy a number of isolated outposts in northern areas of Helmand, most notably the district centers of Sangin, Musa Qala, Naw Zad, and Gereshk. When British troops arrived in Sangin on 25 May, they met little resistance, but the deployment was not quickly followed up by information operations and RRA activities. Rather, while British troops simply occupied the town, the Taliban conducted their own information operation, telling locals that the British had come to strangle the opium trade. It was not long before shooting started and a cycle of escalation took shape. In mid-June, the Taliban attacked in force. Taliban fighters formed into larger formations, and the sledgehammer of airpower was needed to prevent the British from being overrun. The towns that British troops had been sent to protect, develop, and govern were being destroyed. Captain Docherty could only lament that

> we had all these study days before deploying, looking at how we dealt with the Malaya insurgency of the 1950s and how we were going to use the same strategy of first creating these secure zones or ink-spots around the main locations of Lashkar Gah and Gereshk and then move out. The whole focus was supposed to be not high-intensity fighting but construction of a nation-state. Instead we've deviated spectacularly from the plan and scattered in a meaningless way across northern towns of Helmand. To withdraw from these now would be seen as defeat, but the only way to survive is to increase the level of violence.[73]

British forces thwarted Taliban attacks throughout the summer of 2006 and pushed the resistance to northern Helmand, but it had all been much more violent than envisaged. Establishing security was clearly part of the requirement for NATO troops in the south, but the scale of fighting was counterproductive to the RRA agenda. Indeed, for most of 2006 the Taliban successfully countered RRA in Helmand, with both sides bringing destruction, discordance, and dissimulation. The on-again, off-again coalition of disgruntled locals, village Taliban, main-force infiltrators from Pakistan, and opium traders was an alliance that might take years to wear down, coerce, persuade, and break up.[74] It was certainly going to take a lot longer than the three-year deployment that was initially planned. The war escalated again in 2007 and 2008, and even though Taliban fighters continued to suffer disproportionate losses, it was unclear whether and when such resistance could ever be tamed.

The Future of the US-NATO Mission in Afghanistan

How, then, could the Pushtun south and east be more reconciled and assimilated into a new order? The big questions remain about the transition from RRA to long-term governance. Although the Bonn process had set up a system of governance—and the entire US and NATO effort was premised on making its writ run across the country—the characters of the Kabul government and its security forces were not conducive to bridging the RRA-governance gap. The penetration of Kabul by warlords and selfish bureaucratic interests meant that there were no such things as a national government and security forces; the ANA was the best hope, but even it was likely to malfunction if it was not closely supervised by Western troops. Indeed, to the extent that Kabul was able to expand its writ in the south and east, this sometimes meant simply replacing one set of warlords with another set of Kabul-licensed warlords or self-interested bureaucrats. Westerners rarely understood this Afghan brand of politics, and thus whenever Western forces paved the way for Kabul's governors and policemen, there was a real danger that they were actually creating conditions for an insurgency. The constant rotation of some NATO troops, with the tour for British troops being perhaps only six months, also undermined the ability to properly understand and supervise RRA.

Warlords and selfish insiders were an insidious influence as far as the US-NATO mission was concerned, but this was the Afghan way—and Hamid Karzai was simply not in a position to supersede their influence in Kabul or their security and social functions throughout Afghanistan. Having already expedited the creation of a system of governance, going back to substantially reform it was always going to be difficult because it was protected by those who benefited from it. Although it was possible to scope out some sort of reckoning with warlords and insiders as a precursor to major reforms in the system of governance, it was probably more realistic to talk about very gradually redefining the terms of trade among President Karzai and his government, its selfish insiders, and the provincial warlords.[75] Taking on the warlords and insiders risked opening new fronts of conflict, especially in the north and west, and such a move might not be possible at least until the mounting insurgency in the south was contained.[76] The alternative to a strategy of trying to grind out an attritional victory in the south, make RRA work, and reform the system of governance was to leave Afghans to their own devices—perhaps with the United States and NATO occasionally intervening to tip the balance of power as well as to set the parameters of some sort of bargaining process with the Taliban or individual members. In an article in the *Military Review* in late 2005, Major Andrew M. Roe of the British Army argued the reality was that the United States and NATO had little choice but to scale back aspirations and work with realities on the ground.[77] Local militias and fiefdoms were a fact of life in the country, and the most effective response was to vet and integrate them as arms of the Kabul government. Similarly, accepting big warlords as provincial governors (i.e., where they were not already) might be a way of creating more effective local governance as well as gradually reforming behaviors. Once responsibilities had been conferred, then militia commanders might be slowly encouraged to meet a number of performance criteria. Of course, whether warlords could be tamed and civilized by means of benchmarking was another matter! Some might be. For others, especially at lower levels, NATO forces and the ANA might ultimately have to coerce compliance or threaten to alter the balance of local tribal forces. It was all likely to be a fiendishly complicated bargaining process, and drawing in acceptable elements from the Taliban was likely to be even trickier. With whom could bargains be struck? Who should continue to be targeted? Were deals sustainable? The big question about the Taliban, however, was how could it be reconciled and assimilated? The potential for top-down reconciliation with Taliban leaders was unclear. Hamid Karzai might express a preparedness to talk to Taliban leaders, but given the deep ideological differences and movement's apparent momentum, it seemed unlikely that talks with the leadership of the organization could be successful in the foreseeable future. In the meantime, US and British strategy involved an attempt to reconcile and assimilate the Taliban as individuals by detaching (by means of force and bargaining rewards) members of the Taliban in Afghanistan from the leadership cadres in Pakistan. Whether this approach could be successful remained to be seen. Afghans were apt to defect back and forth, and by 2008 the momentum of the insurgency was overpowering the Allegiance Program.

The strategy of individual assimilation might also have had unintended effects: focusing strikes on Taliban leadership targets ran the risk of making the Taliban 4GW-like—fragmenting it, putting the leadership of smaller groups into the hands of younger and more radical figures, and making it a much less coherent bargaining partner.

A long period of chipping away at the edges of the Taliban movement might be the only option, although even here the coalition did not entirely appear to be working off the same RRA hymn sheet. In an interview published in the *New York Times* in April 2008, President Karzai chided US and British forces for arresting too many Taliban figures and sympathizers in Pushtun villages, claiming that the threat of arrest and mistreatment was dissuading individual Taliban fighters from returning to Afghanistan to lay down their arms.[78] Karzai also wanted his Western allies to stop using so much firepower in Afghan villages, leading to far too many civilian casualties, when the real problem lay across the border in Pakistan.

Amid the deteriorating security situation in 2008, there was a growing sense that a rethinking was needed. With General David Petraeus, one of the architects of the so-called surge in Iraq, becoming commander of US Central Command (with Afghanistan in his area of responsibility), an Afghanistan surge was in the cards. Speaking at the Royal United Services Institute in London in October 2008, NATO's Supreme Allied Commander–Europe, General John Craddock of the US Army, reflected the admission that the United States and NATO had so far failed to provide sufficient troops, that the civil follow-up to military operations was inadequate and "disjointed," and that the Afghan government had to do much more to reform itself and its forces.[79] On the ground, a surge would involve more troops; the immersion of US, NATO, and Afghan forces in the communities they hoped to secure; and a more concerted effort to bargain away local resistance to the troop presence, including by means of hiring and empowering local militiamen. Of course, whether the general success of the Iraqi surge could be repeated in Afghanistan remained to be seen. The United States and NATO would have to rustle up tens of thousands more troops to surge and rotate while also committing more money and personnel to train and mentor Afghan security forces. Craddock himself perceived some "wavering" among the NATO allies; indeed, his comments came shortly after reports of a surge of pessimism among British officials and commanders in Afghanistan about the mission.[80] Many of the other NATO contributors—notably Canada, Germany, France—were similarly skeptical about the prospects for the war, and accordingly reluctant to commit additional forces to it. Above all, a successful surge in Afghanistan would require—as it had in Iraq—the need to bargain with adversaries to produce results. In Iraq, the United States managed to leverage growing differences among foreign jihadists and local tribes and nationalists. Although all sorts of differences of interest and perception existed within the Taliban movement, it remained to be seen whether those differences could be leveraged into an operational-level breakthrough. With the Afghan Taliban dominant in the insurgency in the south, Al-Qaida and other foreign jihadists did not represent the kind of challenge to the locals as they had in Iraq. That being said, the Pakistani Taliban and other insurgent forces in Pakistan's North-West Frontier Province were probably more vulnerable to this kind of intelligence-information warfare leveraging, although the job of doing this largely fell to Pakistani security forces. At the same time, even if individual or small groups of Taliban could be turned, their loyalty could not necessarily be guaranteed going forward. Any progress might be difficult to sustain in the long run.

The United States and its NATO allies had a tangle of intractables to sort out. In an article in *The Sunday Times* in June 2008, Simon Jenkins perceived the "cascade of hypotheticals" required to prevail in Afghanistan, observing that

> Victory would be at hand "if only" the Afghan Army was better, if the poppy crop were suppressed, the Pakistani border sealed, the Taliban leadership assassinated, corruption eradicated, hearts and minds won over. None of this is going to happen. The generals know it but the politicians dare not admit it. . . . We forget that the objective of the Afghanistan incursion was not to build a new and democratic Afghanistan. It was to punish the Taliban for harbouring Osama Bin Laden and to prevent Afghanistan from becoming a haven for Al-Qaeda training camps. The former objective was achieved on day one; the latter would never be achieved by military occupation.[81]

From the perspective of 2009, there was really no end in sight to it all.

Notes

1. Bob Woodward, *Bush at War* (New York: Simon and Schuster, 2002), esp. chapter 6, 75–92.
2. UN Security Council Resolution of 12 September 2001 and UNSC Resolution 1373 of 28 September 2001, www.un.org/docs/scres/2001/sc2001.htm.
3. US Secretary of State Colin Powell to the 9/11 commission, 23 March 2004, http://govinfo.library.unt.edu/911/hearings/hearing8/powell_statement.pdf.
4. For details on the planning process, including the respective roles of the Pentagon and CIA, see Woodward, *Bush at War,* chapter 6, 75–92.
5. Richard A. Clarke, "Right War, Wrong War," chapter 11, *Against All Enemies: Inside America's War on Terror* (New York: Simon and Schuster, 2004), xiii, 247–287, 274–275; see also the statement made by US Secretary of State Colin Powell to the 9/11 commission, 23 March 2004, http://govinfo.library.unt.edu/911/hearings/hearing8/powell_statement.pdf.
6. Clarke, *Against All Enemies,* 209–210.
7. Accounts of Jawbreaker's activities in Operation Enduring Freedom can be found in the works of two of its principal participants: Gary Schroen, *First Inside: An Insider's Account of How the CIA Spearheaded the War on Terror in Afghanistan* (New York: Presidio Press, 2007) (Schroen was the initial team leader); and Gary Berntsen and Ralph Pezzullo, *Jawbreaker—The Attack on Bin Laden and Al-Qaeda: A Personal Account by the CIA's Key Field Commander* (New York: Three Rivers Press, 2006) (Berntsen succeeded as team leader). See also Woodward, *Bush at War,* especially chapters 10, 11, 13, 14, 16, 17, 19, and 20.
8. Woodward, *Bush at War,* 317.
9. For an analysis of the Afghan campaign more from the perspective of the US military, see Stephen Biddle, *Afghanistan and the Future of Warfare: Implications for Army and Defense Policy,* report undertaken for the Strategic Studies Institute, US Army War College, Carlisle Barracks, Penn. (November 2002), ix, www.strategicstudiesinstitute.army.mil/pdffiles/PUB109.pdf.
10. Woodward, *Bush at War,* 246–247.
11. Ibid., 238–241.

110 *The Problem of Force*

12. Colin McInnes, "A Different Kind of War? September 11 and the United States' Afghan War," *Review of International Studies* 29, no. 2 (April 2003), 165–184, 180–181.
13. Woodward, *Bush at War,* 252–254.
14. Biddle, *Afghanistan and the Future of Warfare,* 10.
15. For further discussion about defections, see ibid., 16–19.
16. Woodward, *Bush at War,* 310.
17. For further discussion about Operation Anaconda and the battle around Shah-i-Khot, see Biddle, *Afghanistan and the Future of Warfare,* 13–15, 28–33, and 35–36; McInnes, "A Different Kind Of War?" 177; Mark Thompson, "Sudden Warrior," *Time,* 11 September 2002, 70–74, esp. 73–74; Wesley K. Clark (General, ret., US Army), "Flawed Arguments, Flawed Strategy," *Winning Modern Wars: Iraq, Terrorism, and the American Empire* (New York: Public Affairs, 2003), chapter 5, 137–160, esp. 138–139.
18. Comment made in Jason Burke, "The War on Terror," chapter 16, *Al Qaeda: The True Story of Radical Islam* (London: Penguin Books, 2004), 254–276, esp. 255 (Burke is an Al-Qaida expert and was a reporter for the *Observer.* He worked as a field correspondent with the Royal Marines on the 2002 Afghan deployment).
19. Ibid., 256.
20. Bin Laden was last seen in Jalalabad on 14 November 2001. Jason Burke believed that he was likely to be hiding on the frontier south of Khost and north of Quetta. Ibid., 273.
21. Statement of US Secretary of State Colin Powell to the 9/11 commission, 23 March 2004, http://govinfo.library.unt.edu/911/hearings/hearing8/powell_statement.pdf, 15; see also Burke, *Al-Qaeda,* 260.
22. "U.S. Military Readies for Iraq Action," BBC News, 7 August 2002, http://news.bbc.co.uk/1/hi/world/middle_east/2178492; for an analysis of the effectiveness of precision weapons and SOF target designation, see Biddle, *Afghanistan and the Future of Warfare,* 26–37.
23. See David Lamm (Colonel, US Army), "Success in Afghanistan Means Fighting Several Wars at Once," *Armed Forces Journal* (November 2005): 25–27. David Lamm was chief of staff of the Combined Forces Command Afghanistan (CFC-A) as well as a professor of strategy at the National War College, National Defense University, Fort Lesley J. McNair, Washington, DC.
24. For further details on the Bonn political process, see UN Assistance Mission to Afghan (UNAMA), Political Affairs, www.unama-afg.org/about/_pa/political_affairs.htm.
25. "Afghan Factions Sign Landmark Deal," BBC News, 5 December 2001, http://news.bbc.co.uk/hi/engligh/world/south_asia/newsid_1692000/1692695.stm.
26. Lyse Doucet, "Can Hamid Karzai Deliver?" BBC News, 3 November 2004, http://news.bbc.co.uk/1/hi/world/south_asia/3979801.stm.
27. "Afghanistan Holds Landmark Vote," BBC News, 18 September 2005, http://news.bbc.co.uk/1/hi/world/south_asia/4255816.stm.
28. In June 2002, after a six-month stint setting up the operation, British forces handed over an establishment of some 4,500 troops from eighteen nations to a series of other leading contingents, notably from Turkey and Germany. In August 2003, the NATO force had grown to about 6,500 (twenty-six member states). "Turkey Steps in to Lead Afghan Security Mission," *Jane's Defence Weekly* 37, no. 26 (26 June 2002): 2; UN Security Council Resolution 1386 of 20 December 2001, www.un.org/Docs/scres/2001/sc2001.htm.
29. In his testimony to the 9/11 commission, US Secretary of State Colin Powell claimed that 205 schools and 140 health clinics were built or rehabilitated between 2002 and March 2004. The fiscal year 2005 federal budget included a request for a further US$1.2 billion in assistance to Afghanistan, with the aim of rehabilitating a further

275 schools and 150 health clinics by June 2004. Statement of Colin Powell to the 9/11 Commission, 23 March 2004, http://govinfo.library.unt.edu/911/hearings/hearing8/powell_statement.pdf, 20.

30. Figure given by Peter Rodman to the Senate Foreign Relations Committee, 12 February 2003, http://foreign.senate.gov/hearings/2003/hrg030212a.html, 2, 8–9.

31. Figure given by US Secretary of State Colin Powell in "The President's Budget Request for FY 2005," written remarks to the Senate Budget Committee, 26 February 2004, http://budget.senate.gov/democratic/testimony/2004/powell_intlaffairsbudget2005.pdf, 3.

32. Paul Reynolds, "Afghanistan Nation-Building at Critical Point," BBC News, 31 March 2004, http://news.bbc.co.uk/2/hi/south_asia/3582677.stm.

33. From the statement made by the president of the Transitional Islamic State of Afghanistan, Hamid Karzi, to the 59th Session of the General Assembly of the United Nations, New York, 21 September 2001, www.un.org/webcast/ga/59/21.html, 2.

34. "Afghan Army Development Speeded Up," *Jane's Defence Weekly* (16 March 2005): 7.

35. Lamm, "Success in Afghanistan," 25–27.

36. Vance Serchuk, "Innovative Teams Are Building Goodwill at the Grass-Roots Level," *Armed Forces Journal* (November 2005): 23–24; see also Rodman, "Statement to the Senate Foreign Relations Committee."

37. Serchuk, "Innovative Teams," 23–24.

38. Ibid., 24.

39. "Aid Doctors Leave Afghanistan," BBC News, 28 July 2004, http://news.bbc.co.uk/1/hi/world/south_asia/3931995.stm.

40. Andrew North, "Why Afghanistan Remains Work In Progress," BBC News, 30 January 2006, http://news.bbc.co.uk/1/hi/world/south_asia/4656034.stm.

41. Ian Westerman, "Pacifying Afghanistan: Enduring Lessons from CORDS in Vietnam," *RUSI Journal* 153, no. 5 (October 2008): 14–21. (Colonel Ian Westerman of the British Army was the director for Multi-Agency Operations in the UK's Development, Concepts, and Doctrine Centre, Shrivenham. He set up and ran the UK-led multinational PRT in Maimana, northern Afghanistan in 2004.)

42. Ibid., 18–19.

43. Ibid., 20–21.

44. In the first two years of the nation-building efforts in Bosnia and Kosovo, the funds made available by the international community were US$1,390 and US$814 per capita, respectively. It was US$52 per capita in Afghanistan. See Clarke, *Against All Enemies,* 278.

45. For fuller quantitative details on the opium trade in Afghanistan, see United Nations Office on Drugs and Crime (in association with the Ministry of Counter Narcotics, Government of Afghanistan), "Afghanistan Opium Survey 2007: Executive Summary" (August 2007), www.unodc.org/unodc/en/crop-monitoring/index.html, vii, esp. iv, 1, 7, and 8).

46. For some insight into the impact of the drug trade across Afghanistan, see the BBC report following the visit of the Head of the UN Office on Drugs and Crime, Antonio Maria Costa, to Afghanistan in May–June 2004: "Following the Afghan Drugs Trail," BBC News, 4 June 2004, http://news.bbc.o.uk/1/hi/world/south_asia/3774003.stm.

47. Nick Meo and Leonard Doyle, "Afghanistan: A Nation Abandoned to Drugs," *The Independent,* London, 19 November 2004, 1 and 4.

48. Greg Mills, "Calibrating Ink Spots: Filling Afghanistan's Ungoverned Spaces," *RUSI Journal* 151, no. 4 (August 2006): 16–25.

49. United Nations Office on Drugs and Crime, "Afghanistan Opium Survey 2007," 1.

50. "Afghan Drug Lord Handed to US," BBC News, 25 October 2005, http://news.bbc.co.uk/1/hi/world/south_asia/4373744.stm.

51. Barry McCaffrey, "The War We're Winning," *Armed Forces Journal* (November 2005): 17–19, esp. 19.

52. Andrew North, "Losing the War on Afghan Drugs," BBC News, 4 December 2005, http://news.bbc.co.uk/1/hi/world/south_asia/4493596.stm.

53. Mills, "Calibrating Ink Spots," 16–25.

54. Tom Coghlan, "British Make Big Advance in War on the Afghan Poppy," *Daily Telegraph,* 25 April 2008, 18.

55. Lamm, "Success in Afghanistan," 27.

56. Sean D. Naylor, "The Taliban Lost the War in Afghanistan, but Still Bedevils Coalition Efforts to Establish Security," *Armed Forces Journal* (November 2005): 19–23, esp. 22.

57. Anthony Davis, "Afghan Security Deteriorates as Taliban Regroup," *Jane's Intelligence Review* 15, no. 5 (May 2003): 10–15.

58. Ilyas Khan, "Pakistanis Bear Brunt of Bomb Blast," BBC News, 21 September 2008, http://news.bbc.co.uk/1/hi/world/south_asia/7627755.stm.

59. Jason Burke, "The New Taliban," *The Observer,* 14 October 2007, 31–33.

60. Christiana Lamb, "Rogue Pakistan Spies Aid Taliban," *The Sunday Times,* 3 August 2008, 25; for further reporting on the tribal areas, see Ilyas Khan, "The Afghan-Pakistan Military Nexus," BBC News, 10 September 2008, http://news.bbc.co.uk/1/hi/world/south_asia/7601748.stm.

61. See Seth G. Jones, "Pakistan's Dangerous Game," *Survival* 49, no. 1 (Spring 2007): 15–32.

62. Lamb, "Rogue Pakistan Spies Aid Taliban," 25.

63. Ahmed Rashid, "Pakistan Crisis Hits Army Morale," BBC News, 6 September 2007, http://news.bbc.co.uk/1/hi/world/south_asia/6978240.stm.

64. Shaukat Qadir (Brigadier, ret., Pakistan Army), "Pakistan's Waziristan Problem," *RUSI Journal* 153, no. 2 (April 2008): 42–45, esp. 44.

65. Jones, "Pakistan's Dangerous Game," 20.

66. Christiana Lamb, "The Bandits Wait for the British," *The Sunday Times,* 29 January 2006, 25.

67. Christiana Lamb, "US Sends in Its Taliban Tamers," *The Sunday Times,* 28 January 2007, 24.

68. Charles Haviland, "Afghan Bombers Foreigners—UN," BBC News, 8 September 2007, http://news.bbc.co.uk/1/hi/world/south_asia/6985400.stm.

69. Lamb, "The Bandits Wait for the British," 25.

70. For some discussion about the role of Provincial Reconstruction Teams (PRTs), Provincial Development Plans (PDPs), and the system of District and Provincial Development Committees, see David Richards (Lieutenant General, British Army), "NATO in Afghanistan, Transformation on the Front Line," *RUSI Journal* 151, no. 4 (August 2006): 10–14; Mills, "Calibrating Ink Spots," 16–25.

71. Lamb, "US Sends in Its Taliban Tamers," 24.

72. Christiana Lamb, "What a Bloody Hopeless War," *The Sunday Times,* Review, 10 September 2006, 3.

73. Ibid., 3.

74. Jason Burke, "Dam Holds Back Force of the Taliban," *The Observer,* 28 January 2007, 37.

75. Dominique Orsini, "Walking the Tightrope: Dealing with Warlords in Afghanistan's Destabilizing North," *RUSI Journal* 152, no. 5 (October 2007): 46–50 (Orsini

was political officer and head of office in the UN Assistance Mission in Afghanistan in Badakhshan province, 2006–2007).

76. Ibid.

77. Andrew M. Roe (Major, British Army), "To Create a Stable Afghanistan: Provisional Reconstruction Teams, Good Governance, and a Splash of History," *Military Review* 85, no. 6 (November–December 2005): 20–26.

78. Carlotta Gall, "Afghan Leader Criticizes U.S. on Conduct of War," 26 April 2008, New York Times Online, www.nytimes.com/2008/04/26/world/asia/26afghan.html?_r=1&scp=2&sq=Hamid%20Karzai&st=cse&oref=slogin.

79. Caroline Wyatt, "NATO 'Wavering' over Afghanistan," BBC News, 20 October 2008, http://news.bbc.co.uk/1/hi/world/south_asia/7681166.stm.

80. "A Surge of Pessimism," *The Economist,* 18–24 October 2008, 80.

81. Simon Jenkins, "Stop Killing the Taliban—They Offer the Best Hope of Beating Al-Qaeda," *The Sunday Times,* 22 June 2008, 20.

6
Planning the Iraq War

There are good ideas that are well executed, good ideas that are badly executed, bad ideas that are well executed, and bad ideas that are badly executed. With hindsight, it would be difficult to argue that the decision of President George W. Bush to conquer Iraq represented the first of these possibilities. In fact, it was a policymaking disaster that discredited those who instigated it—and it became a human disaster for the people of Iraq. Any debate over the wisdom of the Iraq War, therefore, spans only the last three possibilities outlined above.

The causes of the Iraq disaster are so numerous and so difficult to unpack that the debate will continue for years to come. The analysis below tends toward the fourth possibility cited above: In the general and particular context in which the Iraq War was conducted, the achievement of the desired political objectives was never a realistic possibility. It was a bad idea that was badly executed. The discussion below is an assessment of the general context in which the war was planned and conducted, especially the way in which political and legal factors thwarted an effective planning process. Later, in Chapters 7 and 8, the discussion focuses on how the particular conditions in Iraq meant that strategic success was always improbable, including how flaws in the US war plan exacerbated what were already very poor prospects for success. In the final analysis, the Bush administration's proposition that resistance to a US-ordained political order in Iraq could be subdued—and the country could be transformed into a democracy and a long-term strategic ally—was simply beyond the bounds of possibility in the time frame available.

A Problematic Planning Context

From the perspective of 2009, there seems little doubt that the decision of the Bush administration to undertake regime change in Iraq—and to use whatever military force was necessary to achieve that political objective—reflected a predisposition precipitated by 9/11. Several key figures in the administration had long supported the idea of overthrowing Saddam Hussein. Subsequent evidence, notably the leaked Downing Street memo of 31 January 2003, support the suspicion that the Bush administration had resolved to change the regime by force regardless of the diplomacy then going on.[1] If Iraq hadn't been penciled in after 9/11, then Bush appears to have committed himself to regime change during the first few months of 2002, beginning the evolution that led to the invasion. The US war plan was initially formulated between late November 2001 and June 2002 and sent over to the United Kingdom during the first week of July 2002 for consideration by a select group of British planners.[2] The debate within the Pentagon between advocates of the Generated Start option (a heavier, more prepared deployment) and Running Start (a relatively late, fast, and light deployment) resulted in the so-called Hybrid Plan by August, although this plan would be refined to look more like Generated Start later that year.[3] In September 2002, elements of US 3rd Infantry Division began to preposition in Kuwait and commence training. In late November, a theater headquarters was developed in Qatar, and full-scale wargaming exercises were initiated. By January 2003, therefore, the bulk of the forces required were generated in the region. On 20 January 2003, President Bush signed National Security Presidential Directive 24, which made the Department of Defense the lead institution on Iraq policy, prompting the Pentagon to set up the Office of Reconstruction and Humanitarian Affairs (ORHA) to prepare for the occupation of postwar Iraq.

Although terminating Saddam Hussein's evil tyranny might have been a good idea in principle, the inherent problem was that any use of force to achieve outright political objectives was illegal under international law, specifically article 2(4) of the UN Charter, unless it was enabled by the right of self-defense permitted under article 51 (which clearly did not apply) or authorized by the UN Security Council as part of a so-called Chapter 7 enforcement action.[4] Thus, a legal justification was necessary, with the only available argument being that Iraq had evaded UN-authorized monitoring of WMD over many years and must be brought to account. The legal process in the UN Security Council, however, did not go the way the United States had hoped. UN Security Council Resolution 1441, passed unanimously, threatened Iraq with "serious consequences" for further noncompliance, but it was not unambiguous.[5] Many Security Council members voted for Resolution 1441 precisely as a way to tie the United States and United Kingdom to the UN process, not as an authorization for further military action. Resolution 1441 did not mention the magic words "all necessary means" with respect to enforcement. When Hans Blix, the head of UNMOVIC, the UN's weapons monitoring mission in Iraq, reported to the Security Council on 27 January 2003 and 14 February 2003, he reported finding no WMD but was unable to disprove that Iraq was not cheating. Reasonably,

Blix wanted more time, as did much of the international community. Thus, when the United States and the United Kingdom immediately pushed for a second resolution in search of "all necessary means," there was a major split among the international community. The second resolution—introduced by the United States, the UK, and Spain on 24 February 2003, declaring Iraq to be in breech of Resolution 1441—foundered before a vote was cast; there was to be no specific authorization for the use of force.

The failure to get a follow-up resolution was a body-blow to any legal case: There would be little consensus in the international community about the legality of US military action.[6] Indeed, it must be said, the idea that a powerful state was entitled to invade and conquer another UN member state, based on disputed interpretations of ten-year-old resolutions was contentious, to say the least. Surely, if international law was to have any meaning, an undertaking on such a scale required specific authorization. The transparent reality was that the United States had gone to the international community demanding an exceptional right to use force against Iraq, and when it did not get what it wanted it went ahead anyway. Although Iraq may or may not have been a morally good war, it was difficult to see it as a legally sanctioned war.

Much of the prewar debate about legality generated more heat than light. The debate was soon enmeshed in a tangle of secondary issues about government spin and the media's handling of the issues. Ultimately, the problem of legality was manageable because no one was ever going to hold the United States to account, and US forces were capable of undertaking the proposed military action alone if need be. If President Bush and Prime Minister Tony Blair did nothing else, it was to expose international law for what it really was. In Benjamin Barber's words, it was the "destitute camp follower of the itinerant armies of transnationalism," less a system of impartial law and more a set of hegemonic rules.[7] Yet the issue of legality *was* important, because it raised the level of opposition to the Iraq War and seriously distorted the planning process for the war itself.

Even if Bush and Blair had genuinely believed in the existence and threat of Iraqi WMD, going to war on the basis of noncompliance with UN monitoring always embodied a hypothesis that could neither be proved nor disproved beforehand.[8] Indeed, the risk of being proved wrong was quite a possibility, because UNMOVIC and other intelligence sources indicated that Iraq had only limited WMD and ballistic-missile capabilities: There was no industrial-scale nuclear weapons program, no industrial-scale production of chemical weapons, and possibly fewer than twenty Al-Hussein ballistic missiles.[9] Bush and Blair gambled that hidden WMD existed and would eventually be found, thereby providing post facto legitimacy for going to war: It was a pact with the devil that was eventually to turn sour, and the blow to the legitimacy of the entire Iraq project would be serious indeed.

In an article published in the *Review of International Studies* in December 2005, Richard Falk made the argument that the Iraq War was neither legal nor legitimate.[10] For Falk, even though the NATO operation over Kosovo in 1999 was not authorized by the UN Security Council, it was widely seen as a "principled violation" of the UN Charter because it provided a necessary, effective, and proportionate response to an ongoing humanitarian emergency.[11] Moreover, while the UN did not provide full "rightful authority" for the Kosovo intervention, it was conducted by the next best representative of the international community—the regional organization NATO. By comparison, Iraq ticked none of the boxes, and Falk concluded that

> I would maintain that the position taken by the Bush administration was illegal and illegitimate from the outset, and not susceptible to be legitimated after the fact. At most, the degree of illegitimacy could have been considerably mitigated if large stockpiles of WMD had been discovered together with plans for future wars and if the Iraqi people had overwhelmingly welcomed the foreign forces as liberators. Then, and only then, could one credibly dismiss the resisting elements in Iraq, as was done by Donald Rumsfeld, as "dead-enders."[12]

Thus, the invasion of Iraq could not be seen as a last resort, as a response to an imminent threat or ongoing humanitarian emergency, or as something conducted by an authority any more "rightful" than the Bush administration. Neither would the United States be able to retroactively legitimize the invasion by virtue of its effectiveness. The WMD never existed, or at least was never found, and the gross mismanagement of postwar Iraq after the invasion cast further doubt over whether the United States had done right. It may be possible for illegal actions to become legitimate, but it does not happen very often, and it simply could not have happened with Iraq. The Iraq War was not seen as either legal or legitimate by great swathes of opinion in the United States itself, the Western world, the Middle East, and beyond. Fighting such a highly contentious war of choice in the context of the liberal international order was simply a bad idea.

Doubts about the legal case for war were pronounced among some of America's key allies, notably Great Britain and Turkey, both of whom were anxious to obtain specific UN authorization before committing to war. Bush decided to indulge these concerns, although—as some key Bush aides feared—this significantly complicated the run-up to military action by highlighting political and legal objections. The most immediate effect was that prewar politics in Turkey did not help US-British war planning. The election of the Islamist-tinged government of Recep Erdogan had strengthened the antiwar camp in Turkey. A multibillion-dollar aid package was not enough to buy off Turkey, and a motion introduced in the Turkish parliament allowing for the passage of up to 62,000 Coalition troops was stymied; Turkey insisted upon UN authorization first. In fact, in December, given the likely closure of routes through Turkey, most British forces committed to invading Iraq were pulled out of the proposed northern front and redirected southward—a change that significantly disrupted the generation of British forces in the region and delayed whatever meager planning was taking place for the postwar phase. The largest and most sophisticated division in the US Army, 4th Infantry Division, was also left at sea until it redeployed to Iraq via Kuwait in mid-April 2003.

The need to justify the forthcoming war in terms of eliminating WMD would also seriously distort the planning process. The Iraq War was to be a classic case where the rationale for war—something or other about WMD and Iraqi noncompliance—obscured the real function: to invade, conquer, subjugate, and transform the country. But because this skirted the bounds of international law, US and British policymakers and commanders could not say as much, or allow sufficient discussion on the matter, or make sure that adequate resources were in place beforehand. A few coalition policymakers and commanders, notably in Great Britain, even appeared to fool themselves into believing that the conquest and subjugation of Iraq were quite incidental to the dispute about WMD; the reality was that there was never any serious chance that diplomacy would stop the war from happening.[13]

The general problems caused by the legal uncertainties fed into a number of particular problems relating to the dynamics of the Bush administration. The truth is, war planning is rarely the outcome of a rational assessment of problem and requirement done by competent people. Rather, plans more often emerge through ideological distortion, debates about the allocation of resources, and internal political and bureaucratic processes. A number of particular things appear to have happened within the Bush administration.

First, there was the Pentagon, specifically with respect to mission intent and the decisions about appropriate resourcing to achieve that mission (whatever that was). From today's standpoint, the postwar planning done by US Secretary of Defense Donald Rumsfeld and his Pentagon team appears extraordinarily inadequate. Why? Several possibilities exist. (1) The Pentagon team, or some members of it, knew about the shortfalls in postwar planning but didn't care or think it relevant (they were cynics). (2) They knew about the shortfalls but were simply unable to properly address them for organizational and political reasons (they were frustrated). (3) They simply didn't understand the magnitude of the problem that faced them (they were ignorant and inept). All three can be traced by examining the decisionmaking process, with some of the personalities appearing more cynical, frustrated, or ignorant than others; the balance between cynicism, frustration, and ignorance changed over time as well.

At the outset, despite their neoconservative inclinations to spread freedom around the world, the Pentagon team appears to have been circumspect about what the United States could or should do in postwar Iraq, with Donald Rumsfeld's basic instinct being to prevent the United States from getting too tied down in some colossal nation-building and social work job. As he saw it, the installation of freedom in Iraq would be messy, and it would ultimately be up to the Iraqis. Indeed, the strategic aim that appears to have quietly been fostered was to hand over Iraq to a small group of friendly exiles, led by Ahmed Chalabi, in less than ninety days after the occupation. Rumsfeld appears to have believed that the use of force would be so efficient that it would somehow be decisive (no doubt, by some process of shock and awe), with the attendant hope that things would simply work out. This mix of cynicism and ignorance was to last well into the occupation, with the Pentagon team looking to withdraw the vast bulk of US forces within months of regime change and to limit any involvement of its forces in nation-building. In this respect, there seems to have been a major disconnect between the aspirations of the Pentagon compared to the views held by the other branches of government, including President Bush at the White House, who appears to have understood that the subjugation and transformation of Iraq would require more substantial US engagement. In the aftermath of the invasion, this disconnect manifested in the growing tensions between Rumsfeld's team and the president's de facto envoy in Iraq, L. Paul Bremer, head of the Coalition Provisional Authority (CPA).

Second: The Pentagon's planning process was affected by the problematic political and legal context. For the likes of Vice President Cheney and the team at the Pentagon, the first priority was to get to the point of invading Iraq rather than worrying everybody about all the reasons *not* to do it. Thus, top policymakers were prone to wishful thinking, risk avoidance, distortion of facts, and the promotion of partial and even faulty intelligence to justify the case for war and to prove the viability of the mission. To stay focused—and also doubtless to avoid the inevitable press leaks once contentious debates began within the government—policymakers swept under the carpet all indications of how difficult and expensive the conquest of Iraq was likely going to be. Among the comprehensive studies largely ignored and not disseminated was the State Department's Future of Iraq Project, in addition to a number of studies undertaken by the US Army War College, the Naval War College, National Defense University, the Association of the US Army in cooperation with the Center for Strategic and International Studies, and the Institute for Defense Analysis.[14]

Instead, the White House and Pentagon promoted the expert views of a few Iraqi exiles, especially those associated with Ahmed Chalabi and the Iraqi National Congress (INC), as well as a number of sympathetic academics. The advice was tinged by self-interested agendas and detached from realities on the ground, and it reinforced the already distorted picture that key figures seem to have held. In his speech to veterans on 26 August 2002, for instance, Vice President Cheney expressed the view that "as for the reaction of the Arab 'street,' the Middle East expert Professor Fouad Ajami predicts that after liberation, the streets in Basra and Baghdad are 'sure to erupt in joy in the same way the throngs in Kabul greeted the Americans.' Extremists in the region would have to rethink their strategy of Jihad. Moderates throughout the region would take heart. And our ability to advance the Israeli-Palestinian peace process would be enhanced, just as it was following the liberation of Kuwait in 1991."[15]

This was optimism bordering on simplistic fantasy. Less benign scenarios were not really considered, much less planned for. In reality, even though the vast majority of Iraqis wanted to see an end to Saddam Hussein, most were also ambivalent or hostile to the United States. Many Iraqis despised former US policies, were repelled by its alliance with Israel, and were suspicious about its future intentions.

Third: Planning for Iraq intersected preexisting politics at the Pentagon, in particular Rumsfeld's authoritarian style—he cowed the generals—and his determination to push through the transformation agenda.[16] Rumsfeld's demand was that US forces harness new technologies and techniques, especially through use of airpower, to slim down their overall size and budgets. What transformation meant with respect to Iraq was prolonged haggling between civilian policymakers and military staff over troop numbers as well as the timing for assembling forces in the region. In the end, Rumsfeld would take to vetting each and every unit committed, personally supervising the implementation of the Time-Phased Force Deployment List.[17]

The existing plan for a possible Iraq war—OPLAN 1003-98, last reviewed by General Anthony Zinni in 1998—proposed the deployment of some 380,000 troops, although Zinni's Desert Crossing war game in 1999 indicated that even more might be needed during a postwar phase.[18] Under pressure from Rumsfeld, the commander of US Central Command, General Tommy Franks, reduced force levels in the evolving command estimate to about 275,000 troops—a figure he briefed to President Bush on 28 December 2001—but after further cajoling reportedly told Bush at Camp David on 20 April 2002 that the initial deployment could be 180,000, with a subsequent increase to some 250,000.[19] By August, the debate was between the slimmed-down Hybrid Option (advocating a light and late generation of forces) and the preferred option of the land forces commander, Lieutenant General David McKiernan, the Cobra II plan (allowing for a larger and longer generation of forces). With diplomacy stretching out into the spring of 2003, Cobra II prevailed, but there were still too few troops, and the postwar planning gap had not been bridged. When Army Chief of Staff General Eric Shinseki raised concerns about numbers and planning before the US Armed Services Committee on 23 February 2003, he was firmly rebuffed by the civilian leadership. In his well-sourced account of Iraq planning, *Fiasco: The American Military Adventure in Iraq,* Thomas E. Ricks observed that the way in which Shinseki was slapped down in public and private had a "chilling effect" on further discussion among the senior military staff.[20] In the end, the US invasion of Iraq in March and April 2003 would directly employ only about 145,000 troops: three Army divisions (3rd Infantry, 101st Airborne, and a brigade each from 82nd Airborne and 173rd Airborne Divisions) numbering some 65,000, a large US Marine Corps task force numbering about 60,000, and a British division of about 20,000.[21] US 4th Infantry Division was unable to redeploy in time from the closed route through Turkey.

Fourth: Notwithstanding the problem that it was not a realistic strategic aim to hand over Iraq to a handful of preferred exiles, the Pentagon failed to stand up an organization that was capable of developing a viable concept and practical plan for the occupation and transfer of power. Initially, in the summer of 2002, planning for the postwar phase was given to US Central Command; its planning staff had recently worked on the Afghan campaign, and they were now fully immersed in rewrites of the Iraqi war plan. General Franks appears to have been content to largely delegate the job to a new office in Qatar, Joint Task Force IV (JTF-IV), under US Army Brigadier General Steve Hawkins.22 In Thomas Ricks's account, JTF-IV mistook activity for progress, and it was unable to produce much of actual use. A plan that consisted of thirty-two PowerPoint briefing slides was scarcely enough, with Ricks quoting the deputy chief of plans at US Central Command, Colonel John Agoglia, recalling that "we thought that it would be the core of planning for a post-conflict headquarters. Instead, it was Steve Hawkins and fifty-five yahoos with shareware who were clueless."23

To be fair to the team at JTF-IV, Brigadier Hawkins had received a task, at which he could not help but fail, from policymakers and senior commanders who should have known better. The project was such a colossal undertaking that it demanded a major national strategy, something that JTF-IV was simply incapable of formulating and resourcing. Big ideas about the future of Iraq were involved, but they were not communicated down the chain. Moreover, JTF-IV was an ad hoc body and had few of the capacities (people, expertise, contacts, funding) needed to coordinate a large multiagency effort—and it certainly could not do it from Qatar. Sending off the planning for the most strategic element of the Iraq War to a substrategic level may have doomed the mission to failure from the outset.

By late December 2002, it was clear at Central Command and the Pentagon that JTF-IV was faltering. But it was not until January that the planning lead was shifted to the Pentagon's Office of Special Plans, headed by a neoconservative insider, Douglas Feith. Aside from particular questions that have been raised about Douglas Feith's abilities as a manager, the Office of Special Plans was a highly insular and secretive unit.24 Much of its work was premised on a quick handover to the Pentagon's handful of tame Iraqi exiles, but no one else was ever given the opportunity to sign off on the scheme—not the White House, State Department, CIA, or any US ally. Although no one complained about Feith's flawed planning assumptions prior to the war—such was the reluctance to raise problems—they would not be a done deal in its aftermath. Neither the State Department nor the CIA thought that Ahmed Chalabi and his Iraqi National Congress were a remotely sensible option.

Having seen one ad hoc planning unit (JTF-IV) with inadequate capacities fail, the Pentagon then moved to set up another. On 17 January 2003, Feith called upon Lieutenant General Jay Garner (US Army, ret.) to head up the new

Office of Reconstruction and Humanitarian Assistance (ORHA). After some persuasion, Garner took the job. Garner was a capable and experienced man, but he also had been given an impossible job. Garner's mistake was that even though he realized the situation, he did not do enough to make sure that others did.[25]

In the end, Garner and the ORHA lacked everything needed to succeed. Feith was coy about the ultimate strategic aims, and much of the work being done by the Office of Special Plans, much less anywhere else, was simply not passed along to him.[26] Garner got little more help in formulating a practical plan and resourcing an organization capable of carrying it out. Beside phoning some of his former colleagues, the process of hiring key staff was dogged by a totally inadequate level of resourcing and administration, as well as bitter interagency squabbling. Indeed, Garner's preparedness to think about co-opting the expertise of the State Department and international community may have undermined his position at the White House and Pentagon. Certainly, getting right-thinking people approved by Rumsfeld and Feith slowed the recruitment of expert personnel into ORHA.[27] In the end, Garner himself was not even able to get to Baghdad until 21 April, and within days of his arrival he was phoned by Rumsfeld to be told that ORHA was to be wound up and replaced by yet another ad hoc organization, the Coalition Provisional Authority under L. Paul Bremer, by mid-May.[28]

In his engaging and well-sourced account of US missteps in Iraq, *Imperial Life in the Emerald City,* Rajiv Chandrasekaran speculated that Garner was almost set up to fail. According to Chandrasekaran, "Feith's hope, as articulated to others in the Pentagon, was that without a clear blue print for the political transition, Garner would turn to Chalabi and his band of exiles. Feith would get the outcome he wanted without provoking a fight ahead of time with State and the CIA, both of which regarded Chalabi as a fraud."[29] In other words, politics demanded that circumstances prevailed in which Chalabi and the INC simply emerged as the best alternative. The Pentagon may have feared that if it pressed its pro-Chalabi hand too early, a full-fledged interagency squabble would break out in which the White House might come down on someone else's side. As it turned out, the subsequent installation of Paul Bremer and the CPA would see Chalabi and the INC firmly sidelined. Whatever the truth about Washington politics at the time, the drift from one ad hoc organization (JTF-IV) to another (ORHA) and to yet another (CPA) in the middle of the operation was a prescription for failure.

The Iraq War: March–April 2003

If the US administration faltered when it came to planning for postwar Iraq, the superb armed forces of the United States had an unrivalled capacity to transport its politicians to the point of disaster.[30] The war plan for Iraq encompassed two major components designed to effect the speedy overthrow of Saddam Hussein's regime: an armored maneuver component, and an information warfare component. Because regime change was the principal objective, a prolonged period of attritional softening up by means of airpower was not part of the plan. Bridges over the Tigris and Euphrates Rivers were to be taken intact to allow US land forces to initiate a rolling start, proceeding northward as rapidly as possible.

The US plan was bold. It identified Baghdad as the center of gravity and proposed sending a ribbon of armor across hundreds of miles of desert to storm the capital and thereby initiate the disintegration of Saddam Hussein's regime. In the event, 3rd US Infantry Division's drive to Baghdad—bypassing the complex landscape and population centers of the Euphrates' valley—was the nearest thing to blitzkrieg since World War II. The promise of this armored drive was to achieve disproportionate effects for the resources applied. The speed and violence of the advance would either overwhelm or disable Iraqi forces before they had a chance to develop a defense. A minimal amount of collateral damage, which would have to be fixed later, would be inflicted. The inherent risk of waging such a lightning war was that US forces had to move fast and relatively lightly, with US policymakers and commanders banking on the dissolution of Iraqi resistance once Baghdad had fallen to negate the need for large numbers of infantrymen for mopping-up operations.

Among the most distinctive developments introduced by US forces was an effects-based approach to warfare that synchronized physical effects with cognitive effects. Thus, working alongside precision air strikes and high-tempo armored maneuvers were psychological and information operations designed under the auspices of the director of information operations at US Central Command, Major General Gene Renuart.[31] Indeed, when US strategists talked about shock and awe, they did not necessarily mean that they intended to deliver overwhelming destructive force—that was just one option among a portfolio of other techniques that could be deployed to pressure the opposing force to the point of disintegration.[32] In Iraq, shock and awe was to be much more subtle than it sounded, because the cognitive element of the campaign could reasonably be expected to deliver an unusually high payoff.

Saddam Hussein's regime had long since exhausted any broader appeal in Iraq, with its survival increasingly reliant on the core terror apparatus. The principal task of the information warriors inside the CIA and US military was to get among the core security apparatus, as well as between the core apparatus and the mass of the Iraqi army and population. The Special Republican Guard, and the Fedayeen Saddam paramilitary force under Saddam's son, Uday, were mostly loyal, but it seemed unlikely that the mass of the Iraqi army would fight unless it was closely supervised by the core apparatus. Amid the various personal and clan rivalries that had developed within the Republic Guards

Corps and Iraqi army over the preceding years, its loyalty had become questionable. Information operations set about instigating defections, undermining the will of Iraqi troops to fight, generating intelligence, and persuading ordinary Iraqis to stay out of the way. If the information campaign succeeded, the hold of the core security apparatus would be broken before patriotic impulses against the invasion inclined more Iraqi soldiers and civilians to resist.

In the course of the information operations, the United States dropped countless leaflets, broadcast radio messages, and launched an extraordinary telephone and email campaign that made personal contact with thousands of Iraqis, especially army officers and local notables.[33] The Iraqi opposition and Arabs from other countries were harnessed. Lebanon's former president, Amin Gemayel, was reportedly used to relay the realities of the situation to Saddam Hussein himself, as well as to make contact with other members of the regime and security forces. The Iraqi National Congress organized interpreters, guides, and intelligence-gatherers to infiltrate Iraq and assist US forces. Iraqi National Accord, a group fronted by Iyad Allawi, included many former members of the Iraqi military and security services, and they set about agitating among their contacts in Iraq.

The objectives of the information war appear to have been largely realized: Iraqi commanders were turned and persuaded to do things that hastened the defeat or dissolution of army units; the vast majority of Iraqi troops declined to fight; and the regime was unable to sabotage key parts of the country's infrastructure, notably its oil production and refining facilities. Among the most important achievements of the information war was the penetration of Republican Guard and Special Republican Guard units. The details remain murky, but stories later circulated that senior Republican Guard officers at general staff and divisional levels—even up to the chief of staff of the Special Republican Guard, General Mahar Soufiane al-Takriti—were induced not to fight or to purposely sabotage an effective defense.[34] Republican Guard officers in the field were later quoted as saying that they believed they had been betrayed by superiors. At a national level, the Iraqi regime continued to propagate its messages for a time, but when its television and radio broadcasts were finally extinguished as US forces approached Baghdad the regime simply seemed to fade away.

The armored maneuver component of the US campaign was launched on 20 March 2003. Its start came slightly ahead of schedule—and was slightly more ragged that it might have been—as US forces responded to an intelligence tip that Saddam Hussein was in a house in the Doura Farms complex in southern Baghdad; an air strike was called in but the target slipped away.[35] Once the air war was initiated against command-and-control and other key targets, coalition land forces immediately began their rolling start, moving into Iraq on the night of 21 March (see Figure 6.1). With the coalition having failed to route US 4th Infantry Division and British forces through Turkey, the principal axis of

Figure 6.1 Map of the Iraq War, 2003

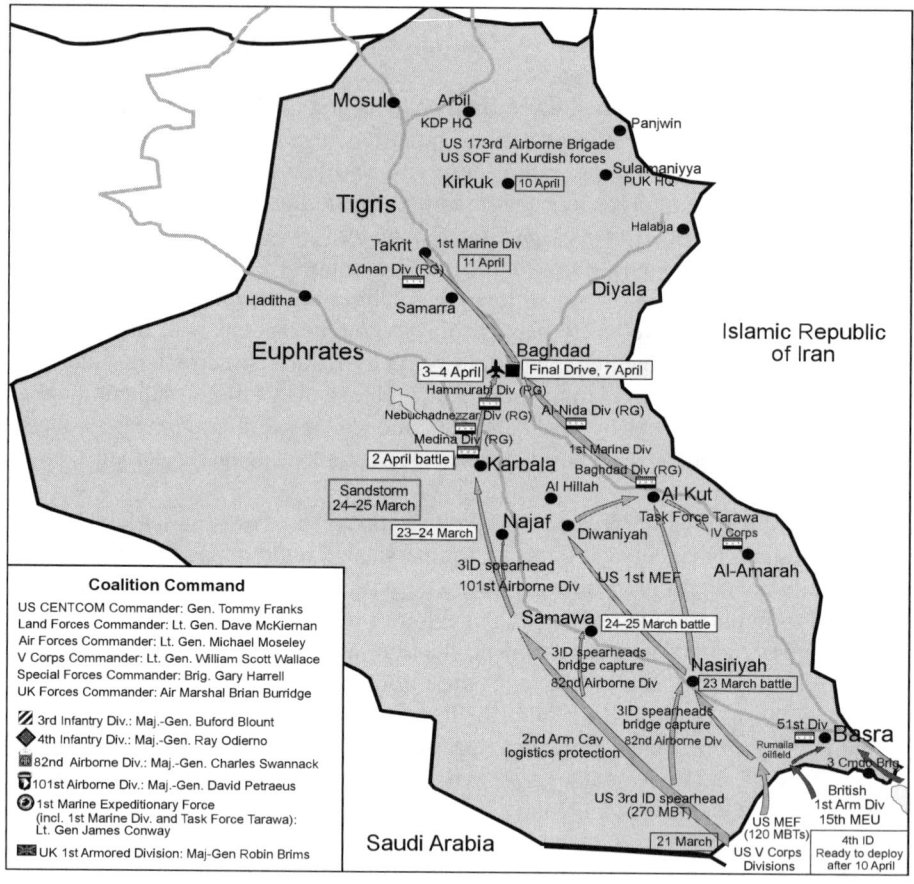

attack was from the south, with 3rd Infantry Division driving on Baghdad while skirting west of the Euphrates Valley, and 1st Marine Division taking the more difficult line of advance up the Tigris and Euphrates Valleys.[36] British forces secured Fao Peninsula and the oilfields near the southern borders, then pushed on to Basra.[37] Within a few hours of the start, elements of the US spearhead were already 100 miles into Iraq.

Iraqi forces were never going to deal with the speed and violence of what was coming. Systematic air attacks meant that Iraqi command and control largely disintegrated within the first week. Many Iraqi commanders were reduced to employing runners. Once out of close contact with higher command, much of the regular army was either passive or quickly began to disintegrate whenever the prospect of contact with coalition forces loomed. The most determined resistance was put up by members of Fedayeen Saddam and the Special Republican Guard, as well as assorted bands of irregulars who often fought from light vehicles. On occasion, these forces focused their resistance, and in a few places they held up US forces for a period. During the fighting in Nasiriyah from 23 March, for instance, US forces lost thirty killed and sixty injured.[38] Iraqi irregulars were also able to take advantage of an inherent problem of lightning maneuver: Sending a fast-moving ribbon of armor to a distant decapitation or incapacitation objective inevitably left enemy troops in the rear area and exposed rear-echelon forces to insurgent-type attacks. Logistics and support troops were killed and captured in a series of incidents, most notably involving the 507th Maintenance Company in Nasiriyah. Iraqi insurgency tactics included suicide bombings, with the first being an attack in Najaf on 29 March 2003 that killed four US troops.[39]

The activities of Fedayeen insurgents had a number of effects. They cast a continued shadow over the Iraqi population and army that slowed the effects of information operations, not least because given the presence of suicide bombers, coalition troops were forced to distance themselves from Iraqi civilians. Insurgent attacks also diverted troops. 101st Airborne Division, including its Apache helicopters, spent more time than envisaged managing the insurgent threat along 3rd Infantry Division's line of advance, and 2nd Armored Cavalry Regiment was also rushed in. Yet while attacks along the line of advance sparked some public debate in the United States and Britain, the level of Iraqi activity was well within tolerable parameters. Insurgent-type attacks in US rear areas did not represent a critical threat to the main line of advance. For the US forces spearheading the advance, it was always better to press on because the real payoff—a quick victory—lay ahead. During the drive to Baghdad, the insurgents had less effect than the weather, and if there was any hiatus along the route it was caused by the huge sandstorm that hit the entire theater from 24 to 27 March.

The Iraq War came to a culminating point as 3rd Infantry Division approached Baghdad from the southwest during the first week of April. The approaches to the city were guarded by a number of Republican Guard divisions. Medina Division held positions to the southwest in the so-called Karbala Gap, the passage of land between the Euphrates River and Lake Razazah to the west; its position threatened something of a bottleneck that could hold up the advance to Baghdad and precipitate a logistics crunch. But with the coalition synchronizing kinetic and information operations, Medina Division was demolished from the air and outmaneuvered on land.[40] 3rd Infantry's passage was not significantly slowed. In fact, the forward positioning of almost all Republican Guard divisions along the approaches to Baghdad, rather than in the city itself, significantly eased the task of disabling them. One must suppose that Saddam was either reluctant to station Republican Guard divisions in Baghdad for fear of a military coup, or lacked the will or ability to turn Baghdad into an urban bastion. On 3 April, the lead elements of 3rd Infantry moved to take Baghdad's international airport.

3rd Infantry Division ended its drive on Baghdad with its fearsome armored probing around the international airport and the west of the city from 6 to 8 April.[41] The Iraqi regime could do little more than commit a few Special Republican Guard units to a disastrous head-on assault against the airport; disorganized irregulars were shot to pieces. As US tanks rolled onto the bridges over the Tigris River in central Baghdad, the clear failure of the Iraqi regime's rhetoric to stop the US advance into the city magnified the shock value. When Saddam fled Baghdad, the fear that the capital might become an urban battlefield, requiring weeks of street-to-street fighting to overcome, quickly faded. Everywhere, the regime simply dissolved. On 9 April, crowds gathered in central Baghdad to begin destroying the symbols of Saddam's rule, with the iconic moment coming in al-Fardus Square, where Marine Corps engineers helped jubilant Iraqis pull down Saddam's monumental statue. 1st Marine Division soon swept into Baghdad from the east, moving on to occupy the heartland of the regime. Tikrit was taken by 14 April. It was over more easily than anyone had imagined.

The Iraq War of March–April 2003 was a triumph for US arms and its concept of warfare. Many of the promises of network-enabled effects-based warfare were realized. Iraqi resistance was overcome, disabled, and dissolved with unprecedented efficiency. US casualties were low for an operation of such scale. When President Bush announced an end to major combat operations on 1 May 2003, US forces had suffered only 138 killed.[42]

However, it must be said that the war exposed Saddam Hussein's regime to be a paper tiger by that time. Decades of war and sanctions had clearly taken a toll, and the regime was scarcely capable of mounting a national defense. The failure to blow up more than a handful of oil wellheads or adequately prepare for the demolition of key bridges over the Tigris and Euphrates Rivers pointed to a drastic failure of planning and capability. Similarly, the use of major formations on the edges of cities rather than in built-up areas was badly misconceived. Bearing in mind the overwhelming power of the juggernaut heading toward them, it was perhaps understandable that most Iraqi soldiers did not want to fight—but the problem was much deeper. The regime had long lost the support of the vast majority of people, and internal cohesion was under severe strain, not least because of the wild antics of Saddam's son, Uday, during the 1990s. Divisions within the regime and security forces gave US information and psychological operations great leverage. The core security apparatus was unable to keep the Iraqi army together, and perhaps only 15 percent of Iraqi security forces put up a fight.

The inability of the Iraqi regime to mobilize the country reflected the general weakness of many Arab regimes. In *Overstating the Arab State,* Nazih

Ayubi argued that states like Iraq were "fierce," but they were not really strong. Ayubi noted that "although they have large bureaucracies, mighty armies, and harsh prisons, they are lamentably feeble when it comes to collecting taxes, winning wars or forging a really 'hegemonic' power block (in the Gramscian sense) or an ideology that can carry the state beyond the coercive and 'corporate' level and into the moral and intellectual sphere."[43]

In short, far too many Iraqis did not believe in their government—or even in Iraq itself. Where the core security apparatus of the regime was absent, the writ of the state did not run, and when the central fiefdom in Baghdad was routed, the entire apparatus of the state simply dissolved. In fact, there was a catastrophic collapse for which coalition policymakers and commanders did not preplan. Saddam Hussein's demise would leave the coalition with a poisoned chalice.

The Debacle of the Follow-On Phase

If the invasion of Iraq was a triumph for US arms, the events that followed would have put a banana republic to shame. The dissolution of the Iraqi state led to a collapse of law and order. Many tens of thousands of Iraqis went on an extraordinary three-week looting spree. The looters didn't merely target government offices and the homes of members of the former regime; they ransacked schools, hospitals, banks, shops, the electric power system, and just about every other corner of public infrastructure. Initially, coalition forces stood and watched, as some were not averse to see Iraqis redistributing some of the ill-gotten gains of the regime. When the magnitude of these events was realized, however, coalition forces had neither the numbers, the expertise, nor the administrative systems to get a hold on matters. Many more military policemen, interpreters, and training and intelligence troops were required—and the looters were able to carry on until there was little left to take. Iraq was already a debilitated third world country, but by the time the looting was over it was utterly wrecked. The chaotic breakdown made the subsequent task of occupying the country much more difficult. The high level of lawlessness was to persist, and it conveyed the impression that coalition troops were not in control.

Iraq was always going to be a hard case: It was a society divided along primordial clan and ethnic lines; it was known for high levels of social violence and lawlessness; it had a deep nationalist, revolutionary, and anti-imperialist tradition in Sunni areas; it was bound to undergo a post-Saddam Islamic revival; it was awash with arms; and it had lengthy and difficult-to-control borders. Post-Saddam Iraq may simply have been beyond the capacity of even the United States to control. And if the occupation was not difficult enough already, the mismanagement of postwar planning sealed the fate. Although there was a logic in making the Pentagon the lead organization in postwar Iraq, its ability to mount such a colossal project was hampered by the failings among its leadership, as well as its institutional culture, lack of appropriate expertise and personnel, and absence of a coherent occupation authority.

The unfolding crisis had all been foreseen. In testimony to the US Senate Foreign Relations Committee on 1 August 2002, Colonel Scott Feil—in his capacity as codirector of the Post-Conflict Reconstruction Project of the Association of the US Army and the Center for Strategic and International Studies—warned that

> the United States needs a strategy for Iraq that integrates post-conflict reconstruction efforts with the political and military campaign to accomplish regime change. U.S. planning efforts should avoid the false dichotomy of conflict and post-conflict operations, and our strategy and operational plans must define a seamless progression of tasks, responsible actors, and the resources applied to those tasks that accomplish the national objective. The planning for post-conflict reconstruction must commence now rather than after hostilities have commenced or, worse, ended.[44]

Feil returned to the Senate on 11 February 2003 and, in presenting the joint study on the future of Iraq, *A Wiser Peace,* alleged that

> the effort to implement procedures and organize resources is still fragmented and there has been more activity than movement. From an American perspective, what is needed is a clear articulation of American goals for Iraq, the delineation of the tasks America expects to accomplish, what America will assist with, and what is expected of coalition and Iraqi partners, and the dedication of resources (i.e. people, equipment and funds) to the effort. America will lead the effort. Difficult as it may be, the U.S. needs to present a plan for comment, review, revision, and implementation. Experience shows that circulating a draft is more effective than asking all concerned to start with a blank sheet of paper. At present the military effort is as nearly ready for post-conflict as it is for the military campaign, and the rest of government is supporting the military preparations for the campaign. But with respect to the post-conflict reconstruction, the U.S. and the international community are still "getting ready to get ready." The President and the Congress need to establish interagency authority and accountability now, and resources need to be pre-positioned. . . . Post conflict reconstruction in Iraq can be successful—if success is adequately defined and if resources match intent. But time is short, the planning process has not kept pace with the military and diplomatic timeline, and the agencies who can resolve some of the outstanding issues are running out of time to do so.[45]

What became clear was that nothing was going to be seamless; indeed, the Pentagon had been working off an effects-map that went only as far as regime change via the destruction of Iraqi armed forces. What lay beyond had been sketched in only the most rudimentary terms by people (led by Douglas Feith) who didn't really know how to draw the map. The effects-map titled "getting to a desired political outcome" was much larger and more complex, and neither

US nor British policymakers and commanders had really wanted to sketch it out, let alone study it, before the journey began. It was only when they got to Iraq that they began to understand the difficulty of the journey ahead and the possibility that it might be impassable after all. The entire prewar planning effort had produced only a substrategic war plan—almost completely focused at the operational level.

Amid the US failure to properly organize an occupation, the international community was scarcely in a position to come to the rescue. The disputed legitimacy of the war dissuaded involvement, and the model of multilateralized intervention developed in the 1990s—which came together in a rather organic way in Bosnia, Kosovo, and Afghanistan—simply did not coalesce in time for Iraq. Important volunteers did not step forward, with the absence of French, German, and other follow-on forces a very big loss—whether or not US policymakers and soldiers realized it. Moreover, to the extent that the UN and NGOs did become involved, they did so in support of US war objectives, and it was not long before they were identified as the enemy by insurgents. When the UN headquarters in Baghdad was demolished by a bomb on 19 August 2003, killing the head of the UN mission, Sergio Viera de Mello, the UN for the most part fled the country. The United States would have to shoulder the burden of occupying and transforming Iraq.

The Iraq War of 2003 had something of the best of times, the worst of times about it. It removed an evil tyranny and gave most Iraqis the chance of a better life. Yet it was done outside any agreed understanding of international law, and to much of the world it looked like self-interested vigilantism. The war also brought tactical and operational art to new heights, demonstrating the supremacy of US arms on a conventional battlefield. Yet the war was conducted within the context of the most problematic strategy since at least Vietnam, and it would leave the United States and Great Britain in a position in which they could be defeated. The prolonged occupation of Iraq would soon squander a great deal of the prestige that the United States and its armed forces had accrued in the post–Cold War, post-9/11 world. Ultimately, the story of the Iraq War was to become a story of what went wrong.

Notes

1. Don Van Natta Jr., "Bush Saw Iraq War as Inevitable," *International Herald Tribune* (28 March 2006); "Bush-Blair Iraq Memo Revealed," BBC News, 27 March 2006, http://news.bbc.co.uk/1/hi/world/americas/4849744.stm.

2. Nora Bensahel, "Mission Not Accomplished: What Went Wrong with Iraqi Reconstruction," *Journal of Strategic Studies* 29, no. 3 (June 2006): 453–473, esp. 454; Wesley K. Clark (General, ret., US Army), *Winning Modern Wars: Iraq, Terrorism, and the American Empire* (New York: Public Affairs, 2003), xvi, 9–10; Tim Ripley, "Planning for 'Iraqi Freedom,'" *Jane's Intelligence Review* 15, no. 7 (July 2003): 8–11, esp. 9.

3. A detailed chronology as well as declassified documents related to the Iraq planning process are available at "Top Secret Polo Step," George Washington University, National Security Archive, www.gwu.edu/~nsarchiv/NSAEBB/NSAEBB214/index.htm.

4. The UN Charter is available at www.un.org/aboutun/charter.

5. UN Security Council Resolution 1441 of 8 November 2002, www.un.org/Docs/scres/2002/sc2002.htm.

6. Having failed to get specific authorization, the US and British governments argued that war was justified anyway because Iraq had failed to fully comply with the conditions set out in various UN Security Council resolutions. The legal argument for the Iraq War of 2003 was set out by the United Kingdom's Attorney-General, Lord Goldsmith, 7 March 2003; see "Legal Basis for Use of Force Against Iraq," 17 March 2003, www.number10.gov.uk/Page3287.

7. Benjamin Barber, "Jihad and McWorld in the New World Disorder," chapter 15 in *Jihad vs. McWorld: How Globalism and Tribalism Are Reshaping the World* (New York: Ballantine Books, 1996), 219–235, esp. 225.

8. Lawrence Freedman, "War in Iraq: Selling the Threat," *Survival* 46, no. 2 (Summer 2004): 7–50, esp. 17

9. Prime Minister, *Iraq's Weapons of Mass Destruction: The Assessment of the British Government,* www.number10.gov.uk/Page271; see also Christopher Bluth, "The British Road to War: Blair, Bush, and the Decision to Invade Iraq," *International Affairs* 80, no. 5 (October 2004): 871–892.

10. Richard Falk, "Legality and Legitimacy: The Quest for Principled Flexibility and Restraint," *Review of International Studies* 31, Special Issue (December 2005): 33–50 (Richard Falk was the Albert G. Milbank Professor Emeritus of International Law and Practice at Princeton University; he was also a visiting professor of global studies, University of California–Santa Barbara).

11. Ibid., 39–40.

12. Ibid., 44.

13. British planning for the Iraq War of 2003 was disjointed for a number of reasons. The uncertain legality meant that some UK policymakers and commanders were reticent about whether the war would happen and whether UK forces would participate in it. It was also difficult to generate forces in the Middle East region: first because they could not be seen deploying before the WMD-related diplomacy had run its course; and second because a reluctant Turkey was blocking the intended deployment to northern Iraq. The UK planning effort was coordinated by a planning cell at the Permanent Joint Headquarters in Northwood. It prioritized the warfighting phase (Phase 3) before addressing follow-on operations (Phase 4). However, because planning and deployment for Phase 3 took longer than expected, due to political-legal sensitivities and Turkey's position, planning for Phase 4 was crowded out. By the time the Northwood cell turned to Phase 4, war was imminent. Moreover, planning was isolated, and the capabilities of other ministries—the Foreign Office, International Development, Treasury, and so on—were insufficiently integrated into an operational plan. The Foreign Office's own Iraqi Planning Unit, which did bring together civilian and military staff, also failed to develop a joined-up national strategy.

14. For a discussion about the planning climate, see Rajiv Chandrasekaran, "A Deer in the Headlights," chapter 2 in *Imperial Life in the Emerald City: Inside Baghdad's Green Zone* (London: Bloomsbury, 2006), 27–40.

15. Speech by US Vice President Dick Cheney to the 103rd National Convention of Veterans, 26 August 2002, American Rhetoric Online Speech Bank, www.americanrhetoric.com/speeches/dickcheney103rdvfw.htm.

16. Bob Woodward, "Breaking the Military Men: How Rumsfeld Won Total Command," *The Sunday Times,* Review, 8 October 2006, 1–3 (extracts from his book, *State of Denial*).

17. Clark, *Winning Modern Wars,* 9 and 17

18. Thomas E. Ricks, *Fiasco: The American Military Adventure in Iraq* (London: Penguin, 2006), 87 (Ricks was the *Washington Post*'s senior Pentagon correspondent at the time).

19. "Top Secret Polo Step."

20. Ricks, *Fiasco,* 96–100. Shinseki became secretary of veterans affairs in President Barack Obama's administration in early 2009.

21. Ricks, *Fiasco,* 117; for more discussion on troop levels, see Clark, *Winning Modern Wars,* 165–167; Larry Diamond, "What Went Wrong in Iraq," *Foreign Affairs* 83, no. 5 (September–October 2004): 34–56, esp. 35.

22. Ricks, *Fiasco,* 79; for further discussion about JTF-IV, see Michael Gordon and Bernard Trainor (Lieutenant General, USMC), *Cobra II: The Inside Story of the Invasion and Occupation of Iraq* (London: Atlantic Books, 2006), 143–146.

23. Ricks, *Fiasco,* 79.

24. Ibid., 76–78; Bob Woodward, *Plan of Attack* (London: Simon and Schuster UK, 2004), 281–282.

25. Bob Woodward, "Prisoners of War," *The Sunday Times,* Review, 8 October 2006, 1–3, esp. 1 (extracts from his book *State of Denial*).

26. Chandrasekaran, *Imperial Life in the Emerald City,* 32.

27. For an account of Garner's troubles in getting the ORHA up and running, see ibid., 27–40.

28. Woodward, "Prisoners of War," 2.

29. Chandrasekaran, *Imperial Life in the Emerald City,* 3.

30. For comprehensive accounts of the conduct of the Iraq War of 2003 (Operation Iraqi Freedom), see Gordon and Trainor, *Cobra II*; Williamson Murray and Robert H. Scales (Major-General, ret., US Army), *The Iraq War: A Military History* (Cambridge, MA: Belknap Press of Harvard University Press, 2003); Anthony Cordesman, *The Iraq War: Strategy, Tactics, and Military Lessons* (Westport, CT: Praeger Publishers, 2003), 592.

31. Andrew Koch, "Information War Played a Major Role in Iraq," *Jane's Defence Weekly* 40, no. 3 (23 July 2003): 5.

32. See Nick Cook, "Cause and Effect," *Jane's Defence Weekly* 39, no. 24 (18 June 2003): 52–57.

33. Ed Harriman, "Treachery: How Iraq Went to War Against Saddam," *The Sunday Times,* Review (11 January 2004), 1–2; BBC1 Television, *Secrets, Spies, and the Iraq War* (broadcast at 9 P.M., 7 April 2004).

34. Those reported turned included Republican Guard generals, Mahar Soufiane al-Takriti and Mahdi Abdullah al-Dulemi. It was rumored that on 7 April 2003 a Hercules transport took off from Baghdad's International Airport taking a group of the most senior turncoats out of Iraq. Harriman, "Treachery," 1–2.

35. Ricks, *Fiasco,* 116–117.

36. A detailed daily account of the land war can be found in "Iraq Analysis," *Jane's Intelligence Review* 15, no. 7 (July 2003), 7–48.

37. For details of British operations in the Iraq War, see Ministry of Defence, *Operations in Iraq: Lessons for the Future,* 2003), foreword by the Secretary of State for Defence, Geoff Hoon, www.mod.uk/NR/rdonlyres/734920BA-6ADE-461F-A809-7E5A754990D7/0/opsiniraq_lessons_dec03.pdf.

38. Andrew North, "Nasiriya Struggles with War Memories," BBC News, 17 June 2003, http://news.bbc.co.uk/1/hi/world/middle_east/2995568.htm.

39. "Misgivings Fade at the City Gates," *The Economist,* 5–11 April 2003, 24–25, esp. 25.

40. A comprehensive account of the battle for the Karbala Gap can be found in Gordon and Trainor, *Cobra II,* especially chapters 14 and 18, 260–281 and 345–373; see also Clark, *Winning Modern Wars,* 61, 66.

41. Gordon and Trainor, *COBRA II,* chapters 19–21, 374–433.

42. Figure given by US commander in Iraq, Lieutenant General Ricardo Sanchez, in an interview with Wolf Blitzer on CNN's "Late Edition," Sunday, 27 July 2003, 1, reproduced by CNN, http://transcripts.cnn.com/TRANSCRIPTS/0307/27/le.00.html.

43. Nazih N. Ayubi, *Overstating the Arab State: Politics and Society in the Middle East* (London: I. B. Tauris, 1995), xiii, xi.

44. Scott Feil, "Post-Conflict Reconstruction," written testimony to the Senate Foreign Relations Committee, 1 August 2002, http://frwebgate.access.gpo.gov/cgi-bin/getdoc.cgi?dbname=107_senate_hearings&docid=f:81697.wais (Scott Feil was the codirector of the joint Association of the US Army and the Center for Strategic and International Studies Post-Conflict Reconstruction Project).

45. Scott Feil, "Security in a Post-Conflict Situation in Iraq," written testimony to the Senate Foreign Relations Committee, 11 February 2003, http://foreign.senate.gov/hearings/2003/hrg030211a.html.

7

What Went Wrong in Iraq?

Lackadaisical planning. The lack of personnel and resources on the ground. The absence of any real capacity to govern effectively. Little would stand in the way of Iraq drifting toward chaos after the US occupation of the country. Nor would the US military be ready to deal with the emergence of Iraq as a front in the wider "glocal insurgency." It would take more than three years for US forces to adapt to the insurgent threat—as well as the global psychological and marketing battle that ensued. Above all, US policymakers had failed to fully appreciate the audacity of what they were proposing to do in Iraq and how difficult it would be to plot the appropriate track to a desired end state. The United States would struggle to synchronize the appropriate emphasis in its policy—specifically the balance between the application of force, RRA activities, and the design of long-term governance—in order to take that track. The failure to plot the right track was a significant element in the Iraq debacle, and it is the subject of this chapter.

The Potential End-States in Iraq

The decision to overthrow Saddam Hussein was bound to unleash all sorts of forces in Iraq of which top US policymakers appear to have been only dimly aware. The Bush administration might hope for the emergence of some sort of democratic Iraq and, on the back of that, construct a new security architecture in the Middle East—but that hypothesis was always speculative. Moreover, because no one had really thought out what the preferred end state would look like, there were always less benign possibilities. In fact, the Iraq project pointed to four potential outcomes in the medium to long terms, which can be summarized as

1. Fundamental democratic reform. With the creation of a democratic Iraq and as a key alliance partner of the United States, Iraq would become the entry point for political and economic reform into the Middle East region. Victory!
2. Partial reform (Sunni-weighted). The minimum reform option was to purge the Iraqi state of former Saddamist elements but reconstitute the existing Sunni-led state. This was the least costly option, but the risk was that nationalist, anti-American, anti-Israeli, and militaristic values would reassert themselves later.
3. Partial reform (Shia-led). The most powerful political forces in post-Saddam Iraq were Shia Islamists, and they stood to be the principal beneficiaries of any rapid or poorly controlled democratization process.
4. The creation of a "strategic cesspit." If an effective democratic government could not be created, Iraq might descend into disorder, verging on civil war. Iraq would become a haven for sectarian militias, criminal mafias, and Islamic militants.

Clearly, although nothing was properly scoped out beforehand, the most desired end state was for something approximating the first potential outcome: victory. As early as his important speech to US veterans on 26 August 2002, US vice president Dick Cheney had set out an extraordinary vision:

> With our help, a liberated Iraq can be a great nation once again. Iraq is rich in natural resources and human talent, and has unlimited potential for a peaceful, prosperous future. Our goal would be an Iraq that has territorial integrity, a government that is democratic and pluralistic, a nation where the human rights of every ethnic and religious group are recognized and protected. In that troubled land all who seek justice, and dignity, and the chance to live their own lives, can know they have a friend and ally in the United States of America.[1]

Any kind of representative government would have to embody a significant degree of power-sharing. Minorities must be protected. Mindful of their Kurdish and other clients, the last thing the Bush administration wanted to see was an Islamic state or ethnic warring between Arabs and Kurds. In addition to some sort of federal-style government, US policymakers were also keen to reform the Iraqi economy and integrate it into the global marketplace. A free economy was to be the bulwark of a free society.

Wishful thinking abounded among the top echelon of the Bush administration, although some differences about means existed, with Donald Rumsfeld at the Pentagon seemingly more circumspect about how far America could directly engineer a democratic Iraq as compared to some of those at the White House. To the extent that President Bush was aware of the likely scale and duration of the project ahead, he appears to have been sold on doing what was necessary to achieve an unambiguous victory.

Achieving fundamental democratic reform implied steering away from the other possible end states; at the outset, the Bush administration appeared most concerned to prevent the old Sunni elite from hijacking the reform process. What was not in the US interest was to get rid of Saddam Hussein only to hand over the country to someone rather like him—only now more difficult to manage. Unless there was a root-and-branch reform of Iraqi politics, it was difficult to imagine that anti-Western and anti-Israeli sentiments would not be reasserted once US forces left. Moreover, the Bush administration was mindful that most of its Iraqi exile-friends were set upon purging the Baathists. Thus, while the Pentagon's ORHA under Jay Garner initially went to Iraq prepared to co-opt some former regime elements in order to effect a rapid transfer of governance (a process he hoped might be undertaken in only ninety days), the White House soon moved on to a more radical path.[2] Garner and the ORHA were abruptly replaced by the CPA, headed by L. Paul Bremer III.

If Garner was pragmatic, Bremer was idealistic. Bremer was personally convinced that the Baath Party was a force for evil in the world and had to be expunged.[3] Bremer's first acts as head of the CPA were to issue two monumental edicts that disbanded the Baath Party (CPA Order No. 1, 16 May 2003) and dissolved the Iraqi army (CPA Order No. 2, 23 May 2003).[4] The top four levels of Baath Party membership were sanctioned. Anyone formerly holding the rank of colonel or above—perhaps 20,000 people or more—was deemed to be a senior party member ineligible to participate in public life, hold a government job, and even draw an appropriate pension. The management of every ministry, nationalized industry, hospital, and university was now liable to be purged.[5] More ominously, some half-million Iraqi men working for the armed forces or Interior Ministry suddenly found themselves jobless. The decisions shocked the ORHA team still in place, but an attempt by Garner and others to persuade Bremer not to pursue such a course fell on deaf ears.[6] Upon his return to Washington, Garner was reported to have taken the matter up with Rumsfeld, but the response was that the decision had been taken—and that was that.[7]

In the light of the Sunni insurgency and its horrors, the decision to dissolve the Baath Party and Iraqi army became highly controversial, and it has become difficult to trace the provenance of the decision. In his well-sourced book *Fiasco,* Thomas E. Ricks reports that a senior unnamed figure in the administration thought that the decisions to disband the Baath Party and Iraqi army actually contradicted prior discussions involving Bush and Bremer, as well as executive decisions made by the president at a war-cabinet meeting on 10 March.[8] The team at the Pentagon—Donald Rumsfeld, Paul Wolfowitz, and Douglas Feith—were also later to point the finger at Bremer, implying that his purge in Iraq was a devolved decision that went much further than intended.[9]

Bizarrely, having been among the principal cheerleaders for regime change, the Pentagon team appears to have been ambivalent about the scale and duration of the military commitment actually involved. Rumsfeld himself, for instance, reportedly believed and hoped that the vast bulk of US troops would be withdrawn from Iraq within three to six months.[10]

In contrast, Rajiv Chandrasekaran's book *Imperial Life in the Emerald City* voices the view that Douglas Feith's Office of Special Plans (partly influenced by Ahmed Chalabi and the INC) had drawn up orders for a broad purge of Baathists.[11] The Office of Special Plans drafted an executive order titled "De-Baathification of Iraqi Society," which prohibited the employment of the top four ranks of Baathists (to the rank of *udu firka*) and contained restrictions on rank-and-file Baathists holding management positions in the public sector. But it seems likely that the motives of Feith and Bremer were different. For Feith, de-Baathification was a prerequisite to the transfer of authority to Ahmed Chalabi and the INC.[12] For Bremer, de-Baathification was a clear statement of intent to Iraqis about the final demise of the Baathist regime and the radical democratization of Iraq that he hoped to preside over.

If Bremer's own account, *My Year in Iraq,* is anything to go by, having privately been given President Bush's writ as a kind of personal envoy, Bremer acted according to the mission intent that he believed had been agreed with the White House.[13] Although Bremer was officially in Rumsfeld's chain of command, his relationship with the president conferred a degree of independence, although Bremer also believed that following predeployment meetings with Rumsfeld and Feith on 9 May 2003 that the purging of Baathists was also the mission intent of the Pentagon.[14] Once in Baghdad, the Iraqi exiles close to administration insiders, notably Ahmed Chalabi and the Kurdish parties, were also quick to impress upon Bremer the necessity of finishing the rout of the Baath Party and Iraqi army.[15] In any event, although President Bush may not have been as immersed in the decisionmaking as might be expected, he acquiesced. The White House allowed the decisions to stand without much review and questioning—and so did the Pentagon. Although the Bush administration rarely seems to have fired on all cylinders, it beggars belief that Bremer could have taken such a major decision without authorization from Washington. Bremer would later say that the actual purge orders were fully reviewed by Wolfowitz and Feith.[16]

The formal dissolution of the Baathist state and its security forces was a historic moment. A completely new political order in Iraq now had to be created. Little had been done to prepare for this; indeed, Bremer's decision completely contradicted the planning assumptions that had informed the approach of US Central Command and ORHA. What followed was an enormous disruption. No system of vetting existed, and CPA officials would soon be spending much time dealing with personnel and vetting matters. It was not as if they had nothing else to do! In time, recruitment practices would vary from place to place until the CPA tried to standardize them, causing yet more disruption. Most important, it left hundreds of thousands of former officials, soldiers, and policemen unemployed. Confusion and delays over the payment of monthly stipends to former soldiers did little to help the situation, and Sunni clansmen were soon turning their minds to alternative livelihood schemes. The decision to let the old state dissolve into history undoubtedly contributed to the buildup of insurgency and organized crime. What it also meant was that substantial numbers of US forces would have to remain in Iraq for years to come to stand up the new political order.

The Two Revolutions

What US policymakers proposed to do—although they didn't quite realize it at the time—was the daunting task of instigating two colossal revolutions in Iraq. The first was a democratic revolution involving the reorganization of governance according to democratic principles; this also implied an end to the primacy of the Sunni Arab minority and the uplifting of Shia Arabs and Kurds. The democratic revolution meant an end to the Iraq that had been known since 1921. For many Sunnis, the transition to Shia and Kurdish preeminence not only cast a huge shadow over their future security but also challenged the very nature of Iraq as an Arab state. A deep nationalist-revolutionary tradition existed in the Sunni community, and some Sunnis were never going to give up *their* dream of Iraq without a fight. For Sunni chauvinists, Shia Arabs were little more than backward pseudo-Persians and stalking horses for an Iranian takeover of Iraq. Many Sunnis also believed, as Ahmed S. Hashim repeatedly heard during his tours of duty to Iraq for the US armed forces, that their community was not in the minority at all.[17] In fact, Sunni Arabs constituted only about 20 percent of the population, compared to Shia Arabs with more than 60 percent. The democratic revolution always carried the risk of producing great violence.

With the United States having torn down the old Iraq, a second revolution was required to forge the right kind of new Iraq—this was the cultural revolution. Iraq had no real tradition of rule of law, democratic politics, and peaceful handovers of power. For thirty years it had been run as a gangster fiefdom, with the principal alternative to Saddamism being some sort of Islamism. Moreover, even though an Iraqi national identity existed—which coalition policymakers and their Iraqi clients determinedly purported to be robust—the underlying DNA of Iraqi society embodied powerful references to family, tribal, ethnic, and religious identities. There were huge questions over Iraqi attitudes to secular values and institutions such as the rule of law, human equality, democracy, accountability among officials, and universal human rights. Beyond the commonalities of clans and religious affiliations, Iraqis did not really trust people from other groups to hold power over them.

Thus, the danger always existed that selfish sectarian interests might seek to subvert the reform process. At a local level, the rule of law and democratic principles meant little to tribal or militia groups. In fact, in the new Iraq getting a public-sector job and equal treatment before the law was often about who you were or whom you knew. At a national level, it was also easy to imagine that the big ethnic and religious groups might discard the idea of an Iraqi nation and a national interest. To initiate the first democratic revolution without instilling a second cultural revolution risked forging a weak state and a façade democracy in which an unstable coalition of Shia Islamists would most likely be the preeminent force.

To instigate an appropriate cultural revolution required reconciling a sufficient mass of Iraqis to liberal political values and practices and liberal-capitalist economics. It was a dauntingly difficult RRA job made all the more improbable by the lack of effective thought and planning beforehand. Notwithstanding the planning gap, whether the United States could ever have successfully instigated the two revolutions was always questionable. Implementing any cultural revolution was a feat that would surely take decades to complete. Moreover, it was inevitable that the violence stemming from the democratic revolution—and the transition from Sunni to Shia and Kurdish preeminence—would spill over into any cultural revolution. And to make matters worse, US policymakers not only sought to democratize Iraq at the point of a gun but also envisaged doing so within an occupation time frame of only twenty-four to forty-eight months.[18] None of it was ever remotely realistic.

The Task Ahead: The Intended Track of the Occupation

The reality of the situation was that the United States was now in a race to reach a desired end state before resistance mounted and the costs of trying to get there became unacceptable to the balance of US public and congressional opinion. One way of trying to make better sense of the dynamics of this race is to look at the occupation in terms of the trinity of policy emphasis set out in Chapter 3. To recap, the trinity of policy emphasis embodies the use of force and provision of security; reconstruction enabling the reconciliation and assimilation of the population and/or enemy combatants to the postwar settlement (the RRA process); and the construction of a viable system of long-term governance.

As the war against the Saddam regime's forces came to an end, the initial emphasis on the use of force evolved. In the first instance, Jay Garner as head of ORHA favored moving quickly from force to governance. With Garner prepared to co-opt elements in the old regime and its security forces, RRA might be expedited (see Figure 7.1, Track A). Of course, the risk of this approach was that while more members of the Sunni community might be reconciled to the new order, others in the Shia and Kurdish community would not.

Figure 7.1 Potential Alternative Tracks of US Policy Emphasis in the Management of Occupied Iraq

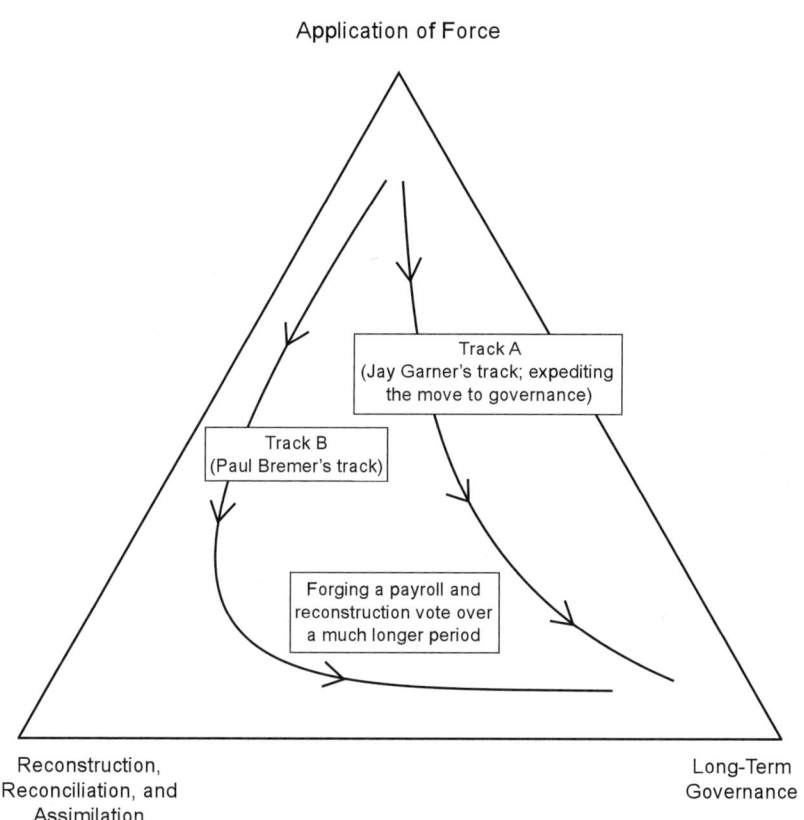

The replacement of Garner and the ORHA by Bremer and the CPA by mid-May 2003 heralded a more radical transformation project, and it meant that the track of US policy would be very different. Less emphasis was put on expediting a system of governance. Instead, what Bremer first set out to do was to create conditions for a more radical reform of governance by fostering a longer and deeper RRA process (see Figure 7.1, Track B). What this meant in practice was the attempt by the CPA to build up a payroll and reconstruction vote before moving on to configure the shape of long-term governance. CPA officials tended to hold to a rational choice/interest-based approach to this RRA process, believing that if jobs were created, pocketbooks filled, consumer experiences enjoyed, and entrepreneurial spirits unleashed, the hearts and minds of Iraqis would follow. Thus, until a sufficiently strong class of stakeholders could be put in place, Bremer intended that the CPA retain as much control over governance as possible. The work done by Garner and his ORHA team to transfer governance to Iraqis, including the creation of an interim leadership group by 15 May 2003, was summarily dismissed.[19] Bremer later recalled his thoughts when first hearing of Garner's plans to expedite the move to governance:

> I knew it would take careful work to disabuse both the Iraqi and American proponents of this reckless fantasy—what some in the administration were calling "early transfer" of power—animated in part by their aversion to "nation building." I mentioned to the President that giving Iraq a stable political structure would require not just installing democratic institutions, but also creating what I called the social "shock absorbers," institutions which form civil society—a free press, trade unions, political parties, professional organizations. These, I told the president, are what help cushion the individual from an overpowering state.[20]

Bremer recalled that President Bush understood and agreed with the arguments for a deeper democratization project. Iraqis would have to wait to get their hands on a system of governance. Above all, Bremer believed that a permanent constitution had to be formulated and put in place before Iraqis could take full responsibility for government.[21] To set up a government without a permanent constitution might just invite the self-interested rigging of the system that would ultimately destroy the democratic ideal he wanted to institute.

Bremer has subsequently attracted an enormous amount of criticism, including from the leadership team at the Pentagon, but in many ways he was right. To topple Saddam Hussein's regime and then promptly leave Iraq was not only grossly irresponsible, it was bad strategy. The intent of waging war is to achieve a political purpose, not to leave the field to some ill-defined and poorly supervised end. Given that the mission intent of the White House was for a radical democratization project, a longer and deeper RRA process really was required to engineer the desired strategic outcome. The track Bremer proposed to take was probably the ideal one given the strategic objective related to governance. However, the entire story of the US occupation, including that of Bremer and the CPA, involved a certain detachment from reality. Although Bremer's track was probably the ideal one in theory, taking that course may never have been realistic in practice. The United States had scarcely prepared for such a long and complex project, and neither the Pentagon, Congress, nor US public opinion were psyched up for it.

The United States and its allies now faced the unenviable task of occupying Iraq for an indeterminate duration (see Figure 7.2). If the principal figures of the Bush administration ever had a sense of the magnitude of what they had taken on, it was not obvious. Iraq was utterly broken. Even if the United States had properly prepared beforehand, Iraq was by far the biggest, most complex, and most risk-laden nation-building job of the post–Cold War years. And things

Figure 7.2 Map of the Coalition Occupation of Iraq, September 2003

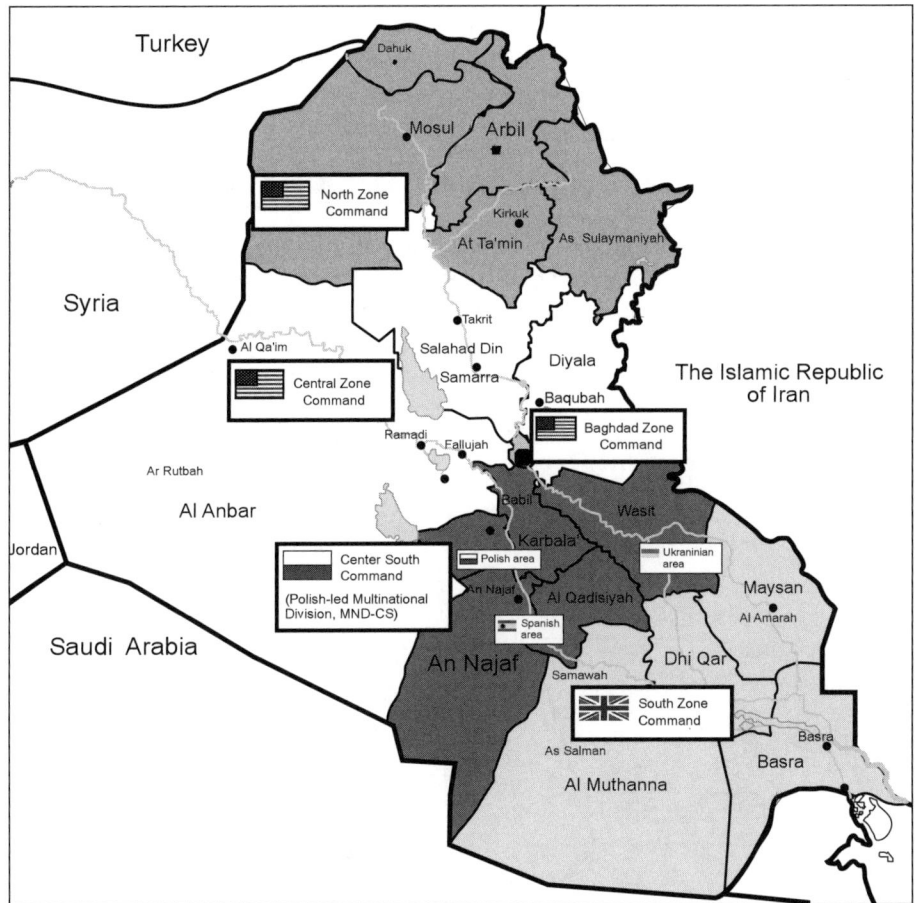

had started so very badly. If Iraqis had ever felt the warm glow of liberation, it was quickly squandered amid the crime wave, mass unemployment, disruption to incomes, and near collapse of utilities and public services. On 18 July 2003, a Pentagon advisory team led by John Hamre—head of the Center for Strategic and International Studies—reported back on a fact-finding mission to Iraq from 26 June to 7 July.[22] The team perceived that some progress had been made but observed that "the enormity of this undertaking cannot be overstated," noting the potential for "real chaos" called for an immediate "turbocharged effort" over the next three months. The turbocharger did not kick in.

The Actual Track of the Occupation

Whatever the intentions of US policymakers, the actual track of the occupation would soon be buffeted by circumstances and radically changed (see Figure 7.3). These changes can be plotted through distinct periods.

Period 1: May–November 2003

The initial period included priming the RRA process, and the development of the Iraqi resistance.

Whether the rational-choice approach adopted by the CPA and US military to RRA was ever viable can be questioned, but in a sense the model was never really tested because US policy was so badly executed. Aside from the lack of manpower and money, the CPA was undermined by unity of command issues. Paul Bremer ran the CPA, but the US military—with Lieutenant General

Figure 7.3 The Actual Track of the US Occupation of Iraq, 2003–2006

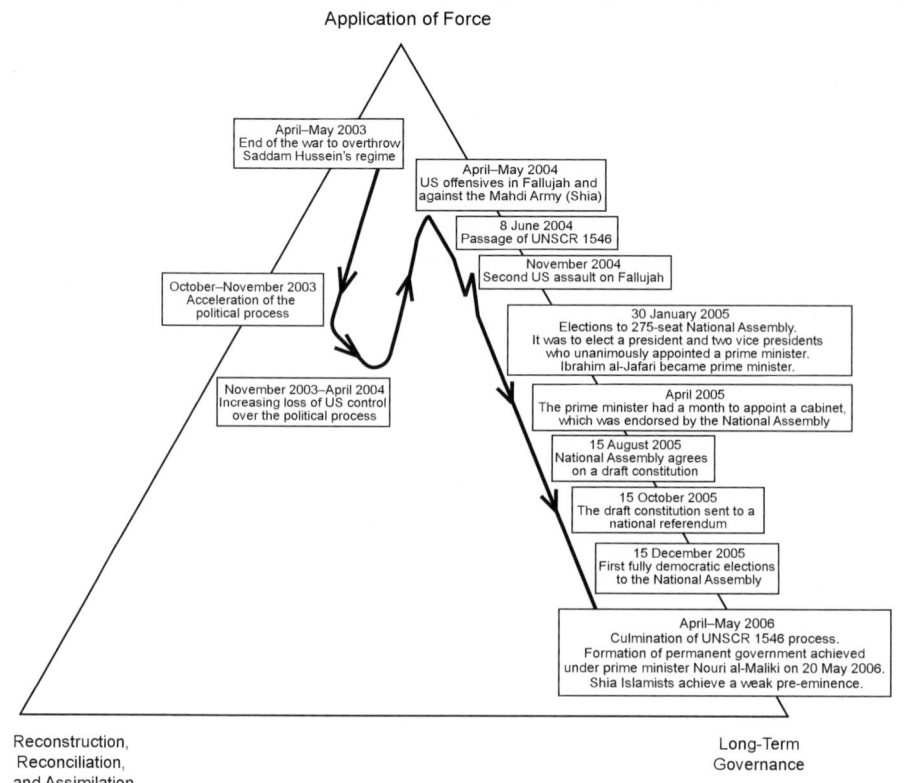

Ricardo Sanchez as commander of Combined Joint Task Force 7—was the dominant power in Iraq.[23] The US military had different priorities; it was interested in security, stabilization, and withdrawal, whereas the CPA was more concerned about its revolutionary reform project. Neither Bremer nor Sanchez had anything like an adequately resourced staff to support their work, with the brief three-month tours of many CPA recruits further frustrating the formation of a competent administration. Bremer and Sanchez may also not have had a sufficiently empathetic personal relationship to bridge the significant organizational and cultural dissonance. It has been widely circulated since that time that both Bremer and Sanchez had aloof personal styles and sometimes exhibited a reluctance to entertain doubts, much less criticism. Bremer was not a popular figure among some senior US officers in Iraq—or with Wolfowitz and Feith at the Pentagon.

The CPA would always struggle to make its writ run across Iraq, and this problem was exacerbated by its physical isolation in the fortified Green Zone in Baghdad. Thus, while Bremer's inclination was to try to centralize authority and policymaking even when coherent decisions were made, it was difficult to enact them. The CPA was widely regarded to be detached from events on the ground and prone to generate a great deal of wishful thinking about progress that it fed back to Washington. Attempts by the Pentagon to verify the CPA's assessments were not welcomed. Notwithstanding issues related to particular personnel, such problems were the inevitable consequence of setting up an ad hoc occupation authority in such little time.

Meanwhile, even though the US military was good at organizing the logistics required for some reconstruction work, it lacked the capability in many civil realms (the local political and social action that might produce reconciliation and assimilation) and much of an ability to harness those in the multilateral community that did. In written testimony to the US Senate Foreign Relations Committee on 23 September 2003, John Hamre offered this view:

> I understand and appreciate Secretary Rumsfeld's view that the Defense Department would overwhelmingly field the assets required for reconstruction, and therefore the Department should have complete authority to undertake the task. In theory, I agree with this point. But, in practice it has not worked. The patterns of cooperation inside the government broke down during the last year. DoD [the US Department of Defense] now has to manage tasks for which it has no background or competence, and it has not been effective in inviting the support of others in the government who have that background and competence. Either DoD needs a new approach for collaboration with others, or the President needs to change the assignment of responsibilities. The challenge of rebuilding Iraq is enormous and our ability to be effective in this effort is being eroded by the bureaucratic struggles here in Washington.[24]

In the same Senate hearings, the US aid and nation-building expert J. Brian Atwood agreed that Pentagon leadership had been problematic:

> DoD's tasking procedures and their coordination protocols do not translate well in a fluid transitional civilian environment. NGOs do not work well under Pentagon "task orders," nor do contractors whose expertise lies in various essential development or humanitarian fields, such as education, healthcare or democratization. Furthermore, DoD has precious few professionals who have worked in foreign cultures. DoD officials tend to approach a transition as if it were a linear task, proceeding mission to mission *ad seriatum*. What is needed are multiple activities undertaken simultaneously—humanitarian relief, reconciliation programs, infrastructure repairs, political and economic development. These are not part of the Pentagon's playbook.[25]

Atwood offered the view that the Pentagon should cede authority to the State Department, USAID, and the UN; all had greater expertise and existing capabilities in development management. But the Pentagon retained its lead.

In the short to medium terms, anyone seeking to progress through the RRA zone in Iraq first needed to do something about rebuilding basic services as well as providing policing, health, and education. Jobs and incomes would follow. Bremer saw the task in terms of three steps: restore basic services; increase the income of the population by paying salaries, offering loans, and restoring the banking system; and privatize and deregulate the largely state-owned economy.[26]

To the extent that the CPA was properly manned, it had been staffed by free-market enthusiasts, with Peter McPherson and, later, Tom Foley put in charge of privatizing the Iraqi economy. Although some initial pain would have to be absorbed by ordinary Iraqis, the CPA hoped that economic reform would be the real driver of RRA in the medium term. The privatizers embarked on a radical project but soon found only patchy support. A few Iraqis saw the opportunities. Many more were opposed, because the likely consequences of privatization and deregulation were a massive shakeout of public-sector jobs, cuts in public subsidies for basic goods and services, price inflation, and foreign ownership of Iraqi businesses. Above all, though, despite all the ideological zeal of the CPA's free-marketers, they simply did not have the capacity to undertake what they advocated. Privatizing an economy the size of Iraq's requires thousands of personnel to assemble data, conduct reviews and site inspections, make valuations, and process a mass of human-resource issues for many tens of thousands of workers; it would also happen in the face of much Iraqi resistance, including violent resistance. Only a tiny handful of CPA staff was in place to formulate and implement the practical plan for their fantastic concept.[27] Some CPA officials soon understood that US authorities simply did not have the power to execute such an extensive privatization program. It was all an exercise on paper.

Although dreams of privatization soon ran into the ground, the CPA did get on more successfully with other economic reforms. A new currency was introduced. Income tax was reduced, and a system was set up to actually collect more of it. Commercial law was progressively modernized. The system of public subsidies was reformed. Import tariffs were abolished. By the autumn of 2003, the CPA's Iraqi clients—by then constituted into the Iraqi Governing Council (IGC)—were induced to consider the introduction of a free-floating Iraqi dinar, a foreign investment law that allowed foreign ownership, the unrestricted right to send profits abroad, and the entry of foreign banks on the basis of equality with the local sector.[28]

But the reality was that an enormous—and improbable—amount of capacity-building was needed to put in the cultural, institutional, and support services necessary to make some sort of free-market capitalism work in Iraq. It would require the consolidation of the rule of law; the drafting of a new regulatory framework; the reconstitution of government; and the provision of public services. To even begin this task would require funds to prime the pump. In September 2003, defense undersecretary Paul Wolfowitz told the Senate Armed Services Committee that an estimated US$50–75 billion was needed to restore basic infrastructure alone.[29] The initial US estimate was backed up in more detail by a joint UN–World Bank report of October 2003, which reckoned that at least US$36 billion was needed in "UN/World Bank sectors" (economic and social development) and another US$20 billion in "CPA sectors" (especially security and governance).[30]

Iraq's oil income was expected to provide a significant proportion of these resources—something that US policymakers took for granted. With the passage of UN Resolution 1483 (22 May 2003), endorsing the fact of US occupation, the UN Development Fund for Iraq (DFI) also became available; it amounted to slightly more than US$20 billion in previously accumulated oil receipts and seized funds.[31] Much of the DFI money was to be handed over to the CPA, US military, and Iraqi clients. However, even though the DFI money covered much of the cost of setting up the occupation authority, it was later reported that much of it was frittered away amid stupendous levels of maladministration, waste, overbilling, and outright corruption.[32] In the month prior to the CPA's handover to the new Iraqi Interim Government in June 2004, for instance, the CPA and US military rushed to spend up to US$5 billion—with US$2.4 billion in freight-sized pallets of hundred-dollar bills being rushed over and handed out without proper accounting—so the money would not have to be turned over to the new Iraqi government itself.

Although spending DFI cash with abandon, the United States was much more cautious about turning over US taxpayer money. In the early days of the occupation, CPA officials realized that despite the inclinations of Pentagon leaders, US taxpayer money would be required to stabilize Iraqi society and prime the economy. The issue was most pressing with respect to the electricity system, with chronic shortages of power raising all sorts of issues. CPA officials would rush to bid for a supplemental appropriation to a bigger bill funding the wars as a whole in Afghanistan and Iraq.[33] CPA officials eventually drew up a reduced list of some US$35 billion of infrastructure reconstruction; mindful of the reaction in Washington, Bremer simply halved it.[34] The "supplemental" was not particularly well constructed, and the US regulatory system would eventually slow the flow of funds to a crawl. Although some US$18 billion in US taxpayer money was made available after October 2003, less than US$1 billion was actually spent in the year that followed. US taxpayers would eventually pledge nearly US$21 billion, although there would be a halt on further allocations in early 2006. The years it could take to get appropriations through the US regulatory framework was a lesson for the future.

Other international donors were similarly restrained. At a donor's conference of seventy countries held in Madrid in October 2003, the Bush administration was reportedly looking for donors to pony up US$30–55 billion; only US$13 billion was pledged for the period 2004–2007, and nothing like these sums was actually forthcoming.[35]

In the event, Iraqis would have to wait for the oil industry (in association with the rises in world oil prices in 2007–2008) to generate the sums required, although corruption and insurgent attacks would greatly slow progress in that sector as well. As of August 2003, Iraqi oil exports were only some 1.3 million barrels per day (mbd) as compared to production of up to 3 mbd before the war.[36] Thus, the draft Iraqi budget for 2004 estimated total revenues at just US$12.9 billion and envisaged development allocations of only US$1.4 billion.[37] In 2005, insurgent attacks on the Iraqi oil industry cost a reported US$6.25 billion in damage and lost earnings, with oil production still at only about 2 mbd; indeed, by December 2005 oil exports would hit a new postwar low of only 1.1 mbd.[38]

As things developed, however, raising enough money appeared to be the least serious of the problems at hand. The use of foreign contractors to lead reconstruction may not have been the best way to get the most RRA bang for the buck. The CPA could quickly point to a number of large-scale projects that might be deemed successful, as well as a number of sectors that were progressing well, notably local government and the schools system. But US authorities struggled to properly supervise the breadth of reconstruction contracts and activities. Foreign contractors and consultants were expensive, and they in turn found it difficult to monitor work supposedly going on in Iraq. Foreign contractors also edged Iraqis out of reconstruction work, thereby limiting the financial and employment gains in Iraq itself, and significant sums earmarked as profit went nowhere near Iraq. Thus, too little was achieved on the ground in the first year of the occupation. Iraqis continued to be plagued by power, water, and oil shortages for years to come, starkly contrasting the rapid restoration of basic services under Saddam Hussein following the Gulf War in 1991. Mass unemployment and poverty remained a pervasive feature of life, with some 60 percent of Iraqis continuing to rely on UN food-rationing.

Above all, it was the rapid deterioration in the security situation that stymied reconstruction and reconciliation. The security crisis affected Iraqis and foreigners alike. In an article published in *Foreign Affairs* in September–October 2004, Larry Diamond (a former senior adviser on governance to the CPA) lamented that

> without some minimum level of security people cannot engage in trade and commerce, organize to rebuild their communities, or participate meaningfully in politics. Without security, a country has nothing but disorder, distrust, and desperation—an utterly Hobbessian situation in which fear pervades and raw force dominates. This is why violence-ridden societies tend to turn to almost any political force that promises to provide order, even if it is oppressive. . . . Insecurity drove the political occupation into a physical and psychological bunker. Already separated from Iraqis by the formidable security around the three-square-mile Green Zone and around the CPA's regional and provincial headquarters, coalition officials began to travel less and less with every passing month. By the early spring of this year, foreign officials and contractors could no longer safely move around the country without an armoured car and a well-armed escort.[39]

Criminal gangs targeted foreign contractors and local entrepreneurs for reasons of profit. Insurgents identified them as the enemy. The kidnappings and murders of foreign contractors and aid staff, as well as local businessmen and ordinary workers, had a big impact. Local businesses that prospered were likely targets for kidnapping, extortion, and outright expropriation. The ability of foreign contractors to make site visits was severely reduced, and a significant proportion of all aid dollars had to be given over to private security companies. By early 2005, some 38,000 private security contractors were in Iraq, and as much as 25 percent of the aid budget was diverted to that purpose.[40] Even so, by the end of 2005 more than 400 foreign contractors had been killed, and US contractors were being squeezed out. The result was that the United States would not be the preeminent external influence in the Iraqi economy in quite the way that some in the Bush administration had hoped. It seemed more likely that the big winners of Iraqi reconstruction would be contracting interests from other regional states, notably Turkey, Iran, Egypt, and the Gulf States.

Besides reconstruction of the economy, the other major consideration in this early period of the US occupation was how to manage the governance question. Although the CPA acted to delay the transfer of governance, the pressure was soon mounting to put something in place. Bremer rejected the advice of the UN special envoy, Sergio Viera de Mello, in June 2003 that direct elections and the formation of an interim government be brought forward. Instead, after tortuous haggling, Bremer constituted the Iraqi Governing Council, a body of twenty-five nominated members (from a list drawn up by US and British diplomats) that first met on 13 July 2003. The IGC embodied the diverse nature of Iraq, with thirteen Shia, five Sunni, five Kurds, one Assyrian Christian, and one Turkmen.

The IGC was given mostly consultative powers, and its principal purpose was to help legitimize CPA rule as well as initiate the kind of dialogue that would eventually be needed to establish a system of governance. The IGC was to have a very mixed record. It was a forum of representation and consultation. It did co-opt the leading political factions. But the IGC was soon being criticized for the performance of individual members and its ultimate political effect. Many of the IGC's leading personalities were the client-exiles of the United States and did not have a local base. The IGC's detachment was reinforced by its isolation within the Green Zone as well as by the amount of time some members spent outside the country. Even when in Iraq, members spent most of their time haggling for partisan advantage. Above all, even though the decision to select the IGC along ethnic and religious lines appeared reasonable—it was probably the best a US proconsul could do to make the IGC a representative body—it nevertheless recognized and institutionalized the sectarian differences.

The reorganization of Iraqi politics along sectarian lines may have been inevitable (see Figure 7.4). Although many pointed to the existence of an Iraqi identity, the CPA does not appear to have been fully attuned to the growing danger of sectarianism—and a number of contradictions in US policy may have speeded the way. The CPA eventually aspired to forge a strong federal-style government, but as Charles Tripp observe, "Whether for practical reasons of local order or because many in the CPA genuinely believed in the decentralization of power, local forms of mediation, organization and power were encouraged to emerge in the provinces. The CPA's efforts to bring about an integration of these trends at the national level, by constructing an authoritative framework for national politics [were] inconsistent, hesitant, and reactive, even if each new initiative [was] presented by Bremer with his characteristic ebullience."[41]

Whether or not US policymakers realized it, the CPA presided over a national politics that was increasingly sectarian but also paralyzed. Mainstream Sunnis were reported to be particularly shocked by the blatantly sectarian nature of the IGC, with the Association of Muslim Scholars pronouncing it to be an illegitimate body.[42] At the same time, away from the frustrating dialogue in Baghdad, the CPA was happy to see its Kurdish allies get on with consolidating an effective regional government, just as it was resigned to seeing allied tribal shaikhs and local militias begin to do the same in Sunni and Shia areas. Indeed, the principal benefit of membership of the IGC was as a grant of authority to grasp political power at a local or regional level.

The Sunni Insurgency

Perhaps the faltering start to the occupation would not have mattered so much if it had not been Iraq. It was a society known for high levels of social violence. It was awash with weapons, and the chaos of invasion had released untold tons

What Went Wrong in Iraq? 151

Figure 7.4 Map of the Ethnic Landscape of Iraq

of munitions into the country. The Sunni community harbored a deep revolutionary and anticolonialist tradition. For the previous thirty years, Iraq had been under the iron grip of a ruthless security apparatus, and its masters now found themselves dispossessed. Maybe the Sunnis were not the good guys, but the US occupation was too insensitive to what it was doing to them. According to the academic and US military adviser Ahmed S. Hashim,

> This assault on Iraqi national identity as shaped by Sunnis could have been mitigated had there been a post-Saddam policy of reconciling the Sunni Arabs to the new order. . . . Instead it could be argued that an insidious set of

policy options were adopted by the Bush administration to deepen this assault on the Sunni Arab community and to ensure its marginalization in a future Iraq where the Kurds and the Shia were the favored partners. These policy options have undoubtedly been key factors in the outbreak and persistence into 2006 of the insurgency. These policies have affected the Sunnis materially and in terms of assaulting and undermining their identity. Many observers have no doubt that this was a deliberate strategy crafted by the policy-makers who gave us the war. However, they did not expect the Sunni Arabs to react the way they did by sparking an insurgency that has a widespread and significant impact.[43]

The United States was always going to face an insurgency in Iraq, and one only had to think about the resilience and duration of Palestinian resistance in the small enclaves of the Israeli Occupied Territories to have guessed how much more serious it might become in Iraq. Yet when coalition forces occupied Iraq, there was little sense quite how time-limited the honeymoon would be and how important it was to hit the right note in responding to the initial signs of resistance.

Although members of the former regime may have played some role in supporting resistance, especially in terms of funding, it seems unlikely that any systematic insurgency plan was put in place beforehand. Notwithstanding the initial euphoria within the coalition, any hope that the killing of Saddam Hussein's sons Uday and Qusay in July 2003 or the capture of Saddam himself in December 2003 might cause the insurgency to peter out quickly proved unfounded. The genesis of the insurgency could really be found in bands of Sunni townspeople who came together because they believed it to be their patriotic duty to defend their communities and resist occupation.[44] Many insurgents appeared to be driven by a new Islamo-patriotism that merged old Baathist references to Arab nationalism and social justice with a more genuine Islamism. A myriad of local Islamist groups emerged. Other Islamists soon arrived from elsewhere, with foreign jihadists infiltrating from Syria, Saudi Arabia, and Jordan. Networks of former soldiers and secret police also introduced higher levels of organizational and technical expertise. Affronted tribal groups authorized insurgent acts.[45] Organized criminals added to the mix. The insurgency was organizationally diffuse, but the collective mission was to resist the occupation by killing Americans and thereby forestall whatever the United States had planned for Iraq; whatever else Sunni insurgents wanted was rather unclear at this stage.

The insurgency soon began to take a toll on US forces. Before President Bush announced the end of major combat operations on the flight deck of the USS *Abraham Lincoln* on 1 May 2003, US losses amounted to some 138 killed. Between 1 May and the end of July, sporadic attacks killed more than 100 additional US troops.[46] Losses ran at around thirty to forty killed per month until November 2003, when they increased to eighty.

The US Response to the Insurgency

The US response to the insurgency was to feed the cycle of escalation. US forces reflexively sought to decisively defeat resistance. The commander in Iraq, Lieutenant General Sanchez, set the tone, articulating the mission in terms of killing or capturing terrorists, defined as Baathist dead-enders and foreign jihadists. With most US forces prioritizing force protection and defeating terrorists, they were prone to heavy-handedness. Thousands of doors were kicked in, the inhabitants terrorized and humiliated. US attempts to stamp their authority upon communities by means of aggressive patrolling were also liable to be counterproductive. Far too many Iraqis were killed by passing patrols without proper discrimination, relatives left to literally pick up the pieces and wonder what had happened. No one was keeping count, but it seems likely that hundreds were killed by US troops on the basis of better safe than sorry. A few US soldiers may have gone out to do more sinister things. Killed Iraqis often had friends and relatives who believed that it was their duty to defend the honor of the dead.

US forces adapted, but it would take time to turn around their ingrained culture and practice. In a controversial and much-cited article published in *Military Review* in 2005, a British officer with experience of coalition operations, Brigadier General Nigel Aylwin-Foster, observed that even though US forces had impressive attributes, they were weighed down by their "big army" organization, as well as a culture that was predisposed to "kinetic" operations, technological solutions, a desire to try to impose too much control over the environment, and a certain self-righteousness stemming from high moral purpose.[47] The US chain of command does seem to have been imbued with ideological tendencies that inclined officers to communicate overoptimistic analyses up and down the chain of command. The United States had gone out on a limb in Iraq, and information indicating that things were not going well was not welcomed. US policymakers and soldiers often conspired to fool themselves. Moreover, even though US forces had peace support capabilities, they tended to be devolved to special forces and civil affairs units. In the early days, some regular soldiers did not believe in winning hearts and minds, and those who did often had little idea about putting it into practice.[48] Further problems followed on Sanchez's watch. Amid a background of poorly targeted roundups of Sunni men, the Abu Ghraib prison abuse scandal broke. It would be difficult to imagine that Iraqis could be presented with a worse example of mishandling and disrespect.

The way in which small-scale follies and tactical actions could have operational- and strategic-level effects was no better demonstrated than by an incident in Fallujah on 28 April 2003, when US troops fired upon a demonstration, killing up to twenty townspeople and wounding many more.[49] Suddenly, US forces found themselves party to a clan war in Fallujah—and later in nearby Ramadi, too—with vengeful locals sustaining gun and grenade attacks against them throughout May 2003. The handover of the area to the US Army's 4th Infantry Division under Major General Ray Odierno may not have helped matters.[50] A cycle of escalation took shape, with US cordon-and-search operations enraging residents even more; the city eventually became so dangerous that US forces effectively withdrew, leaving the town to gathering bands of insurgents. What happened in Fallujah was important because it became one of the key nodes for more organized insurgency in the summer of 2003, including the integration of former regime elements, mainstream Islamo-patriots, and foreign jihadists. Eventually, US forces would have to practically destroy Fallujah in order to save it!

The Gathering Forces of Resistance

The arrival of foreign jihadists added a dangerous new force. Many came from Saudi Arabia, Yemen, Syria, and Jordan. Those operating in Iraq at any given time probably numbered in the hundreds rather than the thousands, but they played a disproportionately large role given their force size. Foreign jihadists came in through various Islamist networks, but the Al-Qaida–affiliated franchise Jama'at al Tawhid waal-Jihad (later renamed Tanzim al-Qa'idat al-Jihad fi Bilad al-Rafidain—Al-Qaida in Iraq) led by Abu Musab al-Zarqawi was a beacon for the most violent fighters. At first, times were tough for the jihadists, but al-Zarqawi and others could call upon support networks that stretched back as far as Europe, and they eventually built up well-armed and -organized forces.[51]

US commanders initially put an optimistic spin on the arrival of the jihadists. Lieutenant General Sanchez even promulgated the idea that Iraq could be seen as a context—a kind of flypaper—in which the Islamic international could be brought to battle and defeated; but it was a dangerous thing to wish for.[52] The foreign jihadists radicalized local struggles, introducing extreme tactics with great psychological impact. Their ability to pace a stream of suicide bombers was of operational- and strategic-level importance. A series of car bombings in August 2003—a police graduation ceremony, the Jordanian Embassy, the UN headquarters in Baghdad, the Red Cross headquarters, and one in Najaf that assassinated the leader of the Supreme Council for the Islamic Revolution in Iraq (SCIRI), Ayatollah Mohammed Bakir Hakim—changed the tenor of the entire insurgency. US forces put tremendous efforts into tracking down the jihadists; notwithstanding some serious attrition, they remained resilient throughout 2004, 2005, and 2006. Until the pacing of suicide bombers could be stemmed, it was difficult to see how the United States could get on with any meaningful RRA program.

The other organized forces that came into the battle were the remnants of the former regime. Networks of army officers and secret police were bound to coalesce after the overthrow of Saddam Hussein. Many doubtless became involved in mafia-style criminality, with robbery, kidnapping, protection rackets, gun-running, and general smuggling operations becoming the foundation of a new power base. Organized crime was also involved in cutting deals with cadres of insurgents as well as directly conducting attacks on coalition forces and the civil infrastructure. Furthermore, despite the fact that former regime cadres were involved in the insurgency early on, increasing numbers of former officers probably entered the fray as time went on. The events in Fallujah may have provided the push. The US clearance operations that devastated that town during March–April and November–December 2004 produced outright rage, and in the aftermath the intensity and sophistication of the insurgency increased markedly, especially in Baghdad and the north.[53] Thus, although US forces eventually achieved a tactical-level victory in Fallujah, the unintended consequences in Iraq and beyond were counterproductive.

The numbers involved in the Sunni insurgency remain unclear, but early US estimates of about 5,000 insurgents significantly understated the problem, partly because coalition officials were determined to cast the insurgents as a few Saddamist dead-enders and foreign extremists.[54] The reality was that support for Islamo-nationalist resistance was widespread among the Sunni community (more than 5 million people), and many tens of thousands were either insurgents or active supporters. More than 90 percent of insurgents were Iraqi. Moreover, the coalition was not facing a finite number of insurgents who could eventually be tracked down. Rather, by 2005 the insurgency appears to have built up to an establishment of perhaps 15,000–20,000 activists, and it could call upon reserves to replace any losses.

Rolling up the insurgents was complicated by their highly diffuse nature. Until a degree of organizational consolidation took place beginning in the autumn of 2004, there were reportedly more than seventy distinct paramilitary groupings active in the Sunni insurgency (although these would eventually coalesce into about a half-dozen).[55] In Baghdad alone in mid-2004, for instance, there were at least twelve autonomous groups, with different groups specializing in particular kinds of attacks or activities.[56] The participation of some insurgents and groups was also sporadic, with some entering and exiting the war for purposes that were largely known only to themselves. Ahmed S. Hashim noted that this fluidity was particularly prominent in rural and tribal areas, where insurgents

> whose geographic scope, functional specialization and motives for fighting are often limited to a very specific grievance or set of grievances. Some members may be part-timers who literally come and go, or who may even move to another group that is somehow part of or connected with the insurgent network.

Others hold jobs (indeed, in the Iraqi insurgency some fighters work in the very state institutions or structures that the insurgency has been trying to topple) and engage in the insurgency as a hobby, albeit, a serious, if not deadly, one to which they turn up when required.[57]

Forms of organization between insurgent groups varied considerably from the more hierarchical (especially former Baathist cadres) to the highly devolved.

Sunni insurgents would be formidable foes. Obtaining arms and war materials was not as serious a constraint as in many other insurgencies. Insurgent groups were often led by men with many years of experience as soldiers and secret police. They knew the ground and were capable of conducting intelligence and counterintelligence operations. Their capacity to co-opt and coerce Sunni neighborhoods was often much greater than that of the coalition, and this superiority would persist until 2007–2008. Insurgent techniques developed rapidly with lessons learned and disseminated by word of mouth and by modern media. The inept were soon killed; the more expert persisted. Early in the occupation, close-quarter gun and grenade attacks were responsible for inflicting most US casualties, but it did not take long for the insurgents' most dangerous weapons—the roadside bomb, the car bomb, and the heavy mortar—to appear. In 2004 alone, nearly 12,000 IED incidents were counted.[58] US forces adapted to the IED threat, but with so many attacks, the losses mounted.[59] The number of US troops killed in Iraq passed the 1,000 mark in September 2004; and it passed the 2,000 mark in October 2005.[60]

Period 2: November 2003–June 2004

This important period included a changing track, and the acceleration of Iraqization.

In early November 2003, Lieutenant General Sanchez dismissed the increase in insurgent attacks as "strategically and operationally insignificant."[61] Sanchez was wrong. True, insurgents could not defeat US forces in open battle—but that was hardly the point. Like all insurgencies, the real dynamic was the ability to sustain subversive activities versus the endurance of the conventional power. The insurgents were testing US willpower as well as stymieing the CPA's attempts to orchestrate an RRA process. In fact, the buildup of the Sunni insurgency was a prelude to the progressive sacrifice of US strategic objectives in increments. As US forces and Sunni insurgents fought to a stalemate, it would be Shia Islamists who would emerge as the real victors.

The ebbing of US objectives (the desired end state) began during October–November 2003. By September, both the White House and Pentagon had begun to exert more pressure on a skeptical Paul Bremer to get on with handing over more governance to Iraqis. A plan devised by Wolfowitz and Feith to expand the IGC and give it a bigger role was much in play.[62] US National Security Adviser Condoleezza Rice (who later replaced Colin Powell as secretary of state) was also becoming more involved. Rice appointed a former US ambassador, Robert Blackwill, as the National Security Council (NCS) coordinator for Iraq in August 2003, and on 6 October she moved to establish a new NSC task force, the Iraq Stabilization Group (ISG).[63] The ISG marked a significant turning point in Washington, with the Pentagon and Bremer losing much of their sway over Iraq policy.

Following a series of high-level meetings in Washington between 27 and 29 October, Bremer responded to the pressure by beginning to talk about giving Iraqis a "path and timeline" for the transfer of governance as well as speeding up the training of the new Iraqi Security Forces (ISF).[64] Then, amid a growing sense of crisis, partly fueled by concerns about resourcing a big rotation of US troops due for spring 2004, Bremer again flew to Washington to discuss the situation on 10 and 11 November; upon his return to Iraq it became clear that the decision had been taken to markedly accelerate Iraqization.[65]

On 15 November, Bremer made the surprise announcement that the CPA— expected to remain in place for another eighteen months—was to be wound up within six months and replaced by a "sovereign" Iraqi government by 30 June 2004.[66] The Transitional Administrative Law (TAL)—effectively an interim constitution and bill of rights—would have to be written by 28 February 2004. Bremer also envisaged that a transitional government would be chosen by a constitutional assembly, probably to be selected by a system of electoral colleges, which would resemble town hall–style caucuses at which local headsmen were likely to have significant influence.[67] In addition, the UN would be encouraged to play a greater role in negotiating and legitimizing the handover of governance. The insurgency had completely altered the track of US policy (recall Figure 7.3).

The trick now was to shape institutional arrangements that could maintain stability and produce a relatively favorable outcome. The subsequent negotiations were extraordinarily difficult, with Bremer having to reconcile differing views over the provisions of the TAL as well as forestalling the insistence of a Shia bloc (fronted by Iraq's most senior Shia clergyman, Grand Ayatollah Ali Sistani) that direct elections underpin the writing of any new constitution and the political process to introduce it, rather than the more tempered and balanced system of electoral colleges envisaged by US officials.[68] Sistani was also eager to see the process completed as rapidly as possible. With the cooperation of a new UN special representative, Lakhdar Brahimi (whose appointment Bremer initially opposed), Bremer managed to parry the difficult issues related to Islam and regional autonomy in the negotiations over the TAL and achieved a degree of acquiescence over the mechanics of the process. Sistani was eventually pacified, and Brahimi (and, effectively, Bremer) got on with choosing the members of the new interim government.[69] Whether this bargaining inside the Green Zone represented true strategic progress for the United States was another matter. Events on the ground were still developing.

Besides negotiating with Iraqis involved in the political process, the runup to the formation of the transitional government would also see Bremer directing the use of force to shape the broader political context, especially through an attempt to suppress those Iraqis most implacably hostile to it. Two targets presented themselves. First, something had to be done to contain the growing Sunni insurgency, especially in Fallujah, a city that was slipping beyond US control. Second, the ambitions of Muqtada al-Sadr—the young Shia cleric who had inherited his family's great name—were a major challenge.[70] The assassination of the SCIRI chief Ayatollah Mohammad Baqr al-Hakim in a car bombing in Najaf on 29 August 2003 had opened the way for al-Sadr. He mobilized the so-called Mahdi army (Jaish al-Mahdi) and set about trying to intimidate his way to the top of the Shia community with a populist, Arab-centric platform that called for the establishment of an Islamic state and articulated open hostility to the United States.

Bremer had wanted to confront the Sunni and Shia challengers earlier but was constrained by the caution of some in Washington and the US military as well as the British. Bremer first moved against the Sadr movement and the Mahdi army. Following a series of inflammatory articles in the organization's newspaper, *al-Hawza,* US troops forcibly closed it down on 28 March 2004 and arrested one of al-Sadr's key lieutenants, Mustafa Yaqoubi. Violence flared in many Shia areas, with the Mahdi army moving to take over the center of Najaf, including its famous mosque. No one in the CPA or US military had really prepared for such a widespread reaction, and US forces were quickly immersed in the operation without really scoping it out. At a press conference on 8 April 2004, Lieutenant General Sanchez outlined the aim to "continue to attack to destroy this disruptive force and to kill or capture its membership and its leadership. . . . Let there be no doubt we will continue the attacks until Sadr's influence is eliminated and Sadr's militia is no longer a threat to Iraq and its citizens. . . . We will not let a small group of criminals and thugs control the destiny of this country. We will not let terrorists inspire and create sectarian violence."[71] US forces moved against the Mahdi army in Najaf and Baghdad, which led to heavy fighting throughout April. The Madhi Army was too inexpert and poorly equipped to offer the kind of resistance that some Sunni insurgents were capable of mounting. Its members fought it out, but many hundreds of al-Sadr's hapless foot soldiers were shot down.

Then, just as violence was flaring in Shia areas, things came to a head with the Sunni insurgents. The killing, mutilation, and public exhibition of four US private security contractors from the Blackwater company in Fallujah on 31 March 2004 enraged both Washington and Bremer, precipitating a major offensive, Operation Vigilant Resolve, against the town beginning on 5 April. Despite the advice of the US commander responsible for the impending operation, Lieutenant General James Conway (USMC), Washington and Bremer were determined to show who was in charge.

The scale of the fighting on two fronts led to a real sense of crisis. More than 130 US troops were killed in April 2004.[72] However, it soon became clear that the political context was not conducive for the decisive use of force. With Bremer's already difficult governance negotiations in danger of completely going off the rails (and off the timetable already agreed upon), both offensives would have to be brought to a premature end, although US forces would return to finish the job in Fallujah during October to November 2004. By 8 April, the lengthening list of Sunni politicians imminently threatening to resign from the IGC and quit the entire political process—as was the UN's interlocutor, Lakhdar Brahimi—was too much for Bremer to resist.[73] Bremer later recalled that he had had no choice but to suspend the offensives because the likely

> chain of events would leave us with a rump Governing Council, and with no way to persuade any respectable Sunni to rejoin it. The CPA, by itself, without the UN, would have to cobble together an interim government. But if we did this quickly, in order to preserve the June 30 deadline, the resulting government would have minimal credibility in the eyes of the Iraqi public. Moreover, it was very unlikely such a government could adequately prosecute the war and prepare for election. Therefore to lose both the Governing Council and the UN would mean losing the June 30 date, with no clear way to get a credible political process revived and no idea of how long that would require. . . . Failing to stick to the June 30 date would call into question the entire November 15 Agreement and the interim constitution, in particular the provisions for elections. If we missed the June 30 date, it would be impossible to hold elections as scheduled in January 2005. This would almost certainly provoke a major crisis with Sistani, who had reluctantly agreed to the UN's reengagement, and had only eventually come to understand that despite his problems with parts of the TAL, the document provided the only path forward.[74]

Lieutenant General Conway was outraged by what had happened; having been sent in against its advice, the Marines Corps was convinced that it was only a few days away from clearing the town.

Similarly, with few Shia politicians in Baghdad wishing to join the company of Saddam Hussein as the slayer of yet another al-Sadr, Bremer was eventually forced to bargain. The Sadr movement scaled back its activities but quietly got on with consolidating its influence. Thus, in many ways the period from November 2003 to June 2004 marked the moment in which the strategic objectives of the United States began to slip away. Indeed, as Iraqis took up the invitation to create a new political system, US and British forces were set to become essentially third-party bystanders in someone else's game.

Period 3: June 2004–December 2005

This period included the transfer of governance, the emergence of Shia primacy, the sacrifice of US strategic goals, and the descent into violent chaos.

As Iraq hurtled down the road toward governance, the CPA's ability to call the shots progressively decreased. Bremer's proposal for a system of indirect elections to the new interim government was effectively blocked by Ayatollah Sistani. His concern was that indirect elections might conspire to deny the Shia community its just desserts. With Sistani refusing to meet US officials in person, Bremer initially tried to push on in the face of his demands, but such was his prestige that he could not be ignored. The Shia politicians of SCIRI and Al-Dawa involved in the political process simply could not go on without Sistani. The UN special envoy, Lakhdar Brahimi, was harnessed to do a deal, and while the United States went on to short-circuit the negotiations—including installing a close ally, Iyad Allawi, as the new prime minister—it was only able to keep most Shia politicians on board by accepting the principle of direct elections for the rest of the process. With Shia Muslims accounting for around 60 percent of Iraq's population of some 25 million, direct elections were bound to make Shia Islamist parties the principal political force. The United States was hoist on its own democratic petard.

The political process rolled out after June 2003 was defined by the passage of UN Resolution 1546 (8 June 2004).[75] This Security Council resolution set down a timetable for the accelerated political process and enhanced the role of the UN in working out the transitional and final institutions (recall Figure 7.3). The schedule was very tight, and all sorts of issues were pending: the distribution of authority between local and central governments; the control of the oil industry and its revenues; and the role of Islam in the political and legal system. On the ground as well, frictions on the frontiers among different communities, notably around Baghdad, Samarra, and Kirkuk, were also becoming explosive.

The reality was that the United States had begun the handover of Iraq to a weak coalition of Shia Islamists who were not acceptable to the Sunni community. National Assembly elections in January 2005 and December 2005 would put the Shia Islamists of the United Iraqi Alliance (UIA) coalition in charge.[76] In January 2005, the UIA received roughly 48 percent of the vote, whereas Bremer's payroll and reconstruction vote, represented by the secular-inclined party list led by Iyad Allawi, got up to only 14 percent.[77] With the UIA attaining 140 seats of the 275-seat National Assembly, it had the majority it needed to appoint the prime minister. After a period of intraparty squabbling, a leading Al-Dawa Party official, Ibrahim Jafaari, was appointed prime minister.

In the subsequent National Assembly elections in December 2005, the UIA remained the largest group, but with only 128 of the 275 seats in parliament it entered power-sharing talks over the formation of a government and the finalization of a permanent constitution.[78] Months of paralysis followed. Sunni and Kurdish factions opposed the continued premiership of Jafaari. It was supposed to take no more than six weeks to choose a prime minister and appoint a cabinet, but it was not until late April 2006 that Jafaari agreed to step down in favor of his Al-Dawa Party colleague, Nouri al-Maliki. The subsequent talks in May related to forming a cabinet were also fraught with problems, and it was not until 20 May 2006 that al-Maliki was able to present his national unity cabinet to parliament.[79] Nevertheless, the creation of a national unity government was a major step forward, and al-Maliki also went on to make the right kinds of noises (as far as the United States was concerned) about dealing with the growing problem of unofficial militias.

The problem was that al-Maliki was in little better position than Jafaari to deal with the militias or much else, for that matter. Shia politics was divided, and the government as constructed was inherently weak. As one of the leading British academics on Iraq, Toby Dodge, noted

> The government and cabinet the new electoral process delivered are unfit for the purpose of rebuilding the Iraqi state. The weakness of a prime minister in a system dominated by parties has directly undermined the coherence of the government. The cabinet, instead of acting as a vehicle for national unity and state building, has become a mechanism for dividing up the spoils. If the ministers that al-Maliki appointed are answerable to anyone, it is to their party bosses, not the prime minister or the electorate. The ministries these politicians now run have become personal and party fiefdoms. At best, scarce government resources are diverted to build party constituencies, with each minister clearing out the payrolls of their ministries to appoint friends, followers and faction members. At worst, with little or no cabinet responsibility or administrative oversight, this system encourages both personal and political corruption. . . . The way that electoral mandate was delivered in 2005 has directly hindered the government's main and crucial task: the rebuilding of the Iraqi state. Instead the cabinet has become highly fractured. Locked away within the fortified Green Zone in the centre of Baghdad, politicians quickly became removed from the everyday concerns of a population struggling to survive in the midst of an increasingly bloody civil war. The new government has followed the path of its predecessor and become mired in the incestuous politics of zero-sum party competition. The state, both coercively and administratively, is still largely irrelevant to the lives of ordinary Iraqis, hastening Iraq's further descent into inter-communal strife and collapse.[80]

In the short to medium terms, the mainstream Shia parties that coalesced around Ayatollah Sistani, including SCIRI and Al-Dawa, were resolved to be pragmatic and cooperative. Sistani himself articulated a moderate Islam that accepted a degree of separation between religion and state. But the United States had begun handing over Iraq to people who could scarcely be regarded as natural allies. Shia politics was divided over personalities and issues, but to sum up the breadth of Shia Islamist opinion: Most wanted an Islamic legal system; most were suspicious or hostile to the United States, the United Kingdom, and Israel; and many had longstanding relations with the Islamic Republic of Iran. Although many Shia Islamists accepted the principle of constitutional multi-ethnic-multifaith politics, quite a few aspired to the ideal of an Islamic state.

Thus, the decision of the Bush administration to press on with the Iraqization of governance before a payroll and reconstruction vote had been developed represented a huge leap into the dark. An Iraq in the hands of Shia Islamists, even if very divided among themselves, was most unlikely to be a beacon of political and economic reform, much less a pillar of some new US-ordained security architecture in the Middle East.

The sudden bypassing of RRA on the road to governance also left too few Sunnis reconciled to the situation. In fact, the battle lines of a savage sectarian war were forming up from mid-2004, especially around Baghdad. With some Sunni jihadists waging a campaign of terrorism against the ISF and Shia civilians, it is scarcely surprising that a dirty war soon got under way. Shia militias played their part in the escalation. The Interior Ministry—controlling the police, National Guard, and other paramilitary forces—also developed a distinctively Shia character and was penetrated by the influence of Shia militias, notably SCIRI's Badr Organization.[81] As the bodies of hundreds of Sunni men began turning up on the streets of Baghdad and elsewhere, there was little doubt that members of the ISF were involved in kidnappings, tortures, and murders. The discovery of 170 abused and starving detainees in a secret prison in the Jadiriya district of Baghdad in mid-November 2005 was the tip of the iceberg.[82] A sectarian bloodbath followed in 2006.

Accelerated Iraqization was never a panacea. Although it is true to say that harnessing local forces is an essential element in any COIN campaign, the way that some US and British policymakers presented it as *the* solution during 2003–2004 was far too glib. Properly recruiting, equipping, training, educating, deploying, and mentoring enough ISF units was a painstaking business. It proceeded at a frustratingly slow pace throughout 2004 and 2005, but it was still done too quickly to prevent the sectarian divisions then emerging in Iraqi society from being transposed into the ISF.[83] A national ethic was not properly institutionalized. Above all, the preeminence of Shia factions soon meant that the ISF was full of people who acted primarily on behalf of the Shia community and particular militia groups, notably the Badr and Mahdi armies. Indeed, when US forces took their Shia trainees into Sunni areas, or established the conditions for Iraqi police and soldiers to enter those areas, they often primed new resistance.

And it all got much worse on 22 February 2006, when a terrorist gang blew up much of the al-Askari Mosque in Samarra—the location of the tombs of the revered tenth and eleventh Shia imams, Ali al-Hadi and al-Hasan al-Askari, and the place where the twelfth imam, Mohammed al-Mahdi (the Hidden Imam), was believed to have gone into occultation in 878—destroying its golden dome. Shia were truly outraged, and even though Iraq avoided an all-out civil war for the time being, the scale and brutality of sectarian violence grew sharply. Few had expected Iraqi society to fragment with quite so much violence. Some of the kind of torture and murder unleashed by sectarian death squads beggared belief.

In a briefing paper published in May 2007, Gareth Stansfield painted a grim picture.[84] Iraqi society had completely fractured, leaving the state as only one of several statelike actors. The fracturing had taken place not only among the three major divisions of Sunni, Shia, and Kurds but also within the main groups, too: There was not one civil war but several civil wars. Violent conflicts were breaking out among sectarian groups, within sectarian groups, among old and new forms of political organization, and over control of particular geographical areas. The surrounding regional powers had thoroughly penetrated these cleavages and were intent on influencing the developments. Iraq stood on the edge of an abyss.

Notes

1. US Vice President Dick Cheney, to the 103rd National Convention of Veterans, 26 August 2002, American Rhetoric Online Speech Bank, www.americanrhetoric.com/speeches/dickcheney103rdvfw.htm.
2. Thomas E. Ricks, *Fiasco: The American Military Adventure in Iraq* (London: Penguin, 2006), 103–106; see also Rajiv Chandrasekaran, *Imperial Life in the Emerald City: Inside Baghdad's Green Zone* (London: Bloomsbury, 2006), 56–60.
3. L. Paul Bremer (with Malcolm McConnell), *My Year in Iraq: The Struggle to Build a Future of Hope* (New York: Simon and Schuster, 2006), 38–39.
4. Ricks, *Fiasco*, 43–44, 158–162.
5. Bremer, *My Year in Iraq*, 40–41.
6. Ricks, *Fiasco*, 159.
7. Bob Woodward, "Prisoners of War," *The Sunday Times*, Review, 8 October 2006, 1–3, esp. 2 (extracts from his book *State of Denial*).
8. Ricks, *Fiasco*, 158.
9. Bremer, *My Year in Iraq*, 235–236; Ricks, *Fiasco*, 163, 179, 235–236.
10. Ricks, *Fiasco*, 106.
11. Chandrasekaran, *Imperial Life in the Emerald City*, 77–79.
12. Ibid., 86–88.
13. Bremer, *My Year in Iraq*, 11–12.
14. Ibid., 39; see also L. Paul Bremer, "How I Didn't Dismantle the Iraqi Army," *New York Times*, 6 September 2007, www.nytimes.com/2007/09/06/opinion/06bremer.html.
15. Bremer, *My Year in Iraq*, 58; Ricks, *Fiasco*, 160, 163; Bremer, "How I Didn't Dismantle the Iraqi Army."
16. Bremer, *My Year in Iraq*, 57, 224.
17. Ahmed S. Hashim, *Insurgency and Counterinsurgency in Iraq* (London: C. Hurst, 2006), 74, 80 (Ahmed S. Hashim was a professor of strategic studies at the US Naval War College and served in Iraq between 2003 and 2005 within the US military command).
18. Information contained in US Central Command planning documents, released by the National Security Archive, National Security Archive Electronic Briefing Book no. 214; see PowerPoint slides for Phase IV, www.gwu.edu/~nsarchiv/NSAEBB/NSAEBB214/index.htm.
19. Woodward, "Prisoners of War," 2.
20. Bremer, *My Year in Iraq*, 12.
21. Chandrasekaran, *Imperial Life in the Emerald City*, 182–184.

22. "'Time Running Out' to Secure Iraq," BBC News, 18 July 2003, http://news.bbc.co.uk/1/hi/world/middle_east/3076531.stm.

23. Sanchez was commander of US 1st Armored Division as it moved into Iraq in mid-May 2003. Assuming control in Baghdad, Sanchez was subsequently handed command of the US V Corps, which became the organizational core of the US occupation. He became a three-star general.

24. John Hamre, "Iraq: Next Steps—How to Internationalize Iraq and Organize the US Government Efforts to Administer Reconstruction Efforts," written testimony to the Senate Foreign Relations Committee, 23 September 2003, http://foreign.senate.gov/hearings/2003/hrg030918a.html (John Hamre was president and chief executive officer, Center for Strategic and International Studies, Washington, DC).

25. J. Brian Atwood, testimony to the Senate Foreign Relations Committee, 23 September 2003, http://foreign.senate.gov/hearings/2003/hrg030918a.html 1–7, 5 (J. Brian Atwood was dean, Hubert H. Humphrey Institute of Public Affairs, University of Minnesota–Minneapolis).

26. Chandrasekaran, *Imperial Life in the Emerald City,* 68.

27. Sourcing the CPA's economic managers (notably Tim Carney and Glenn Corliss), Rajiv Chandrasekaran's *Imperial Life in the Emerald City* describes an illuminating meeting between the CPA's three-man economic team and German consultants. Upon hearing that the CPA had a mere three-man team to initiate the privatization agenda, the German consultants told them that East German privatization had been managed with a staff of 8,000 and that they should not even bother starting in Iraq. Chandrasekaran, *Imperial Life in the Emerald City,* 131–132 (for a broader discussion of the CPA's attempts to reform the Iraqi economy, see esp. chapters 6, 8, and 12).

28. L. Paul Bremer, written testimony to the Senate Foreign Relations Committee, 24 September 2003, http://foreign.senate.gov/hearings/2003/hrg030924a.html, 1–8, 5.

29. Paul D. Wolfowitz, US Undersecretary of State for Defense, written statement to the Senate Armed Services Committee, 9 September 2003. Available at the website of the Senate Armed Services Committee, http://armed-services.senate.gov/e_witnesslist.cfm?id=899, 1–15, esp. 5.

30. UN/World Bank, *United Nations/World Bank Joint Iraq Needs Assessment* (October 2003), www-wds.worldbank.org/external/default/wdscontentserver/wdsp/ib/2007/12/26/000020953_20071226134206/rendered/pdf/419690english011assessment01public1.pdf.

31. UN Security Council Resolution 1483 of 22 May 2003, www.un.org/Docs/scres/2003/sc2003.htm.

32. The Special Inspector-General for Iraqi Reconstruction (SIGIR) was set up by act of Congress. The SIGIR uncovered many cases of misuse of monies and corruption. Extensive details about the SIGIR and its work can be found at www.sigir.mil/.

33. For fuller discussion, see Chandrasekaran, "A Yearning for Old Times," chapter 8 in *Imperial Life in the Emerald City,* 165–188.

34. Chandrasekaran, *Imperial Life in the Emerald City,* 177.

35. "In Search of a New Resolution," *The Economist,* 13 September 2003, 23.

36. UN/World Bank, *Joint Iraq Needs Assessment,* vi.

37. Ibid.

38. "Oil Attacks Costing Iraq $6.25 Bn," BBC News, 19 February 2006, http://news.bbc.co.uk/1/hi/ business/4729178.stm; "Iraq Oil Exports Hit Post-War Low," 2 January 2006, BBC News, http://news.bbc.co.uk/1/hi/business/4574954.stm.

39. Larry Diamond, "What Went Wrong in Iraq," *Foreign Affairs* 83, no. 5 (September–October 2004): 34–56, esp. 37–38 and 39 (Larry Diamond was a senior adviser within the Coalition Provisional Authority).

40. Boris Johnson, "Out of the Ashes," *The Spectator,* 19 March 2005, 12–13, esp. 13.
41. Charles Tripp, "State-Building in Iraq," *Review of International Studies* 30, no. 4 (October 2004): 545–558, esp. 548.
42. Hashim, *Insurgency and Counterinsurgency in Iraq,* 75.
43. Ibid., 346.
44. For some insight into the emergence of the insurgency, see Scott Johnson, "Inside an Enemy," *Newsweek,* 18 August 2003, 16–17. Reporting for *Newsweek* from Iraq, Johnson became one of the leading early sources on Sunni insurgent groups in Iraq. Another of the early sources was the Australian journalist Michael Ware.
45. Hashim, *Insurgency and Counterinsurgency in Iraq,* 104–107.
46. Figure given by the US Commander in Iraq, Lieutenant General Ricardo Sanchez, in an interview with Wolf Blitzer on CNN's "Late Edition," Sunday, 27 July 2003, 1, reproduced by CNN, http://transcripts.cnn.com/transcripts/0307/27/le.00.html; fuller figures on coalition losses in Iraq can be found at "The US Military Death Toll in Iraq," BBC News, 25 October 2005, http://news.bbc.co.uk/1/hi/world/americas/4376392.stm; Iraq Coalition Casualty Count (icasualties.org), http://news.bbc.co.uk/1/hi/world/americas/4376392.stm; and Iraq Body Count, www.iraqbodycount.org.
47. Nigel N. F. Aylwin-Foster (Brigadier, British Army), "Changing the Army for Counterinsurgency Operations," *Military Review* 85, no. 6 (November–December 2005): 2–15 (Nigel Aylwin-Foster served in the Coalition Command in Baghdad between December 2003 and November 2004).
48. See Peter Maass, "Professor Nagl's War" (interview with Major John Nagl), *New York Times Magazine,* 11 January 2004, http://query.nytimes.com/gst/fullpage.html?res=9902E6D61531F932A25752C0A9629C8B63&scp=1&sq=the+counterinsurgent&scp=1&sq=Peter%20Maas,%20The%20Counterinsurgent&st=cse.
49. "Bush Firm Despite Iraq Attacks," BBC News, 1 July 2003, http://news.bbc.co.uk/1/hi/world/middle_east/3034254.stm.
50. For one view of 4IDs operations at the time, see Ricks, *Fiasco,* 142–143.
51. Hashim, *Insurgency and Counterinsurgency in Iraq,* 140–141.
52. From the interview of Sanchez by Wolf Blitzer, CNN, 27 July 2003.
53. Hashim, *Insurgency and Counterinsurgency in Iraq,* 46–47.
54. Fareed Zakaria, "Job One: Solve the Sunni Problem," *Newsweek,* 24 November 2003, 21.
55. By early 2006, the main Sunni groups were Tandhim al-Qaeda fi Balad al-Rifidayn (Al-Qaeda in Iraq, led by Abu Musab al-Zarqawi), Al-Jaish al-Islami fil-Iraq (the Islamic Army in Iraq), Jaish Ansar al Sunna (the Partisans of the Sunna Army), Jaish al-Mujahidin (the Mujahidin Army), Jaish Muhammad (Muhammad's Army), and Harakat al-Muqawama al-Islamiya fil-Iraq (the Islamic Resistance Movement of Iraq). Adam Ward, ed., "Negotiating with the Iraqi Insurgency: Dilemmas and Doubts," *IISS Strategic Comments* 12, no. 1 (February 2006), www.iiss.org/publications/strategic-comments/past-issues/volume-12---2006/volume-12---issue-1/; see also Hashim, *Insurgency and Counterinsurgency in Iraq,* 170–176.
56. Greg Grant, "US Begins to Counter IED Threat in Iraq," *Jane's Defence Weekly* 42, no. 11 (16 March 2005): 5.
57. Hashim, *Insurgency and Counterinsurgency in Iraq,* 154.
58. Grant, "US Begins to Counter IED Threat," 5.
59. In 2005, the United States spent US$150 million to counter the IED threat. In 2006, the US administration provided another US$3.3 billion. The performance of US forces in the field improved significantly, with nearly half of all IEDs planted being found and defused. The casualty rate per IED was cut in half. Information provided in George W. Bush, "President Discusses Freedom and Democracy in Iraq," speech given

at George Washington University, Washington, 13 March 2006, http://merln.ndu.edu/archivepdf/iraq/WH/20060313-3.pdf.

60. For fuller details of US losses, see "The US Military Death Toll in Iraq," BBC News, 25 October 2005, http://news.bbc.co.uk/1/hi/world/americas/4376392.stm; Iraq Coalition Casualty Count (icasualties.org), http://news.bbc.co.uk/1/hi/world/americas/4376392.stm; and Iraq Body Count, www.iraqbodycount.org.

61. "Iraqi Handover to Be Speeded Up," BBC News, 2 November 2003, http://news.bbc.co.uk/1/hi/world/middle_east/3233601.stm.

62. Bremer, *My Year in Iraq,* 170–172.

63. Chandrasekaran, *Imperial Life in the Emerald City,* 212–215.

64. "Iraqi Handover to Be Speeded Up," BBC News, 2 November 2003, http://news.bbc.co.uk/1/hi/world/middle_east/3233601.stm.

65. Bremer, *My Year in Iraq,* 226–227 and 236–237; Ricks, *Fiasco,* 255; Chandrasekaran, *Imperial Life in the Emerald City,* 220–230.

66. For further discussion on the November 2003 acceleration in the political process, see Diamond, "What Went Wrong in Iraq," 47; Toby Dodge, "A Sovereign Iraq?" *Survival* 46, no. 3 (Autumn 2004): 39–58; Tripp, "State-Building in Iraq," 545–558, 548–549.

67. Bremer, *My Year in Iraq,* 210–211 and 227.

68. Ibid., chapters 10 and 11, 267–285 and 286–308.

69. For further discussion, see Chandrasekaran, *Imperial Life in the Emerald City,* 229–230, 272–274.

70. Muqtada al-Sadr's father was Ayatollah Muhammad Sadiq al-Sadr. He was murdered in 1999 probably on the orders of Saddam Hussein.

71. From a Coalition Provisional Authority briefing by Lieutenant General Ricardo Sanchez, Commander, Coalition Ground Forces, Baghdad, 8 April 2004, www.cpa-iraq.org/transcripts/20040409_sanchez_finish-full.html.

72. "The US Military Death Toll in Iraq," BBC News, 25 October 2005, http://news.bbc.co.uk/1/hi/world/americas/4376392.stm.

73. Bremer, *My Year in Iraq,* 332–333.

74. Ibid., 333.

75. UN Security Council Resolution 1546, 8 June 2004, www.un.org/Docs/sc/unsc_resolutions04.html.

76. Oliver Poole, "Friend of Iran Poised for Power," *Daily Telegraph,* Wednesday, 23 February 2005, 14.

77. Ibid., 14.

78. In the 15 December 2005 poll for parliament, the Shia-led United Iraqi Alliance took 128 of 275 seats (10 short of a majority), Kurdish parties took 53, the main Sunni Arab grouping took 44, the Iraqi Accord Front took 44, and the Kurdistan Islamic Union took 5. "Iraq Leaders Set for Tough Talks," BBC News, 21 January 2006, http://news.bbc.co.uk/1/hi/world/middle_east/4633916.stm; see also "Guide to Iraqi Political Parties," BBC News, 20 January 2006, http://news.bbc.co.uk/1/hi/world/middle_east/4511450.stm.

79. "Who's Who in Iraq's New Cabinet," BBC News, 22 May 2006, http://news.bbc.co.uk/1/hi/world/middle_east/5000750.stm.

80. Toby Dodge, "The Causes of US Failure in Iraq," *Survival* 49, no. 1 (Spring 2007): 85–106, 97–98.

81. One of SCIRI/Badr's leading figures, Bayan Jabr, served as minister of interior until the end of May 2006. Jabr's tenure was marked by the increasingly brutal behavior of Shia death squads operating both inside and outside the ISF. Ibid., 92.

82. "Iraq Detainees Found Starving," BBC News, 15 November 2005, http://news.bbc.co.uk/1/hi/ world/middle_east/4440134.stm; "US Demands Iraq Protect Prisoners," BBC News, 25 December 2005, http://news.bbc.co.uk/1/hi/world/middle_east/4559332.stm.

83. For some insight into the challenges of standing up Iraqi forces see Carl D. Grunow (Lieutenant Colonel, US Army), "Advising Iraqis: Building the Iraqi Army," *Military Review* 86, no. 4 (July–August 2006): 8–17 (Grunow completed a twelve-month attachment as senior adviser to a new Iraqi armored brigade in June 2006).

84. Gareth Stansfield, *Accepting Realities in Iraq,* Middle East Briefing Paper (London: Chatham House, May 2007), MEP BP 07/02, 1–12, www.chathamhouse.org.uk/research/middle_east/papers/view/-/id/501/.

8
The Surge Experiment in Iraq

The accelerated move to governance initiated during October–November 2003 culminated with the election of the new National Assembly in December 2005, an occasion for some elation among coalition leaders. But in fact there was little to be happy about. Iraq was in chaos. Suicide bombers struck almost at will, and Shia death squads were roaming the streets. The system of government was weak, and corruption was endemic. The Iraqi state was incapable of dealing with the breadth and enormity of the problems. The country was now in the hands of people who were not natural allies of the United States, its values, and its regional interests. US public and congressional opinion was restive, and the Democratic Party's control of the House and the Senate following the November 2006 US elections threatened serious complications. Things could not go on like this.

Although President Bush continued to talk about victory, the best that the United States could now expect was a greatly suboptimal outcome. The question really was this: How could US forces be withdrawn from Iraq with at least a modicum of credibility and honor? If Iraq was to avoid outright civil war and the existence of the system of governance that had been established safeguarded, then the United States had little choice but to return to RRA with a view toward suppressing the level of insecurity, reconciling hostile parties to a peace process, reconstituting an Iraqi national identity, and persuading key parties to make further compromises over governance. As Iraq descended into worsening chaos in 2006, the Bush administration initiated a significant rethink, and US policymakers and commanders would go on to develop a far more coherent approach to managing the insurgency and the RRA zone.

The yawning RRA gap was to be closed by simultaneously developing top-down and bottom-up reconstruction and reconciliation (see Figure 8.1). The top-down element was indicated in the *National Strategy for Victory in Iraq*, published in November 2005, setting out a series of performance benchmarks

Figure 8.1 The Surge and Closing the Reconstruction, Reconciliation, and Assimilation Gap, 2006–2008

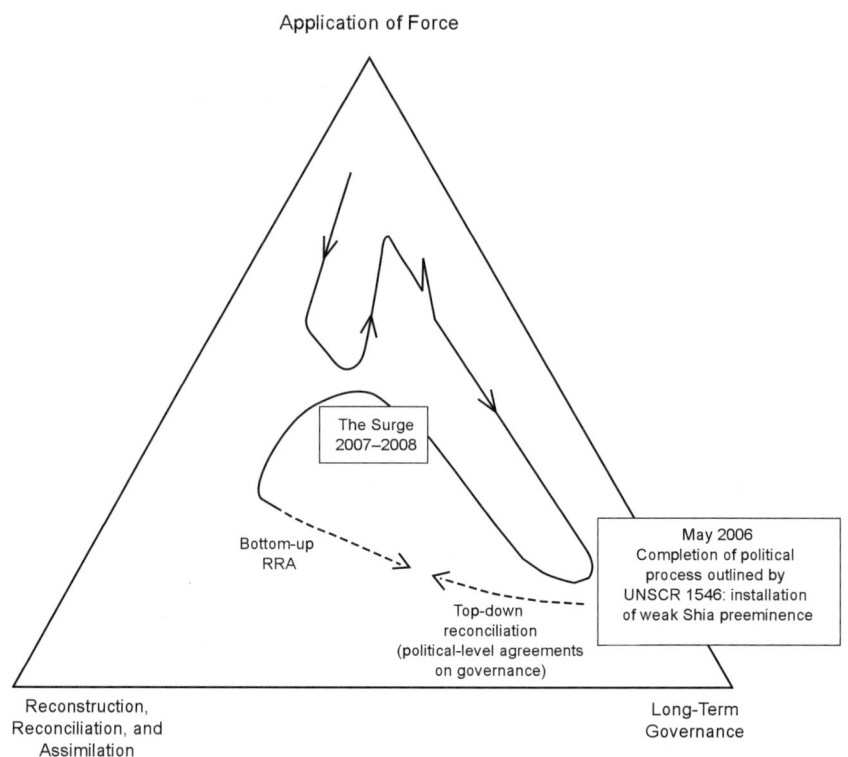

for the Iraqi government in such areas as economic development, constitutional progress, tackling corruption, oil-revenue sharing, and purging militias.[1] The US Congress, as a condition of continued funding, would later go on to refine the idea, introducing eighteen benchmarks mostly related to the performance of government and the attainment of the compromises.

Top-down reconciliation was to be a difficult business. Although the forging of a system of governance under Paul Bremer's stewardship was an achievement of some magnitude, the process was not finished when Bremer left Iraq. Major constitutional issues had yet to be resolved, and the government hardly worked according to existing constitutional and legal rules. The governing coalition led by Nouri al-Maliki was weak and thoroughly penetrated by political groups that maintained armed militias. Amid the context of the Sunni insurgency, al-Maliki was in no position to gain control over the government, parliament, ISF, and militias. No one could expect a breakthrough as long as the security situation was so poor. With the state unable to provide peace and security across Iraq—much less reliable services and jobs—the various communities could scarcely be blamed for relying on militias for security and welfare. To create the conditions for top-down reconciliation, something first needed to be done about the provision of security for the population at a local level.

The provision of greater security was a key aim of a new bottom-up approach. Once additional security was established, it might be possible to undertake sufficient RRA work at a local level to progressively co-opt more communities into the political process. The bottom-up element was to be driven by two major developments. First, in what would be a startling turnaround, the United States would embrace the possibilities of bargaining with the enemy, notably with tribal forces, Baathists, and Islamo-patriots in the Sunni insurgency, as well as with the Mahdi army in Shia areas. Above all, the United States would increasingly leverage the inherent tensions within the ranks of the Sunni insurgency. Second, the bottom-up element was given added impetus by the development and implementation of a new COIN approach that would require a so-called surge of additional US troops and their immersion within local communities in a way not really seen in Iraq. Increasing the level of local security in this way promised to facilitate a close-quarter RRA campaign that was better supervised and controlled. In fact, the combination of enhanced bargaining and unit immersion would prove to be a powerful one.

The Battle for the RRA Zone: 2004–2008

In the four years after the US occupation, the Sunni insurgency was extremely successful in contesting the RRA zone. The insurgents were diffusely organized and thoroughly immersed within Sunni communities, and this made them resilient to the US military response. But diffuseness was a double-edged sword. The insurgents were difficult to root out, but their capacity to mount operations was sometimes only limited and sporadic. A degree of organizational convergence did take place beginning in the autumn of 2004—notably with the development of umbrella organizations such as the Higher Command of the Mujahideen in Iraq, the Army of Muhammad, the Islamic Army of Iraq, and the Partisans of the Sunna Army—but it remained rather loose. If the Sunni insurgency was organizationally diffuse, then there were also increasing internal frictions about operational practice and mission concept. Beyond wrecking the US occupation and trying to forestall a Shia takeover, it was unclear whether the various Islamo-patriotic, nationalist, tribal, jihadist, and mafia-type groups had any common political objectives. The attempt of the Association of Muslim Scholars to set itself up as the political arm of the insurgency proved insufficiently authoritative, and a number of meetings between insurgent leaders in September 2004 would reportedly fail to produce a common vision.[2]

Eventually, the differences among Sunni insurgents would undermine even a minimum level of coherence. Above all, many Iraqi tribal groups—and some Baathists and Islamo-nationalists—would fall out with the more militant jihadists over the tactics of suicide bombings and videotaped beheadings; how far the killing of Shia civilians and the provocations against the Shia community should go; who ran Sunni neighborhoods; and the extent to which the Sunni community should participate in the US-sponsored political process. A bitter internal dispute over Sunni participation in the National Assembly elections of January and December 2005 and the constitutional referendum of October 2005 was the catalyst for disintegration. Sunnis were faced with some stark choices after the elections. The government established was dominated by Shia, and the continuance of an insurgency against both US forces and those of the Shia-dominated government and militias seemed likely to simply perpetuate the isolation of Sunnis and the consolidation of Shia preeminence. Many Sunni insurgents appear to have become convinced that they could no longer wage war against both the United States and Shia at the same time and that a contingent alliance with US forces was now necessary. In the first instance, tribal forces and nationalists would seek US support in their growing conflict with Al-Qaida and, thereafter, to improve their security and bargaining position in the broader political process.

Although US policymakers and Shia politicians were reticent about dealing with Sunni insurgents throughout 2005 and 2006, an opportunity to split the Sunni insurgency against itself had surfaced for the first time.[3] Al-Qaida in Iraq had seriously misplayed its hand. Its repulsive tactics and attempts to exert too much control over the mission concept and organization of the insurgency were disastrous. A key moment came with Al-Qaida in Iraq's murder of Shaikh Bazi al-Risha and one of his sons in a dispute over control of parts of the Baghdad-to-Amman road, prompting another of his sons, Shaikh Abdul Sattar, to seek money and help from the local US commander.[4] It was not long before local Iraqis and jihadists set about killing each other in what amounted to a full-scale civil war within the Sunni insurgency.

The United States was initially reluctant to support former insurgents but eventually could not resist the opportunity. The local tribes organized themselves, forming the Salvation Council for Anbar, fronted by Shaikh Abdul Sattar and Shaikh Faisal al-Goud, and were supplied with money, equipment, operational support, and the promise of political access. Local militiamen were recruited into officially ordained police and paramilitary groups, and in direct cooperation with US forces they began a systematic purge of jihadists. The war between the tribes and jihadists was a fierce one, and tribal elements did not have it all their own way. Many tribal leaders, including Abdul Sattar, were killed.[5] But the tribal forces had a presence across Anbar that made it increasingly difficult for Al-Qaida in Iraq to immerse itself in the landscape.

The impetus behind the so-called Anbar Awakening would later spread to other areas of Iraq in what would become an Iraqi revolt against foreign influences, with even native members of Al-Qaida in Iraq joining concerned local citizens groups (the force was later to be named Sons of Iraq) and being authorized and supported by the coalition around Baghdad and in Diyala Province.[6] Al-Qaida in Iraq was chased from many places. It was a tremendous change in fortune. The United States had penetrated and induced change across the complex networks of the Sunni insurgency in a major operational-level breakthrough.

It must be said, however, that co-opting tribal and Islamo-nationalist elements within the Sunni insurgency meant a potential tradeoff between short-term and long-term aims. Arming and institutionalizing Sunni militias might help chase off Al-Qaida in Iraq in the short term, and give some local Sunnis a greater stake in the new order, but it would ultimately leave groups of armed Sunnis who were far from reconciled to the final order of governance. Indeed, it might simply bolster an enhanced system of Sunni warlordism that would either remain largely beyond the control of the Shia-led national government or would have to be later confronted by the government. It looked to be risking an even worse civil conflict in the future. Many mainstream Sunni insurgents also remained reluctant to negotiate as long as the United States did not announce a date for its departure from Iraq.

The Genesis of the Surge

US armed forces had gone into Iraq without a clear sense of the battle ahead, but once it became engaged the considerable intellectual firepower that existed within the US military eventually swung into action. Drawing on prior British and French experiences as well as their own in Vietnam and Iraq—notably the lessons of the Civil Operations and Revolutionary (later Rural) Development and Support (CORDS) program in Vietnam—US officers started to formulate cutting-edge ideas about contemporary COIN operations that they would test in Iraq.[7] Such thinking soon started to appear in US military journals, notably the US Army's *Military Review* and the US Navy's *Proceedings*. Senior officers like Generals Peter W. Chiarelli (US Army), Thomas Metz (US Army), David Petraeus (US Army), James Mattis (USMC), James Amos (USMC), Jack Keane (US Army, ret.) and Robert Scales (US Army, ret.) and Colonels John Nagl (US Army) and H. R. McMaster (US Army) were the best-known thinkers in the new wave of COIN and culture-centric warfare. A number of mid-level and more junior officers also made significant contributions.

The leading thinker and practitioner of the new wave was David Petraeus. As commander of 101st Airborne Division during the aftermath of the 2003 invasion, Petraeus had run a relatively stable regime in Mosul, and he had returned to Iraq to expedite the training of the ISF. Following his second tour,

Petraeus headed up an elite team at the Doctrine Division of the Combined Arms Center in Fort Leavenworth, Kansas, which incorporated much of the new COIN thinking in the joint US Army/Marine Corps field manual (*FM 3–24*) published in December 2006.[8] What emerged was a number of important ideas: full-spectrum operations (FSO); unit immersion; and the importance of the battalion in COIN operations.

In an article published in the July–August 2005 issue of *Military Review*, Major General Peter W. Chiarelli (US Army) and Major Patrick R. Michaelis (US Army) gave an account of the concept and practice of FSO in Iraq.[9] FSO required the simultaneous implementation of five streams of activity: combat/kinetic; training local forces; providing essential services; promoting good governance; and the development of economic pluralism and long-term job opportunities (premised on market principles). In addition, it was vital to tie all five streams together with information operations (IO) designed to maximize the positive persuasive effects over target audiences, especially fence-sitters (the center of gravity in COIN) and to prevent the enemy from manipulating the story. Chiarelli and Michaelis noted that "unless coalition-initiated projects were methodically thought through and publicized, insurgents would claim credit for the results, using posters, graffiti, or even sermons to inform the people they were the ones responsible for improvements."[10] Doing positive things was not enough. Reconstruction activities had to be interpreted in the right way to win hearts and minds. The Chiarelli-Michaelis article could also cite cases in which the provision of local services and economic pluralism had had a real impact on the level of insurgent activity. In this sense, it was IO that turned reconstruction activities into reconciliation and assimilation. Trials of FSO were undertaken in Sadr City in Baghdad and on the western border of Iraq beginning in May 2005, with the town of Tal Afar becoming something of a model.[11] US forces moved to clear, hold, build, and persuade.

In fact, the various aspects of IO were increasingly seen as central to the operational art. In an article published in the May–June 2006 issue of *Military Review*, a group of US officers led by Lieutenant General Thomas Metz reviewed former failures in Iraq, notably the failed attempt to clear Fallujah in April 2004 (Operation Vigilant Resolution), observing that this had happened because "steps to prepare the information battlefield, including engaging numerous and varied Iraqi leaders, removing enemy information centers, and rapidly disseminating information from the battlefield to worldwide media were not woven into the plan."[12] If US forces were to achieve operational-level success, it was vital that US operations be kept under a so-called information threshold—the point at which the enemy or its de facto allies were able to interfere with US operations with their own IO in the local, national, and international arenas. Raising the information threshold was a precursor to using higher levels of force—if that was required to establish security—as well as fending off the enemy's attempts to interfere with RRA-type activities.

What US forces needed to do in Iraq was mass effects across the realms of IO (psychological operations, deception, operational security, electronic warfare, and computer network operations) at both the local and national levels. During the period 2003–2005, the capacity of US forces to do this was limited, especially at the local level. At the outset of the occupation, US forces tended to locate themselves in large defendable firebases from which they projected combat power. The problem was that this isolated US troops from locals, stymieing the development of properly supervised close-quarter IO. To the extent that US forces were in touch with locals, it was commonly in the form of sweeping through neighborhoods inside armored vehicles. Insurgents were far more immersed and thus were in a better position to physically dominate communities as well as win the intelligence and information wars. Based on previous experiences in Vietnam and Iraq, the solution that presented itself was the concept and practice of unit immersion organized at the level of the battalion.

In an important article, Lieutenant Colonel Douglas A. Ollivant (US Army) and Lieutenant Eric D. Chewning (US Army) argued that, notwithstanding the efforts of civil affairs and special forces, it was the regular maneuver battalion (about 600 men) that was the best level at which to organize immersed COIN operations.[13] The battalion was the largest unit in which its commander was in direct and continuous contact with the population. Ollivant and Chewning argued that

> our thesis is simple: The combined arms maneuver battalion, partnering with indigenous security forces and living among the population it secures, should be the basic tactical unit of counterinsurgency (COIN) warfare. Only such a battalion—a blending of infantry, armor, engineers, and other branches, each retrained and employed as needed—can integrate all arms into full-spectrum operations at the tactical level. . . . Smaller conventional forces might develop excellent community relations, but they lack the robust staff and sufficient mass to fully exploit local relationships. Conversely, while brigades and divisions boast expanded analysis and control capabilities, they cannot develop the street-level rapport so critical for an effective COIN campaign. Unconventional forces are likewise no panacea because the expansion of Special Operations Command assets or the creation of stability and reconstruction or system-administration forces will not result in sustainable COIN strategies. Recent experience in Iraq affirms previously forgotten lessons: "Winning the Peace" requires simultaneous execution along the full spectrum of kinetic and non-kinetic operations. While political developments in Iraq and the United States might have moved past the point at which our suggested COIN solution would be optimal, we argue that the maneuver battalion should be the centerpiece of the Army's future COIN campaigns.[14]

Unit immersion might expose US troops to higher risks in the short term, but the medium- to long-term payoffs might mean that it was a price worth paying.

The development of new tactical-level ideas (practice at point of contact) was also to be complemented by new operational-level perceptions about the context in which the US military was acting. By 2006, US commanders like David Petraeus and Ray Odierno had come to understand that they were not simply involved in an insurgent war; rather, they were in the midst of a putative civil war in a highly complex social setting. In looking beyond the immediate demands of containing the Sunni insurgency, it became clear that the causes of instability and subversion were much wider and included things like sectarianism, Shia assertiveness and extremism, Kurdish expansionism, the fragmentation and disempowerment of Sunnis, criminality, the nature of the weak state, and external subversion.[15] US authorities in Iraq needed to better appreciate how they were constantly being played by various actors within that complex social setting. What was needed was more objectivity. As Emma Sky, the special adviser to Lieutenant General Ray Odierno, commander of Multinational Corps Iraq beginning in late 2006, wrote the following in April 2008:

> It was recognized that the conflict in Iraq was a struggle between different communities for power and resources—and not simply an insurgency. We acknowledged that the government was part of the problem. Iraq was a fragile state with weak legitimacy. Certain elements of the government were using the institutions of state for sectarian purposes. Insurgent groups, criminal gangs and militias of political parties were filling the "ungoverned space." Significant numbers of Iraqis disputed the legitimacy and outcomes of the process that had brought the ruling parties to power.[16]

When Lieutenant General Odierno was deployed to Iraq in late 2006, he brought with him a small team of strategists and conflict-zone experts that became known as the Initiatives Group. The team got on with trying to understand the complexity of the real drivers of instability and with identifying the appropriate responses. At last, US commanders had put together tactical approaches and operational understandings to deal with Iraq more effectively. It was now a question of properly testing the hypothesizing.

The Surge of 2007–2008

The experiment with FSO and unit immersion was the last throw of the dice for the United States in Iraq: It has become known to history as the surge. The plan stemmed from the work of a distinguished panel led by Frederick W. Kagan and General Jack Keane (US Army, ret.) under the auspices of the American Enterprise Institute. In a report titled *Choosing Victory,* Kagan and Keane insisted that the United States could still win in Iraq but admitted that the strategy of relying on the political process (the transit to governance) to eliminate the insurgency had failed.[17] According to Kagan, America's own military efforts to establish security had also been "reactive, sporadic, under-resourced and ephemeral."[18] A new approach was required that took on board the new COIN thinking and committed the appropriate resources to make it work. What was now needed was to surge additional US troops into Baghdad and Anbar Province with the aim of focusing on the provision of security to the population; clearing and holding Sunni and mixed areas with a view toward immersing US units within them; building and policing security walls between hostile communities where necessary; more closely partnering and supervising the ISF; boosting the resources available for reconstruction and reconciliation activities in cooperative neighborhoods; and inducing the Iraqi government to reform itself. In the event, the Baghdad security plan (Fardh Al-Qanoon) would also see the development of the Baghdad Operations Command, which coordinated the national army and local police forces under the leadership of Lieutenant General Abud Qanbar. It would become easier to work with the ISF.[19]

The Kagan-Keane report estimated that nine US combat brigades were needed for key areas in Baghdad.[20] With five US combat brigades already in Baghdad, the surge required another four brigades (about 20,000 troops total).[21] With an enhanced reserve and additional troops for Anbar Province, at least 30,000 more were required during a period of some eighteen months for the plan to come to fruition; only such a deployment could really test the hiding places of the insurgents. Kagan believed that initial preparation, clearance, and holding operations would take ninety days from the beginning of the surge and then much of 2007 to consolidate control in Baghdad. Expanding security to the key areas of Anbar, Diyala, and north to Mosul would then take a good part of 2008.[22] It seemed unlikely that US forces would be able to fully hand over the operation to the ISF for at least eighteen to twenty-four months after its commencement.

President Bush bought in to the basic concept of the Kagan-Keane plan. On 10 January 2007, Bush addressed the nation to announce the dispatch of five more brigades (21,500 troops, later expanded to 24,000) mostly to Baghdad to "help Iraqis clear and secure neighborhoods, to help them protect the local population, and to help ensure that the Iraqi forces left behind are capable of providing the security that Baghdad needs."[23] US forces would put much more effort into partnering ISF units as well as embedding advisers within Iraqi units. The surge would be followed by the expansion of the Provincial Reconstruction Team program, with new PRTs paired with brigade combat teams, thereby giving enhanced authorities and resources to local RRA activities. In reality, the number of PRTs grew from ten to twenty-five in 2007, although filling the hundreds of additional PRT posts would be challenging.[24] Bush also moved to replace the existing military commander in Iraq, General George Casey, with one of the gurus of the new approach—Lieutenant General David Petraeus.[25]

Back on Track? Assessing the Utility of the Surge

During the period 2007–2008, the surge delivered significant benefits at the tactical level and promised operational-level progress. The progress report to the US Congress presented in mid-September 2007 by General Petraeus and Ambassador Ryan Crocker reflected a growing level of cautious optimism.[26] A decisive number of Sunnis appeared to have turned against Al-Qaida in Iraq in Anbar and Diyala. The insurgent sanctuaries of Fallujah, Ramadi, and Baqubah were mostly cleared, as were the Baghdad districts of Adhamiya, Ameriyah, Arab Jabour, Abu Ghraib, and Ghazaliyah. The most startling turnaround was in Anbar, where some 12,000 Sunni militia members had been hired, with the number of insurgent attacks plummeting from 1,350 in October 2006 to only some 200 by August 2007.[27] By the beginning of 2008, there were some 130 Concerned Local Citizens groups across the Sunni areas of Iraq, employing some 80,000 personnel.[28] The last of Al-Qaida in Iraq's major urban strongholds was in Mosul, but with US and Iraqi forces conducting Operation Lion's Roar in May 2008, that city was also cleared by July 2008.[29]

By the autumn of 2007, the level of violence was down significantly. Predictably, US forces had initially taken higher losses, with April, May, and June 2007 each seeing more than 100 US troops killed, but the casualty figures dropped to thirty-eight killed in October 2007 and twenty-three killed in December.[30] Assessing the number of Iraqi casualties was more difficult, but the AFP news agency, quoting sources from the various ministries, estimated that 554 were killed and 333 more bodies found in October 2007 (many of which may have been killed in the previous month); this was down from 2,000 violent deaths in the month of January 2007.[31] Something approaching normal life could be seen developing in parts of Baghdad, Anbar, and Diyala.[32]

Although signs of progress on the ground were unmistakable, it remained difficult to conclude that the surge represented lasting operational-level and strategic-level progress. To his credit, General Petraeus was cautious about doing so. The level of violence was down, but there were a number of potential explanations for this. Most ethnically mixed areas had already been cleansed of their minorities, and so there was less for the militia death squads to do in the short term. Sunni militants and the Mahdi army were avoiding conflict and waiting out the surge. And the co-opting of Sunni militia members was possible only as long as US forces were in the lead and the money to pay the shaikhs and individual militias continued to flow (some shaikhs were being subsidized with tens of thousands of dollars, and individual tribal police reportedly received about $370 per month).[33] In other words, the surge was temporarily suppressing the symptoms of a simmering sectarian conflict that might spark back into life as soon as the surge had run its course.

The surge was also conducted in a broader political context that casts doubts over its ultimate strategic utility for two reasons. First, by 2007–2008 the will of the United States to push on in Iraq was a factor very much in play. President Bush had managed to hold the line in 2008, with the surge widely interpreted as one last chance for success in Iraq before a significant scaling back had to be undertaken. Iraq had done much to wreck the Bush presidency, and the next president would have to make concessions to public and congressional pressures. It threatened to become a replay of Vietnam. After years of fumbling the COIN campaign in Vietnam, the United States had eventually come up with an organization, as well as tactical and operational practices (the CORDS and Phoenix programs), that promised to defeat the insurgency—but it all came too late. Time ran out on the US involvement before CORDS and Phoenix could fully come to fruition, with the programs ultimately providing the exit strategy for the United States.

Second, the strategic utility of the surge was questionable because of the Iraqi context. The point was to create conditions under which the conflicting Iraqi parties might be able to close the RRA gap (bottom up and top down), but this ultimately depended on the willingness and ability of a Shia-led government and the Sunni community to come to terms. Beyond the Iraqi government embracing the RRA process, what the United States also needed, in order to turn the surge into lasting strategic utility, was a political deal that consolidated the US-Iraqi alliance and a long-term status-of-forces agreement. Nouri al-Maliki was probably the best partner that the United States could expect in Iraq, but there were real doubts about his will and capacity to deliver. US concerns about al-Maliki were highlighted in a leaked memorandum dated 8 November 2006 to President Bush and his national security team by National Security Advisor Stephen J. Hadley following a trip to Baghdad. In relation to a meeting between Hadley and al-Maliki on 30 October, Hadley noted that

> we returned from Iraq convinced we need to determine if Prime Minister Maliki is both willing and able to rise above the sectarian agendas being promoted by others. Do we and Prime Minister Maliki share the same vision for Iraq? If so, is he able to curb those who seek Shia hegemony or the reassertion of Sunni power? . . . Despite Maliki's reassuring words, repeated reports from our commanders on the ground contributed to our concerns about Maliki's government. Reports of non-delivery of services to Sunni areas, intervention by the prime minister's office to stop military action against Shia targets and to encourage them against Sunni ones, removal of Iraq's most effective commanders on a sectarian basis and efforts to ensure Shia majorities in all ministries—when combined with the escalation of *Jaish al-Mahdi's* (JAM) killings—all suggest a campaign to consolidate Shia power in Baghdad. While there does seem to be an aggressive push to consolidate Shia power and influence, it is less clear whether Maliki is a witting participant. The information he receives is undoubtedly skewed by his small circle of Dawa advisers, coloring his actions and interpretation of reality. His intentions seem good when he talks with Americans, and sensitive reporting suggests he is trying to stand up to the Shia hierarchy and force positive change. . . . But the reality on the streets of Baghdad suggests Maliki is either ignorant of what

is going on, misrepresenting his intentions, or that his capabilities are not yet sufficient to turn his good intentions into action.[34]

For all the doubts about al-Maliki, the Bush administration had little alternative but to believe—or hope—that al-Maliki's problem was his capacity (rather than willingness) to do the right thing. The hope was that the surge might sufficiently strengthen al-Maliki to allow him to press ahead with a number of key RRA and governance-related reforms: the extension of government health and education services to Sunni areas; the reorganization of his parliamentary bloc and the end of his association with the Sadr movement; the reshuffle of his cabinet to bring in more nonsectarian Shia, Sunni, and Kurds, especially technocrats; a new requirement that all government officials renounce violence; a shakeout of his personal staff; the suspension of corrupt Iraqi police officers; the institution of a more robust program of embedding coalition forces into the Ministry of Interior; and a determined push on a range of governance issues.

The problem was that al-Maliki's incentive for taking the considerable risks involved in the reform agenda was weak, and the reality was that he was not some impartial arbiter of Iraq's national interest. Al-Maliki was deeply immersed in Shia politics and in the business of consolidating Shia preeminence. He was a leading member of the Shia Islamist party, Al-Dawa, which often relied on the Sadr movement for parliamentary support as well as for fending off the other main Shia faction, the Supreme Council for the Islamic Revolution in Iraq, and its Badr militia. Again, it all threatened to be a replay of Vietnam, a war that the United States was fundamentally unable to win because it could not engineer a stable or viable system of governance in South Vietnam capable of turning the use of force and hearts-and-minds operations into lasting political outcomes.

The questions about the political context in which the surge was taking place were reflected in the Petraeus-Crocker benchmark reports to the US Congress in July and September 2007.[35] The Iraqi government continued to have an "unsatisfactory" opaque record with respect to most of the key RRA and governance benchmarks. However, the September report was more optimistic, arguing that top-down reconciliation, despite the failure to meet formal benchmarks, was happening in practice. The report noted that

> while key national legislation has not yet passed, the objectives of such laws are in some ways already being achieved. For example: there is no revenue sharing law, and yet significant oil revenues are being distributed by the central government to the provinces in an equitable manner. There is no provincial powers law, and yet the provincial governors and councils are making decisions on budget expenditures through engagement with the central government and ministries and are providing essential services for their constituents. There is no amnesty law, and yet immunity is being granted to many

former insurgents, who in turn are being recruited to join legitimate security institutions. There is no de-Ba'athification reform law, and yet more than 45,000 former Ba'athist members of the old armed services have been granted pensions or even restored to active duty or government service. Amnesty or de-Ba'athification laws were assumed necessary to drive a wedge between national elements of the largely Sunni insurgency and al-Qaida. In fact, Sunnis in record numbers are turning against al-Qaida, reclaiming their communities, and turning towards the central government for additional resources. These are precisely the "effects" the benchmarks were intended to produce, even if the formal benchmarks themselves have not been met. In the coming months, our strategy will increasingly focus on helping the Iraqis knit together this new "bottom-up" progress with the "top-down" political process. It will still remain vital for Iraq's national government to codify what is happening in practice through formal legislation over time.[36]

The argument made in the September report was plausible; bearing in mind the kind of violence that had been unleashed, any progress was bound to be slow and grudging. Iraqi legislators did eventually begin to grind out a number of more formal agreements, notably enacting a de-Baathification reform law on 12 January 2007. The passage of the Accountability and Justice Law promised to see thousands of dismissed former lower-level and mid-level Baathists reinstated to their jobs, although higher officials and members of the security services could still expect to be pensioned off or even tried for past crimes.[37] Following a tumultuous session of parliament on 12–13 February 2008—in which Shia legislators temporarily walked out and the Sunni speaker, Mahmoud al-Mashhadani, threatened to move for a dissolution of parliament—a package of legislation relating to the passage of a proper budget, a limited amnesty for detainees, and a provincial law defining the relationship between Baghdad and local authorities was also put through.[38]

But the various Iraqi parties remained reluctant to clarify and formalize some of the big RRA and governance issues, and even if and when key measures could be passed, it was unclear what effect they would have in practice. It would be a brave former Baathist indeed who turned up to work in a ministry or public agency penetrated by the Mahdi or Badr armies. Moreover, it was also possible that the agreement of more formal legislation in Baghdad might not only lead to the curtailing of informal kinds of cooperation but also open up new conflicts as well. For instance, new laws outlining provincial powers risked sparking an Arab-Kurdish conflict, as well as secessionist maneuvering in the Shia south. The formal enactment of an oil- and oil revenue–sharing law might ignite a simmering Sunni-Kurdish conflict around Kirkuk. The role and enforcement of Islam throughout society begged all sorts of contentious questions.

The fact was that Iraqi society had disintegrated into sectarian solidarity groups, and overcoming the zero-sum thinking that went with that was a tremendous barrier to bridging the RRA gap. Too few Iraqis liked or trusted

182 The Problem of Force

people in other groups, and major parties remained reluctant to make concessions on the division of resources and power—especially if they were definitive and permanent. Expediting the move to a system of governance during the period 2003–2005 had locked in sectarian politics—a weak central government under a nervous Shia preeminence; Kurdish inclination for separatism; and a dispossessed, resentful, and fragmented Sunni community—and once that happened it was going to be difficult to go back and reengineer a new settlement. It would be wrong to say that RRA in Iraq was impossible, but it certainly wasn't going to happen anytime soon.

Thus, while the surge strategy (and associated hiring of Sunni militias) achieved a necessary suppression of violence, it was not sufficient to produce a timely reworking of the system of governance. Little could be done about this before the November 2008 US presidential elections, with the Republican candidate, John McCain, running against Democrat Barack Obama. Prior to that election, the Bush administration's priority was to maintain as much peace and order as possible. The hiatus masked a festering reality that was described by Steven Simon, who dismissed the conventional wisdom that the surge had worked:

> Unfortunately, such claims misconstrue the causes of the recent fall in violence and, more important, ignore a fatal flaw in the strategy. The surge has changed the situation not by itself but only in conjunction with several other developments: the grim successes of ethnic cleansing, the tactical quiescence of the Shiite militias, and a series of deals between US forces and Sunni tribes that constitute a new bottom-up approach to pacifying Iraq. The problem is that this strategy to reduce violence is not linked to any sustainable plan for building a viable Iraqi state. If anything, it has made such an outcome less likely, by stoking the revanchist fantasies of Sunni Arab tribes and pitting them against the central government and against one another. In other words, the recent short-term gains have come at the expense of the long-term goal of a stable, unitary Iraq. . . . Despite the current lull in violence, Washington needs to shift from a unilateral bottom-up surge strategy to a policy that promotes, rather than undermines, Iraq's cohesion. That means establishing an effective multilateral process to spur top-down political reconciliation among major Iraqi factions. And that, in turn, means stating firmly and clearly that most US forces will be withdrawn from Iraq within two or three years. Otherwise, a strategy adopted for near-term advantage by a frustrated administration will only increase the likelihood of long-term debacle.[39]

The surge strategy had failed to create the conditions for a long-term Sunni-Shia peace agreement. Worse, in the short to medium terms, renewed violence loomed unless an accommodation could be made between the government and Sunni militias, but Shia politicians and commanders were resistant to the idea of formalizing the power of Sunni militias, and the government planned to absorb only some 20 percent of Sunni militia members into the forces of the state.[40]

At the same time, there was the question of the Sadr movement and the Mahdi army in Shia areas—and how far coalition forces sensibly could go in suppressing it. The major military operation authorized by the Maliki government against the Mahdi army in Basra and Baghdad during March and April 2008 was a significant moment. After street fighting that killed hundreds, and despite the initially poor performance of the national army, the ISF (with US support) eventually managed to break the Mahdi army's hold on the streets of Basra and to impose more control in Sadr City. It was a major advance, but the issue was far from resolved. Indeed, the Sadr movement might increasingly come to resemble Lebanon's Hezbollah; a mass political movement, but with its militia reorganizing itself into a smaller and better-disciplined, -trained, and -equipped force. For Shia parties that continued to rely on US assistance, notably SCIRI and Al-Dawa, the Sadr movement represented not only a continuing armed threat but also a major political challenge.

One of the most significant effects of Sadr's political influence was to cut down the Maliki government's wiggle room when it came to a long-term political alliance and status-of-forces agreement with the United States. With the prospect of national elections in 2009, and with the Sadr movement making the populist call for an end to the US presence, al-Maliki and SCIRI had to make concessions to public opinion. The US-Iraqi negotiations in 2008 over a longer-term alliance agreement can be described only as difficult. A whole range of tricky issues—permanent legal immunity for US troops and contractors, authority to initiate military operations, and control of Iraqi airspace—had to be agreed, and al-Maliki was loathe to put anything other than another interim deal before the Iraqi parliament.[41] Although SCIRI also believed for contingent reasons that US help was still needed, it also voiced support for the principle of a full US withdrawal.[42]

In the end, the "status-of-forces agreement" and longer term "strategic framework agreement" worked out between the al-Maliki government and United States in November 2008 reflected the fact that the Iraqis had largely got their way in the tough negotiations.[43] The agreements authorized the presence of US forces in Iraq until 2011 but made it clear that all future operations were to be authorized and coordinated with Iraqi authorities (with US forces losing their authority to conduct targeted raids on Iraqi properties without an Iraqi court order and coordination with Iraqi authorities); members of US forces and private contractors were to become subject to Iraqi justice outside their bases; US forces were to begin withdrawing from Iraq's populated areas from mid-2009 and begin to hand over their bases; and the surveillance and control of Iraqi airspace was to be immediately handed over to Iraq. It was all indicative of the basic fact that few Iraqis (other than Kurds) saw the United States as a natural ally; even fewer wanted Iraq to host US military bases in the long run. The system of electoral politics in Iraq meant that these basic inclinations were fed into government policy.

In Sum

The surge experiment was reason for some optimism that US forces had found a formula for contemporary COIN operations. The combination of full-spectrum operations, unit immersion, and leveraging differences within the insurgency's ranks undoubtedly delivered significant tactical- and operational-level progress. The question for future operations was this: What had been the most important factor in the success? Full-spectrum operations and unit immersion? The bargaining element? Of course, the two sides of the coin were related, and unpacking their relative importance is a difficult thing to do, but at first glance the bargaining element looked to be more important. Certainly, it is difficult to believe that immersed US forces could have stuck it out in Sunni neighborhoods for as long as required if Sunni tribal forces, nationalists, and Islamo-patriots had not decided to strike deals with them.

The other point to make about the surge strategy was that even if it turned the tide against foreign jihadists, it seemed unlikely that winning this battle could deliver stability to Iraq, much less a strategic-level victory for the United States. US forces could not supervise the bottom-up RRA process at such close quarters indefinitely, and top-down reconciliation looked like a long process over which US policymakers had limited influence. By the time of the surge, probably the best end state that the United States could achieve was to foster the survival of a unitary Iraqi state capable of suppressing jihadists as well as warding off some of the influence of Iran. In early 2009, the will and ability of future Iraqi governments to do this remained questionable. Moreover, the bottom line was that Iraq had been put into the hands of an unstable coalition of Shia Islamists. Even if the United States could convince al-Maliki or someone else to restructure governance and agree to some sort of alliance, it was too late to redefine the fundamental character of Iraqi politics. Iraq would not be a stable and unified country. It would not be seen as a model of democratic governance that anyone else in the region would want to follow. It would not be a reliable ally of the United States. It would not become the centerpiece of some new US security architecture in the Middle East. If war is about achieving strategic goals and desired end states, then the Iraq War had been lost long before.

Notes

1. *National Strategy for Victory in Iraq* was prepared by the National Security Council (November 2005), www.washingtonpost.com/wp-srv/nation/documents/iraq nationalstrategy11-30-05.pdf.

2. Ahmed S. Hashim, *Insurgency and Counterinsurgency in Iraq* (London: C. Hurst, 2006), xxviii, 201–206.

3. Adam Ward, ed. "Negotiating with the Iraqi Insurgency: Dilemmas and Doubts," *IISS Strategic Comments* 12, no. 1 (February 2006): www.iiss.org/publications/strategic-comments/past-issues/volume-12---2006/volume-12---issue-1/; Kim Sengupta, "Shia

Accuse US Forces of Appeasing Insurgents as Attacks Kill 11 Soldiers," *The Independent,* Saturday, 7 January 2006, 29.

4. Steven Simon, "The Price of the Surge: How US Strategy Is Hastening Iraq's Demise," *Foreign Affairs* 87, no. 3 (May–June 2008): 57–76, esp. 63.

5. "Iraqi Insurgents Kill Key US Ally," BBC News, 13 September 2007, http://news.bbc.co.uk/1/hi/world/middle_east/6993211.stm.

6. Local Sunni forces were coordinated by the Force Strategic Engagement Cell within the US Commander's headquarters (under General Petraeus) in Iraq. In 2007, it was headed by a British officer, Major General Paul Newton, and Donald Blome, a senior assistant to the US ambassador, Ryan Crocker. See Michael Gordon, "The Former-Insurgent Counterinsurgency," New York Times Online, 2 September 2007, www.nytimes.com/2007/09/02/magazine/ 02iraq-t.html, 13.

7. For insight into the lessons of CORDS, see Robert M. Cassidy (Lieutenant Colonel, US Army), "Winning the War of the Flea: Lessons from Guerrilla Warfare," *Military Review* 84, no. 5 (September–October 2004): 41–46; Montgomery McFate and Andrea Jackson, "The Object Beyond War: Counterinsurgency and the Four Tools of Political Competition," *Military Review* 86, no. 1 (January–February 2006): 13–26; Dale Andrade and James H. Willbanks (Lieutenant Colonel, ret., US Army), "CORDS/Phoenix: Insurgency Lessons from Vietnam for the Future," *Military Review* 86, no. 2 (March–April 2006): 9–23; Ross Coffey (Major, US Army), "Revisiting CORDS: The Need for Unity of Effort to Security Victory in Iraq," *Military Review* 86, no. 2 (March–April 2006): 24–34; John Nagl (Lieutenant Colonel, US Army), *Learning to Eat Soup with a Knife: Counterinsurgency Lessons from Malaya to Vietnam* (Chicago: University of Chicago Press, 2005), xxix, 164–166.

8. Doctrine Division of the Combined Arms Center, US Army and Marine Corps, "Social Network Analysis and Other Analytical Tools," appendix B in Field Manual 3–24, *Counterinsurgency,* Headquarters Department of the US Army (December 2006). The 282-page document was drawn up under the supervision of Lieutenant General David Petraeus and General James Amos (USMC). For a brief outline and discussion of the rewriting process, see John A. Nagl (Lieutenant Colonel, US Army), "An American View of Twenty-First Century Counter-Insurgency," *RUSI Journal* 152, no. 4 (August 2007): 12–16.

9. Peter W. Chiarelli (Major General, US Army) and Patrick R. Michaelis (Major, US Army), "Winning the Peace: The Requirement for Full Spectrum Operations," *Military Review* 85, no. 4 (July–August 2005): 4–17 (Peter Chiarelli was US 1st Cavalry Division commander in Baghdad area in 2004); for another account of the practice of full spectrum operations, see John R. S. Batiste (Major General, US Army) and Paul R. Daniels (Lieutenant Colonel, US Army), "The Fight for Samarra: Full-Spectrum Operations in Modern Warfare," *Military Review* 85, no. 3 (May–June 2005): 13–21.

10. Chiarelli and Michaelis, "Winning the Peace," 15.

11. "Iraq-US Assault Hailed a Success," 22 September 2005, BBC News, http://news.bbc.co.uk/1/hi/ world/middle_east/4271250.stm; Marie Colvin (interview with Colonel H. R. McMaster), "Leaving Now Is Not the Way Out of Iraq," *The Sunday Times,* News Review, London, 29 July 2007, 5.

12. Thomas Metz (Lieutenant General, US Army), Mark Garret (Lieutenant Colonel, US Army), James Hutton (Lieutenant Colonel, US Army), Timothy Bush (Lieutenant Colonel, US Army), "Massing Effects in the Information Domain," *Military Review* 86, no. 3 (May–June 2006): 2–12.

13. Douglas A. Ollivant (Lieutenant Colonel, US Army) and Eric D. Chewning (Lieutenant, US Army), "Producing Victory: Rethinking Conventional Forces in COIN Operations," *Military Review* 86, no. 4 (July–August 2006): 50–59; see also Ralph O. Baker (Colonel, US Army), "A Brigade Combat Team Commander's Perspective on Information Operations," *Military Review* 86, no. 3 (May–June 2006): 13–32.

14. Ollivant and Chewning, "Producing Victory," 50–51.
15. Emma Sky, "Iraq 2007—Moving Beyond Counter-Insurgency Doctrine: A First-Hand Perspective," *RUSI Journal* 153, no. 2 (April 2008): 30–34, 30.
16. Ibid., 30.
17. Frederick W. Kagan, *Choosing Victory: A Plan for Success in Iraq—Phase I Report,* available at the American Enterprise Institute, www.aei.org/publications/pubID .25396/pub_detail.asp.
18. Frederick Kagan, "Send More Troops to Baghdad and We'll Have a Fighting Chance," *The Sunday Times,* 24 December 2006, 14.
19. Sky, "Iraq 2007," 30–31.
20. Frederick W. Kagan and Jack Keane (General, ret., US Army), "The Right Type of 'Surge': Any Troop Increase Must Be Large and Lasting," *Washington Post,* 27 December 2006, reprinted at www.aei.org/pub.ID25356/pub_detail.asp.
21. Kagan, *Choosing Victory,* 15.
22. Kagan, "Send More Troops to Baghdad," 14.
23. From a transcript of a speech by President George W. Bush, "George W. Bush: Address to the Nation on the Troop Surge in Iraq," 10 January 2007, www.americanrhetoric.com/speeches/wariniraq/gwbushiraq011007.htm.
24. Figure given in the statement of Ambassador Ryan C. Crocker, US Ambassador to the Republic of Iraq, before the Senate Committee on Foreign Relations, 11 September 2007, http://foreign.senate.gov/hearings/2007/hrg070911a.html, 9.
25. "Iraq Unveils New Security Plan," 14 February 2007, http://news.bbc.co.uk/1/hi/world/middle_east/6358517.stm.
26. *Benchmark Assessment Report,* 14 September 2007, submitted consistent with Section 1314 of the US Troop Readiness, Veterans' Care, Katrina Recovery, and Iraq Accountability Appropriations Act 2007 (Public Law 110-28), www.online.wsj.com/documents/WHBenchmarkreport0914.pdf.
27. Ibid., 5; also from figures given by General David Petraeus (Commander, Multinational Force–Iraq) in his report to the US Congress on the situation in Iraq, 11 September 2007, before the Senate Committee on Foreign Relations, http://foreign.senate .gov/hearings/2007/ hrg070911a.html.
28. Figure given by President George W. Bush in his State of the Union address to the US Congress, 28 January 2008, www.georgewbush-whitehouse.archives.gov/news/releases/2008/01/20080128-13.html.
29. Marie Colvin, "Iraqis Lead Final Purge of Al Qaeda," *The Sunday Times,* 6 July 2008, 1 and 26–27.
30. Iraq Coalition Casualty Count, http://icasualties.org/oif.
31. "Deaths in Iraq 'Continue to Fall,'" BBC News, 1 November 2007, http://news.bbc.co.uk/1/hi/world/middle_east/7073160.stm.
32. David Smith, "Packed Classes Hint at Peace in Battered Iraq," *The Observer,* 11 November 2007, 19.
33. Marie Colvin, "Sunni Sheikhs Turn Their Sights from US Forces to Al Qaeda," *The Sunday Times,* 9 September 2007, 28–29.
34. The text of the Hadley memo is available at New York Times Online, www.nytimes.com/2006/11/29/world/middleeast/29mtext.html.
35. *Initial Benchmark Assessment Report,* July 12, 2007, submitted consistent with Section 1314 of the US Troop Readiness, Veterans' Care, Katrina Recovery, and Iraq Accountability Appropriations Act 2007 (Public Law 110-28), http://online.wsj.com/documents/finalbenchmarkReport.pdf; see also *Benchmark Assessment Report,* 14 September 2007.
36. *Benchmark Assessment Report,* 14 September 2007, 6.

37. "Bush Praises Iraqi Baathist Law," BBC News, 13 January 2007, http://news.bbc.co.uk/1/hi/world/middle_east/7185602.stm.

38. "Iraqi Deputies Pass Landmark Bills," BBC News, 13 February 2008, http://news.bbc.co.uk/1/hi/world/middle_east/7243434.stm.

39. Steven Simon, "The Price of the Surge," 57–76, 58.

40. Patrick Cockburn, "A New Dawn? Patrick Cockburn in Baghdad," *The Independent*, Extra Supplement, 15 February 2008, 2–6, esp. 6.

41. Qassim Abdul-Zahra and Sebastian Abbot (Associated Press), "Iraq Raises Idea of Timetable for US Withdrawal," ABC News, 9 July 2008, http://abcnews.go.com/print?id=5320314.

42. Ali al-Mashakheel and Nick Schifrin, "Iraqis Protest Long-Term U.S. Military Presence," ABC News, 30 May 2008, http://abcnews.go.com/print?id=4965451.

43. "Agreement Between the United States of America and the Republic of Iraq on the Withdrawal of United States Forces from Iraq and the Organization of Their Activities During Their Temporary Presence in Iraq," www.mnf-Iraq.com/images/CGs_messages/security_agreement.pdf; "Strategic Framework Agreement for a Relationship of Friendship and Cooperation between the United States of America and the Republic of Iraq," www.mnf-Iraq.com/images/CGs_messages/strategic_framework_agreement.pdf.

9
Whither the War on Terror?

Five years into the Global War on Terror, it would be difficult to argue that it had produced anything other than mixed results. The war in Afghanistan during 2001–2002 was a triumph for the United States and its allies, grievously damaging the Al-Qaida organization in its Afghanistan refuge. The Taliban regime was overthrown, the training camps in which Al-Qaida could network at close quarters among other cadres of Islamists were closed down, and what was left of Al-Qaida was sent scurrying into hiding. Its principal leaders, Osama bin Laden and Ayman al-Zawahiri, escaped, but many of their associates would soon be killed or captured. The vast global policing effort that followed 9/11 also did much to bring Al-Qaida under a reasonable degree of control. But the decision of the Bush administration to reorient the main effort in the war on terror toward Iraq was a fateful one. With Iraq, US terror strategy intersected the existing crisis besetting US management of the post-1991 Middle East. The conquest of Iraq would thereafter make the war on terror synonymous with a hugely ambitious effort to reshape the politics of Iraq and the security architecture of the Middle East region.

The Iraq-plus war on terror was badly conceived and executed. The troublesome tyranny of Saddam Hussein was removed, but the United States failed to muster the required concepts and capabilities in time to turn the application of force into a useful strategic outcome. The Iraq project was beyond even the powers of the United States. Iraq was not transformed in the desired way, and the conflict became a colossal revivalist meeting, recruiting tool, and training ground for Islamic jihadists. Al-Qaida leaders could only have dreamed of such folly. By 2007–2008, US forces had come up with a more successful approach, but it seemed unlikely that a strategic victory would ever emerge. The effects of the renewed war in Afghanistan were scarcely more controllable, with the growing political instability in Pakistan being a serious side effect.

The sprawling agenda of the post-2003 war on terror meant that it was much more difficult to make assessments about the success and failure of US strategy. To make the war on terror a success, the Bush administration now needed to make progress with three missions:

1. defeat Al-Qaida and diminish the threat posed by violent Islamic militancy across the world;
2. rebuild a security architecture in the Middle East capable of enhancing the geopolitical position of the United States and its key allies as well as disempowering adversaries, principally Iran and Syria; and
3. begin the longer-term process of "draining the swamp" in the Middle East and Muslim world by addressing unresolved geopolitical conflicts as well as dealing with some of the political and economic causes of popular disillusionment and militancy.

If US policymakers imagined a generation-long project to make the Middle East a better place, then the three missions were certainly relevant, but the bar marking success was now impossibly high. Notwithstanding the particular abilities of the Bush administration to marshal the understanding and skill to achieve such ambitions, it seemed unlikely that any US administration could now achieve, or be seen to achieve, victory in the war on terror. President Bush was hoist on his own petard. The situation was well summed up as early as 2003 in a paper written by Jeffrey Record for the Strategic Studies Institute at the US Army War College. Record lamented that

> the administration has postulated a multiplicity of enemies, including rogue states; weapons of mass destruction proliferators; terrorist organizations of global, regional, and national scope; and terrorism itself. It also seems to have conflated them into a monolithic threat, and in so doing has subordinated strategic clarity to the moral clarity it strives for in foreign policy and may have set the United States on a course of open-ended and gratuitous conflict with states and non-state entities that pose no serious threat to the United States. . . . Most of the GWOT's declared objectives, which include the destruction of al-Qaeda and other transnational terrorist organizations, the transformation of Iraq into a prosperous, stable democracy, the democratization of the rest of the autocratic Middle East, the eradication of terrorism as a means of irregular warfare, and the (forcible, if necessary) termination of WMD proliferation to real and potential enemies worldwide, are unrealistic and condemn the United States to a hopeless quest for absolute security. As such, the GWOT's goals are also politically, fiscally, and militarily unsustainable. . . . Accordingly, the GWOT must be recalibrated to conform to concrete U.S. security interests and the limits of American power. The specific measures required include deconflation of the threat; substitution of credible deterrence for preventive war as the primary vehicle for dealing with rogue states seeking WMD; refocus of the GWOT first and foremost on al-Qaeda, its allies, and homeland security; preparation to settle in Iraq for stability over

democracy (if the choice is forced upon us) and for international rather than U.S. responsibility for Iraq's future; and, finally, a reassessment of U.S. military force levels, especially ground force levels. . . . The GWOT as it has so far been defined and conducted is strategically unfocused, promises much more than it can deliver, and threatens to dissipate scarce U.S. military and other means over too many ends. It violates the fundamental strategic principles of discrimination and concentration.[1]

In short, the war on terror had quickly become a sprawling, overhyped mess, and if the initial objective was to defeat Al-Qaida, then there were now many contradictions in US strategy.

The problems with the strategy were reflected by the situation on the ground. The US National Intelligence Estimate in July 2007 perceived that the US homeland actually faced a growing threat of terrorism.[2] Al-Qaida was regenerating its structure in the safe havens of Pakistan's tribal areas and could be expected to deploy some of the techniques developed in Iraq elsewhere. The technologies and openness of globalization in association with the inspirational stories of struggle emerging from the war on terror itself enabled new growth. Al-Qaida continued to recruit new functionaries and foot soldiers everywhere, but the threat appeared to be growing most in Europe. The National Intelligence Estimate observed that

> the spread of radical—especially Salafi—Internet sites, increasingly aggressive anti-U.S. rhetoric and actions, and the growing number of radical, self-generating cells in Western countries indicate that the radical and violent segment of the West's Muslim population is expanding, including in the United States. The arrest and prosecution by U.S. law enforcement of a small number of violent Islamic extremists inside the United States—who are becoming more connected ideologically, virtually, and/or in a physical sense to the global extremist movement—points to the possibility that others may become sufficiently radicalized that they will view the use of violence here as legitimate. We assess that this internal Muslim terrorist threat is not likely to be as severe as it is in Europe, however.[3]

The sprawling agenda of the war on terror also threatened new instabilities. Isolating the Asad regime in Syria promised a number of geopolitical paybacks, notably forcing Syria's withdrawal from Lebanon, but that too was not necessarily a bad thing for Islamic militants. A more fractious Lebanon opened space for militant groups to operate, and the principal alternative to the Baathist regime in Syria was some version of the Muslim Brotherhood. Isolating and debilitating the Hamas regime in Gaza might or might not induce them to rein in their violent resistance and rejoin the US-sponsored peace talks, but it also perpetuated a conflict that was among the principal factors of Muslim dissatisfaction about the world. Moving to roll back the Islamic Republic of Iran was another possible step for the war on terror, but it was very difficult to predict the unintended consequences of military action against it. The post-2003 war on terror had promised to deliver more, but it was also laden with much more risk.

In Search of More Effective Strategy

Notwithstanding the difficulty of the mission embarked upon, US policymakers and commanders made some serious mistakes in the conduct of the war on terror. The modus operandi during the war on terror's first years was counterterrorism; it aimed to physically defend against the threat, and defeat it absolutely, by means of the killing or capture of Qaida activists and their allies. But as John Mackinlay argued in the *RUSI Journal* in December 2007, such an approach was too narrow, and what was really required was a global counterinsurgency strategy that prioritized the causes of political subversion.[4] However, a global COIN strategy was much more conceptually and physically demanding, with Mackinlay offering the view that

> for Mr. Blair and Mr. Bush, terrorism has been a political version of having chicken pox; it looks nasty but there is no real damage to the body. But insurgency is the political equivalent of cancer; it requires horrible surgery and even a successful outcome may impose a change of lifestyle. In politics, as medicine, labelling it as the lesser problem buys peace of mind in the short term. Right now the West is facing a globalized version of insurgency and calling it by its right name, as more and more officials are, is a good start to developing a more successful counter strategy.[5]

Exactly what a global COIN strategy looked like in practice—it would require a fully developed concept, organization, practical plan, and leadership—was yet to be fully understood, written up, or implemented. Mackinlay's view was that Al-Qaida would be best countered by designing a collective form of organization that lessened the US-centric character of the war on terror and was better able to develop international consensus and coordination across the military and civil realms.[6] A consistent plan with respect to international inclusion, human rights, and legal practice was needed in order to gather allies as well as be more responsive to the concerns of Muslim audiences.

Outlining the need for a collective plan and organization was easier said than done. As the arguments over NATO burden-sharing in Afghanistan demonstrated, for instance, the development of collective solutions would have to overcome the unpopularity of the war on terror in Europe and the skepticism of some European governments about US leadership. The big European states were reluctant to sign up for an endless-looking war in which they had so little influence over the concept, the plan, and the organization. Writing in *Journal of Strategic Studies* in August 2005, the US-based Australian counterinsurgency expert David Kilcullen conceded that the bottom line was that "at the global level, no world government exists with the power to integrate the actions of independent nations to the degree required by traditional counterinsurgency theory; nor can regional counterinsurgency programs be closely enough aligned to block all insurgent maneuver. This is particularly true when the enemy—as in this case—is not a Maoist-style mass rural movement, but an insurgency operating in small cells and teams with low 'tactical signature' in the urban clutter of globalized societies."7 Doing what could be done to synchronize the policies and resources of the international community against terrorism was clearly important, but that alone was unlikely to achieve a decisive victory against the global insurgency led by Al-Qaida. In the world of liberal globalization there would always be gaps in governance.

Although it was not impossible that Al-Qaida might simply self-destruct or dissolve almost on its own accord over the next decade or two—and for some that might be the lowest-cost option for managing the threat—a more proactive strategy to purposefully defeat the Al-Qaida insurgency really required a better understanding of its glocal nature (global-level aspirations and mission concept, locally networked and conducted). Specifically, what was needed was an effects-map for describing and potentially disrupting the narratives and networks of the glocal insurgency. Recalling the conceptual map of the narratives and networks of the contemporary Islamist movement outlined in Figure 2.5—embodying the organizational theory of Donald A. Schon—the following comments will suggest what kinds of actions and effects count as tactical, what as operational, and what as strategic on the glocal battlefield of the war on terror.

The Tactical

The tactical includes actions and effects at the point of contact with the enemy.
When the United States took up the war on terror, it initially looked to the same technologies and techniques—the sensors, communication linkups, precision weapons, and effects-based modeling—that had given US forces superiority on the conventional battlefield. The new technologies and techniques undoubtedly conferred tactical advantages—and it was difficult not be impressed when seeing them in action in such places as Afghanistan and Iraq—but they were not to be decisive. The new technologies were still unable to conquer many of the old dilemmas of COIN warfare: how to find a diffuse enemy; how to defend against sporadic and unpredictable attacks; and how to protect and secure the population without becoming too vulnerable.

Although striking against Al-Qaida fighters and their supporters might be an essential element in the war on terror, it was arguable that simply killing or capturing people across the dissipated networks of the glocal insurgency had little more than tactical effect. Most of the functionaries and foot soldiers in a constellation network are not only replaceable; the dynamics of the "learning system" itself were apt to progressively replace them or parallel their activities. Although Al-Qaida had not had to face the death or imprisonment of bin Laden or al-Zawahiri (the ultimate System Negotiator/Leader and Network Manager), it had lost many of its facilitators, brokers, and underground managers: following the Afghan war in 2001–2002, Khalid Shaikh Muhammed (mastermind of 9/11), Abu Zubaydah, Ramzi Binalshibh, Ahmed Khalfan Ghailani, Amjad Farroqi, Naeem Nor Khan, Abu Faraj al-Libbi, and Abu Hamza Rabia; in Iraq, it lost a succession of facilitators and brokers, most notably Abu Musab al-Zarqawi and Khaled Mashhadani.[8] Yet following the loss of significant functionaries, the networks tended to adapt. Indeed, simply increasing the body count and those held prisoner might actually be counterproductive. The martyrs of the jihadic struggle were center stage in Al-Qaida's proselytizing among Muslims.

Although improving military technologies and techniques might one day stack up sufficient tactical-level successes to the point of an operational-level breakthrough, this was an attritional approach for which a tipping point could not generally be anticipated. In fact, perhaps only in Saudi Arabia were the authorities able to wear down Al-Qaida—it lost a series of cell leaders, Ali Abdul Rahman al-Ghamdi, Khalid Al-Hajj, Abdulziz Al-Muqrin, and Younis al-Hayari between 2003 and 2006—to get to the verge of an operational-level disabling of the organization.[9] And the tactical gains made by Saudi security forces were paralleled and consolidated with a much-vaunted deprogramming and rehabilitation effort, notably in a prison facility at Hayar near Riyadh.[10]

In sum, simply improving the technology and techniques of "kill or capture" implied accepting the prospect of a long attritional campaign without a convincing exit strategy. The approach probably implied parrying and containing the threat until Al-Qaida self-destructed or dissolved essentially of its own accord.

The Operational

The operational includes policies, actions, and effects conducted at the level of the battle and campaign that progressively disable the enemy's resistance or persuade it to concede physical position or political aims.

The glocal insurgency was nearly impossible to defeat by kinetic means alone partly because its extent lay beyond any single theater of operations. Indeed, many of Al-Qaida's subversive activities were immersed across the vast globalized realm of cyberspace. Cells of activists might be apprehended at particular times and places, but the superstructure of narratives and networks continued to provide the "potential for glocality" and thus for regeneration. For the counterinsurgent, interfering with Al-Qaida's potential for glocality was what really counted when pitching to reach the operational and strategic levels.

The front line in the war on terror were the glocal networks, and the principal operational-level battle was to undermine those networks with various means. Rather than simply striking at people in the networks, what was probably more important was to alter the functioning of the networks by means of bargaining and other information operations, including intelligence penetration and co-optation. Writing in the July–August 2006 issue of *Military Review*, Thomas X. Hammes had identified the agenda:

> The fundamental rules for attacking a network are different from those used when attacking a more conventional enemy. First, in counterinsurgency it is better to exploit a known node than attack it. Second, if you have to attack, the best attack is a soft one designed to introduce distrust into the network. Third, if you must make a hard attack, conduct simultaneous attacks on related links, or else the attack will have little effect. Finally, after the attack, increase surveillance to see how the insurgency tries to communicate around or repair the damage. As they are reaching out to establish new contacts, the new nodes will be most visible.[11]

The most direct approach to disrupting the glocal network was by means of bargaining with the glocal insurgent's local allies. Quite clearly, the fracturing of the Sunni insurgency in Iraq beginning in 2006 was a classic case of a bargaining-led, operational-level breakthrough.

Direct bargaining with glocal insurgents themselves was more difficult to undertake: Such insurgents might have multiple centers of decisionmaking, hold unrealistic political aims, and be beyond the pale for moral or political reasons. Thus, if the problem was to bargain with multiple adversaries, often without actually talking to them, then it was probably more useful to think less about negotiating and more about inducing malfunctions in the network. If the enemy could not be defeated or directly bargained with, then it had to be penetrated, induced, and transformed. An entire new operational art had yet to be developed to achieve these ends. The starting point might be to understand and act upon the kind of qualitative network analysis outlined by the theorists of organismic and constellation systems (see Chapter 2). As Schon explained in *Beyond the Stable State* (1971), constellation-type networks are vulnerable to poor coordination as well as to frictions arising from the advent of deviant ideas, personalities, and practices among the specialized functionaries.

A new operational art for the war on terror would also have to include a broader effort to draw Muslims, especially potential recruits and other Islamist cadres, as far away as possible from Al-Qaida's zone of networking (recall Figures 2.2 and Figure 2.4). In the context of active geopolitical conflicts, the key battleground for both sides was the RRA zone: reconstruction, reconciliation, and assimilation (see Chapter 3). US and allied forces could draw on an enormous body of experience from past counterinsurgency and peacekeeping operations to develop best practices in the RRA zone. As explained in Chapter 8, US forces would develop a more coherent model in Iraq, packaging full-spectrum operations, unit immersion, and close-quarter IO—and they did seem to be onto something. That being said, Western forces were still far from mastering the RRA zone. Western politicians were not at ease with the money and force levels required to make big RRA operations work. If Afghanistan and Iraq were anything to go by, the scale and complexity of such project management—that is, parceling out and resourcing countless subsidiary tasks while maintaining overall monitoring and coordination—in the time frames available were beyond the capacity of even the US military.[12]

It must also be said that Western military intervention itself in the Muslim world was probably not the best way of keeping Muslim populations and other Islamist cadres away from Al-Qaida. The inherent hostility of many Muslims to the presence of any Western forces anywhere in the Muslim world always risked overmatching the positive things they could do there. In Afghanistan and Iraq, US forces were always going to face major insurgencies regardless of how well or poorly they handled the RRA zone. Al-Qaida could scarcely have wished for better opportunities to glocalize.

The Operational-Strategic Level

The operational-strategic level includes actions and effects that directly achieve the political objectives of the war.

Although it was possible to imagine that stacking up tactical- and operational-level successes might one day deliver a strategic-level victory, Al-Qaida's potential for glocality stemmed from the plausibility of its narratives (stories of oppression, just struggle, triumph, etc.) about the world to disgruntled Muslims. The fact was that there were significant numbers of Muslims and Islamic activists in the world who believed that Islam was in danger, Muslims were under attack, and the United States and its allies were the principal cause of their pain. As long as Al-Qaida's stories remained plausible, it had the potential to regenerate itself wherever it might suffer tactical- or even operational-level defeats. In short, what was required to achieve the strategic defeat of Al-Qaida was its complete detachment from the circles of Islamic geopoliticals and Islamic traditionalists (see Figure 2.2). Once detached from the other gravities of the Islamic movement, it was far easier to imagine that Al-Qaida could be finally defeated by stacking up tactical and operational successes. The big question was how could this be done?

The significance of this narrative has been addressed by a number of thinkers, notably Lawrence Freedman, John Mackinlay, Frank Hoffman, William Casebeer, and Montgomery McFate and Andrea Jackson.[13] In an important paper published in 2006, "The Transformation of Strategic Affairs," Lawrence Freedman argued that

> The role of strategic narratives in irregular warfare is . . . to provide a framework of understanding that can bind a fighting force together. By providing a strategic context it should guide tactical decisions. If this is the case then the challenge for counter-insurgency and counter-terrorism operations is to seek to unbind the enemy force by undermining the strategic narratives. This requires playing on the natural fault-lines within the political movements that spawn terrorist groups in order to aggravate their differences. Such an approach is helped by the familiar tendency of radical movements to fragment into competing factions. These movements are not inherently pragmatic. They deal in ultimate ends and so small divisions over political programmes or current tactics can quickly be magnified into fundamental differences of principle. . . . Such an approach can consider itself successful so long as the insurgents or terrorists are prevented from moving beyond their networked, cellular form.[14]

The problem for the United States and its allies was that Al-Qaida's narrative was resilient because it tended to focus on the grievances and the struggle rather than on the trickier matters of organization and ultimate objective. When Al-Qaida spoke to Islamic geopoliticals and Islamic traditionalists about the grievances and struggle, it could plausibly tell them that it was the United States and its Western allies that were keeping *takfir* Muslim rulers in power, that they were the "Zionist-Crusader alliance" that was invading Muslim lands, and that they were behind a vast cultural assault on Muslim societies. When Al-Qaida stuck to the common enemy and common struggle, it was at its most dangerous. The great mistake in Iraq, of course, was to try to impose a common organizational hierarchy, modus operandi, and objective. Indeed, the pitiless intimidation and murder of other Muslims in Iraq seriously damaged the Qaida brand. By 2007–2008, what had happened in Iraq even sparked a wave of debate among Qaida-associated militants, some of whom now condemned the killings of innocents as a grave violation of Islamic law and questioned Al-Qaida's entire justification for its jihad.[15]

But even though Al-Qaida might self destruct at some point, if the United States and the West actually wanted a proactive strategy, then they needed to find a formula to systematically counter Al-Qaida's narrative. According to Frank Hoffman,

> the counter narrative should provide the central theme for resolving the conflict, delineate the major aspects of the subsequent information operations activities used by friendly forces, and provide general guidance to subordinate components, including the military. The US government continues to struggle with the basics of strategic communications, public diplomacy, public affairs and related information activities in this area. . . . An effective counter narrative will speak to the entire international community, serving to rally international support, isolate support to the insurgency and minimize its attractiveness and viability. . . . The 4GW antagonist is going to talk to multiple audiences with his message, and so too must the counter-narrative. This grand

narrative must be able to deal with the various audiences of the global "deep fight" making the proverbial Three Block War into a Three Screen War, including CNN, Al Jazeera and the BBC.[16]

The possibility that Western states might split apart the different gravities of Islamic militancy by means of some sort of public affairs campaign was a forlorn hope. Although the United States and its European allies paid lip service to the hearts and minds of the Muslim world—and engaging in an intercultural dialogue with mainstream Muslims was doubtless a worthy endeavor—the persuasiveness of this dialogue among the critical Muslim audiences was lacking. Rather than just constructing some empty public affairs line, the grand counternarrative had to be made credible by explaining how some of the real and understandable grievances that were held by far too many Muslim people were going to be addressed. The things involved were big-ticket items in all sorts of ways, but without them it was difficult to see how a truly strategic approach to dissolving Islamic militancy across the world could be developed.

The Geopolitical Element in Breaking the Circles of Islamic Militancy

It was difficult to imagine that any anti-terror strategy could be truly strategic until it began to separate the Islamic globalists and Islamic geopoliticals; to put it bluntly, it was mostly the geopoliticals who were blowing themselves up around the world. A strategic approach was hobbled by the failure to fully recognize and *actually* do something about resolving, rather than just containing, the unending geopolitical conflicts that beset far too many Muslims. In such cases as the Israel-Palestine and Kashmir conflicts, the vast majority of Muslim and Islamist opinion believed that the grievances were real and the struggle was just. Above all, it was difficult to imagine that a concerted geopolitical element could work until an equitable resolution of the Arab-Israeli conflict was *actually* delivered.

The Bush administration sporadically addressed the Israel-Palestine conflict. In 2003, Bush proposed the idea of a road map, in which he even expressed his support in principle for a two-state solution, but it was quickly lost amid the ongoing war on terror.[17] The administration would again make a show of seeking progress during 2007–2008, convening a peace conference in Annapolis, Maryland, in late November 2007. But in the last analysis, Bush was never completely accepting of the centrality of the geopolitical element. From its inception, Bush's war on terror was premised on the idea that it was a fight against evil men who had perverted Islam and simply hated the West because of its freedom and democracy. Although Bush and his chief ally, Tony Blair, were prepared to state that existing geopolitical conflict and deprivation were important, such an analysis was trumped by their determination to deny that Al-Qaida had resulted from the foreign policy of Western states and their allies. Bush himself articulated the view in a speech in November 2005:

> Over the years these extremists have used a litany of excuses for violence—the Israeli presence on the West Bank, or the U.S. military presence in Saudi Arabia, or the defeat of the Taliban, or the Crusades of a thousand years ago. In fact, we're not facing a set of grievances that can be soothed and addressed. We're facing a radical ideology with inalterable objectives: to enslave whole nations and intimidate the world. No act of ours invited the rage of the killers—and no concession, bribe, or act of appeasement would change or limit their plans for murder.[18]

If the West was indeed facing what Francis Fukuyama called "Islamofascism," a term Bush himself used at a press conference at his Texas ranch on 7 August 2006, the only thing that could be done was to root out such evil and simply demand that the Muslim world concede that Al-Qaida's stories were simply wrong.[19] Bush was loath to cloud the moral certainties of fighting the evildoers. Any acceptance of the geopolitical element also threatened to open a Pandora's box of distractions and intractable problems. Clearly, the US administration could hardly just cede its position in Iraq or do much anytime soon about Israel in Palestine, India in Kashmir, Russia in Chechnya, and so on. The last thing that Bush and Blair wanted to do was point the finger at Israel and other partner states about their endless occupations of Muslim lands. It would all look like an acceptance of some culpability.

Thus, the geopolitical approach adopted bore similarities to that advocated by David Kilcullen in his August 2005 article in the *Journal of Strategic Studies*. Kilcullen had rightly argued that only a strategy of "disaggregation" could break the links between the different countries and regional theaters that constituted the phenomenon of the global jihad.[20] But Kilcullen shied away from highlighting the centrality of *resolving* local conflicts and instead tended to see the problem more in terms of managing and isolating the local groups involved in them. Kilcullen observed that "although dozens of local insurgencies contribute to the global jihad, victory under a disaggregation strategy does not demand the destruction of all local insurgents. Rather (systems analysis indicates) counterinsurgency at the systemic level is a matter of de-linking local issues from the global insurgent system, as much as it is about dealing with local insurgents themselves."[21]

Although Kilcullen did concede the possible usefulness of a global CORDS-type campaign and of encouraging reform in Muslim societies, his approach to disaggregation tended to point to better coercion and interdiction as the means to isolate the local from the global.[22] But shying away from resolving the geopolitical conflicts left Al-Qaida's potential for glocality intact. As long as Muslims were besieged and oppressed in such conflicts, Al-Qaida (or some other universalist-globalist platform) could spin their stories and co-opt the pain of local Muslims no matter how well organized the efforts to physically interdict global-local links.

With respect to the crucial Israeli-Palestinian conflict, it would remain irresolvable until Israel's annexation policy in the West Bank was challenged and a reasonable and authoritative Palestinian government could be constructed. In fact, little progress was made on the Israeli-Palestinian conflict in the first five years of the war on terror, with the situation significantly worsening following the election of a Hamas government in Gaza. Hamas's refusal to recognize Israel's right to exist sent Palestinians back toward wretched isolation. Moreover, as the aid spigot was turned off by Israel and the international community, the political contest between Fatah and Hamas broke into outright conflict. The Palestinian unity government collapsed, and Hamas launched a violent overthrow of Fatah institutions in the Gaza Strip. The sight of Islamic militants violently taking power was an unsettling one.

If the parties in the Israeli-Palestinian conflict could not negotiate a settlement on their own accord—and they could not—the only real prospect for conflict resolution was to implement more robust third-party arbitration. What was probably required, as Hussein Agha and Robert Malley argued in *Foreign Affairs,* was an "outside-in" approach that *enforced* a comprehensive, fair, and lasting agreement.[23] But successive US administrations had neither the will nor the ability to intervene in this way.

The Arab-Israeli conflict was a cancer at the heart of regional security, and until someone did something about it the US presence in the Middle East would continue to be synonymous with chronic dissatisfaction. Indeed, one of the dangers of allowing the impasse to continue was that more Palestinians might become so frustrated that the relatively limited aspirations of Hamas-type Islamism—largely confined to Palestine—might be superseded by something more radical. If Hamas was laid low, it was possible to imagine that an Al-Qaida–type platform might gain ground. Islamic Jihad and a number of smaller groups already offered Palestinians an analysis that put the struggle against Israel into the context of a wider struggle against the West and its oppressive power in the world.

Beyond the impasse in the Arab-Israeli conflict, the geopolitical situation in the rest of the Middle East was scarcely more promising. In fact, the attempt by the Bush administration to use force to rebuild the pax Americana in the region had left it a more unstable and unpredictable place. Iraq was teetering on the brink, with the possibility of de facto balkanization. It was possible to imagine the emergence of a number of substate entities in Iraq over which regional powers competed. Iran already looked like a winner in Shia-dominated southeastern Iraq. The emergence of a Kurdish sovereignty was liable to draw Turkish attentions. Any Sunni entity in northwestern Iraq would draw in the Arab powers of Egypt, Saudi Arabia, and Syria. In Syria itself, US hostility to the

Baathist regime of Bashar al-Asad had bolstered support for it in the short term, but the stability of the regime in the longer term was questionable. Although talk of a Middle East dividing into competitive Sunni and Shia spheres, with Iraq, Syria, and Lebanon being the principal fault lines, was premature, the idea of the Arab nation had been torn asunder. The boosted influence of Shia Iran across a swathe of the Arab Middle East played on many minds.

The Political and Social Element in Breaking the Circles of Islamic Militancy

Reducing Al-Qaida's potential for glocality could also be related to a much broader political and social element. The prevalence of so many immoveable oligarchies that restricted socioeconomic opportunity and suppressed reasonable dissent undoubtedly limited the capacity of Muslim societies to progress to a more prosperous and stable future. The fact that many of these authoritarian regimes—the likes of those in Egypt, Saudi Arabia, and Pakistan—were closely linked to the United States and the West gave Al-Qaida the opportunity to tell its stories. The dictators and oligarchies favored by the West fostered an unstable kind of stability.

The principal challenge to the West's allies in the Muslim world was from Islamic traditionalists. Although the traditionalists represented a lesser threat to the West itself—as compared to the Islamic geopoliticals—their local political and social presence was significant almost everywhere in the Muslim world, and in a few places their grievances even primed the idea of overthrowing the government. At the level of society, traditionalists often sought to resist the moral and social threat that the contemporary world posed to Muslim societies. They also objected to the extent to which their governments were tied up with infidel powers, although they naturally tended to see breaking this link less as a matter of waging a global war as Islamicizing Muslim societies and their governance.

Fostering a strategy to squeeze the overlap between the Islamic globalists and Islamic traditionalists would be an undertaking of enormous magnitude, one so large that it was probably less a matter of policy practice than historical process. Certainly, it was scarcely credible to imagine that the Bush administration was capable of designing a kind of giant RRA strategy for the entire Muslim world that might strengthen the capability and popularity of allied Muslim governments as well as reconciling Islamic traditionalists to more modernization and political reform.

The problems of even developing a transnational RRA approach were all too clear. US policymakers had long been aware that the Middle East and Muslim world were overdue for political and social reforms. The democratic revolution that had swept the world since the end of the Cold War had largely bypassed Muslim regions. In the aftermath of 9/11, the debate about reform was reopened, and it was widely understood inside US policy circles that a new deal was required. The United States would have to strike a careful balance, but, at least in a rhetorical sense, Bush had crossed the Rubicon. The language of freedom and democracy pervaded all of Bush's speeches during the first years of the war on terror, and he did not shy away from pointing the finger at Muslim allies.

The new will for reform was announced in a series of speeches and policy documents in 2002 and 2003. The US National Security Strategy of September 2002 listed eight demands for all states. They were the rule of law; limits on the absolute power of the state; freedom of speech; freedom of worship; equal justice; respect for women; religious and ethnic tolerance; and respect for private property. To follow up, the Middle East Partnership Initiative (MEPI) was launched, designed to support educational, economic, legal, and political reform throughout the Arab world. MEPI proposed supporting a range of bottom-up priming activities such as helping banks provide credit to small- and medium-scale enterprises, designing local commercial law to be more sensitive to the needs of private property, and finding ways of increasing political, social, and economic opportunities for women. By fiscal year 2005, the program was providing more than US$70 million for local television and radio programming that was designed to promote an understanding of freedom and free markets.[24] It was hoped that a number of US-backed Arabic and Persian radio and TV stations might counter the negative images of the United States believed to be propagated by some broadcasters, including the big satellite providers Al-Jazeera and Abu Dhabi TV.

Then, in a major speech to the National Endowment for Democracy on 6 November 2003, President Bush set the tone for the Greater Middle East Initiative in the most soaring terms.[25] Bush observed that "freedom honors and unleashes human creativity—and creativity determines the strength and wealth of nations. Liberty is both the plan of Heaven for humanity, and the best hope for progress here on Earth."[26] As far as Bush was concerned, it should be clear to all that Islamic faith was consistent with democratic rule and that "many Middle Eastern governments now [understood] that military dictatorship and theocratic rule are a straight smooth highway to nowhere."[27] Bush urged friends and adversaries alike to reform, and although he accepted the need to be patient as local cultures adapted to democracy, he made it clear that

> sixty years of Western nations excusing and accommodating the lack of freedom in the Middle East did nothing to make us safe—because in the long run, stability cannot be purchased at the expense of liberty. As long as the Middle East remains a place where freedom does not flourish, it will remain a place of stagnation, resentment, and violence ready for export. And with the spread of weapons that can bring catastrophic harm to our country and to our friends, it would be reckless to accept the status quo. . . . The advance of freedom is the calling of our time; it is the calling of our country. From the Fourteen

Points to the Four Freedoms, to the Speech at Westminster, America has put our power at the service of principle. We believe that liberty is the design of nature; we believe that liberty is the direction of history. We believe that human fulfillment and excellence come in the responsible exercise of liberty. And we believe that freedom—the freedom we prize—is not for us alone, it is the right and the capacity of all mankind.[28]

But what did Bush's freedom rhetoric ultimately represent? Clearly, it embodied the idea that liberal democracy was *the* basis of a universal civilization. But was it a genuine mission to actually promote freedom and democracy in the Middle East, or was it the old story of proselytizing to pressure adversaries and justify the use of military power for US national security ends?

The early years of the war on terror did establish a new tone and began to assemble a track record of success. The overthrow of the Taliban in Afghanistan and the institutionalization of a new political system appeared to be a triumph. In the Middle East, the mood for reform met with a mixed response, but there were important moments of progress: the election of a new Palestinian leader after the death of Yasser Arafat; unprecedented elections for local government in Saudi Arabia; elections or institutional reforms in Morocco, Bahrain, Qatar, Oman, Kuwait, and Jordan; and the withdrawal of Syrian troops from Lebanon and the restart of freer parliamentary politics in that country. Of course, by far the most important democratization project was in Iraq. The Bush administration earnestly hoped that a democratic Iraq might offer a model for neighboring countries. The process did give neighboring populations the sight of progress of a sort, although the accompanying chaos also gave antidemocratic forces a point to make, too. In the end, Iraq was scarcely a model that many people would want to follow. Elsewhere, it was clear that it was very difficult to shape or accelerate democratization. The election of a Hamas government in the Palestinian territories in early 2006 was a function of a political process sponsored by the United States.

The official response of Muslim allies to US proselytizing about democracy was also always going to be cool. Following a meeting with Colin Powell in March 2004, for instance, Foreign Minister Prince Saud al-Faisal of Saudi Arabia took the unusual step of putting a shot across US bows in an interview with the official Saudi Press Agency. The prince observed that the Arabs had their own history and could tackle their own problems themselves; he perceived that the Greater Middle East Initiative "included clear accusations against the Arab people and their governments that they are ignorant of their own affairs. . . . Those behind these plans ignore the fact that our Arab people have cultures rooted deep in history and that we are able to tackle our own affairs."[29] Such calls were "made as if we had not been doing anything and had just been waiting for direction from outside."

The limits of democratization among US allies was also on show with respect to Egypt and, later, Pakistan. In both countries, the friendly dictators were not disposed to share power with anyone, let alone with even moderate Islamists. The situation in Egypt, for instance, deteriorated around the time of its parliamentary elections in late 2005. At a speech at the American University of Cairo on 20 June 2005, US Secretary of State Condoleezza Rice urged President Hosni Mubarak to open the door to change:

> We are all concerned for the future of Egypt's reforms when peaceful supporters of democracy—men and women—are not free from violence. The day must come when the rule of law replaces emergency decrees—and when the independent judiciary replaces arbitrary justice. The Egyptian Government must fulfill the promise it has made to its people—and to the entire world—by giving its citizens the freedom to choose. Egypt's elections, including Parliamentary elections, must meet objective standards that define every free election. . . . The day is coming when the promise of a fully free and democratic world, once thought impossible, will also seem inevitable. The people of Egypt should be at the forefront of this great journey, just as you have led this region through the great journeys of the past.[30]

In the event, the elections were marred by widespread unfairness and intimidation as Mubarak's ruling National Democratic Party made sure that the challenge from the Muslim Brotherhood—and any other party as well—was slapped down. Opposition candidates and election workers suffered physical attacks, arrests, and imprisonment by security forces or those linked to the government. Although the Muslim Brotherhood itself was banned from fielding candidates, a significant number squeezed through.[31] And even though US officials were critical of the Mubarak regime's practices, especially against the secular opposition, there was little that could be done to make Mubarak adopt free and fair politics.

The entrenched oligarchy in Egypt was not about to allow significant reforms, and it was very unclear what would happen if and when it did. Indeed, when the United States nudged its Muslim allies toward reform, it did so at its own peril. Reforms were liable to destabilize, and the probable alternatives to the likes of Mubarak, the al-Saud family, and Abdullah were populist Islamists who were less likely to pander to US interests. Until a decades-long RRA program was undertaken to strengthen the capability of allied governments as well as reconcile sufficient numbers of ordinary people and Islamic activists to change, forcing through reform just did not seem sensible, and the Bush administration eventually came down on the side of better the devil you know. Indeed, one of the big lessons from Iraq was that democratization required the synchronous development of two colossal revolutions: first, a democratic revolution that changed the institutional arrangements of governance in order to empower the majority at the expense of ruling oligarchies; and second, a cultural revolution that developed the political software for democracy to function, requiring a transformation of social attitudes to such things as religion, gender, the rights of the majority, the rights of minorities, and foreigners and their values. Initiating the two revolutions unleashed all kinds of suppressed frustrations and furious forces.

Amid a background of ongoing geopolitical conflicts and social-cultural stress, the Bush administration could not reasonably expect its Arab and Muslim allies to press on with major reforms. In the last analysis, although limited reforms were initiated among some allies—and these were worthy—the democratization of Muslim states and societies was going to be such a long process that it was scarcely feasible to count on it as a component of the war on terror. To the extent that countries like Egypt and Saudi Arabia could be reformed, the process would be driven forward by such things as the imperatives of the global marketplace and political and social stability—not by the urgings of the White House. The Muslim world simply could not be manipulated in the ways desired. And the reality was that the idea of "draining the swamp" by means of initiating political, economic, and social reforms was stymied by the existence of so much geopolitical insecurity at the same time.

Whither the War on Terror, Whither War

Bush's war on terror was an attritional war. The attempt to wear down global jihadists—or rather to wait for their exhaustion and boredom—could not provide a time line for conflict termination. Although Al-Qaida might face local defeats, and it was not impossible that it might largely dissolve of its own accord one day, as long as it could plausibly proselytize among disgruntled Muslims around the world, it (or something like it) had the potential to regenerate. A more maneuverist war on terror strategy required the development of the missing geopolitical and political-social-economic approaches outlined above. But barring miracles of diplomacy, the conflicts in Israel-Palestine, Iraq, Chechnya, Kashmir, Afghanistan, Pakistan, Uzbekistan, Somalia, the Philippines, and elsewhere were not about to be resolved any time soon. In fact, for some of the states involved in them, avoiding negotiated resolution was better than seeing the war on terror go on as a limited attrition.

The war on terror would also meander on because it could; or rather, the opportunity for small groups of people to do this sort of thing simply existed in the contemporary world order. The war on terror was the kind of war that stemmed from the configuration of the technologies, open borders, and lax regulation and policing of liberalized globalization. Indeed, although Al-Qaida was the first of the glocal revolutionaries in the post–Cold War world, it was easy to imagine that other global revolutions might one day come into being. Another Islamic universalist-globalist movement was always a possibility, as was a completely new glocal insurgency perhaps driven by environmental and climate-change activists, a new iteration of Marxism, or some globally or regionally extensive ethno-nationalism. It was also possible to imagine that a federation of organized crime interests might one day pose a global-level insurgency-type threat.

It is ironic, then, that one of the greatest threats to the persistence of the glocal insurgency was the possibility that the world of globalization itself might hit a wall. In fact, beginning in the autumn of 2008, the entire architecture of post–Cold War globalization was threatened by a severe economic crisis, which persisted into 2009 and promised darker days ahead. The vast debt-fueled consumer boom that had bought US and British preeminence in the world economy was unraveling, and what lay beyond might be an historic reordering of the world system. If the result of the economic crisis meant that territorial states reasserted themselves, new regulatory systems were imposed, borders went back up, and the hegemonic capacities of the United States further declined, then the factors that shaped the practice of war and its conduct—the use of technology, as well as the nature of the actors and the system—would be different.

The possibility that the world of liberalizing globalization could not last had already been mooted. Writing in the *RUSI Journal* in October 2005, the doyen of British realists, Colin Gray, had warned that the kind of global cooperation and interdependency that had taken shape under the benign hegemony of the United States was but a brief golden moment, and history was bound to return to things as usual, that is, the logic of self-interested states and great power rivalry.[32] Indeed, contemporary globalization had hastened the onset of resource and environmental crises that would prompt humankind to increasingly look to the organizing power of the state in search of security and scarce resources. In terms of the effect on the future of warfare, the reemergence of a more bordered and state-centric world might well be a case of back to the future, in which the interstate regional war and the limited wars and proxy wars of great powers might well make a comeback (the existence of nuclear weapons and other factors would probably continue to preclude open warfare between great powers). In short, war and warfare might go back up the scale (recall Figure 1.1), although only toward the middle of the spectrum. It was difficult not to wonder whether the Russia-Georgia war of August–September 2008 did not portend things to come.

From the perspective of 2009, it is perhaps too soon to identify a new era of interstate war and warfare, much less describe the actual dynamics of the balance of power that might develop within it.[33] Although Thomas Malthus might have the last laugh one day, there are powerful forces (outlined in Chapter 1) that continued to work against the resumption of interstate war in the world. As long as the global economy did not completely disintegrate and US military preeminence endured, then the dominant idiom of conflict in the international system was likely to remain between the forces of liberalizing globalization and its asymmetric discontents.[34] Many aspects of globalization also could not be put back in the box, and thus the potential for glocal insurgency would persist even if other kinds of war and warfare returned to the world system. The phenomenon of the glocal insurgency would last as long as globalization endured.

Notes

1. Jeffrey Record, "Bounding the Global War on Terrorism," written under the auspices of the Strategic Studies Institute, US Army War College, Carlisle, Pennsylvania, December 2003, www.globalsecurity.org/military/library/report/2003/record_bounding.pdf, v–vi (Jeffrey Record joined the Strategic Studies Institute as a visiting fellow in August 2003; he was a professor in the Department of Strategic and International Security at the USAF's Air War College in Montgomery, Alabama).

2. Office of the Director of National Intelligence, *National Intelligence Estimate: The Terrorist Threat to the US Homeland* (July 2007; see Press Releases, 17 July 2007), www.dni.gov/ /press_releases/20070717_release.pdf, 1–7.

3. Director of National Intelligence, *National Intelligence Estimate*, 7.

4. John Mackinlay, "Counter-Insurgency in Global Perspective—An Introduction: Politicans Need to Understand Insurgency," *RUSI Journal* 152, no. 6 (December 2007): 6–7. See also David Kilcullen, "Countering Global Insurgency," *Journal of Strategic Studies* 28, no. 4 (August 2005): 597–617, esp. 606 (David Kilcullen was at the Land Warfare Studies Center, Duntroon, Canberra, and later became the chief strategist in the Office of the Coordinator for Counter-Terrorism, US State Department, Washington, DC).

5. Mackinlay, "Counter-Insurgency in Global Perspective," 6.

6. John Mackinlay, *Defeating Complex Insurgency: Beyond Iraq and Afghanistan,* Whitehall Paper 64 (London: Royal United Services Institute, 2005), especially chapter 4, 53–61.

7. Kilcullen, "Countering Global Insurgency," 607.

8. Jason Burke, *Al-Qaeda: The True Story of Radical Islam* (London: Penguin Books, 2004), 259–260; Gordon Corera, "Key Al Qaeda Player Seized," BBC News, 4 May 2005, http://news.bbc.co.uk/1/hi/world/south_asia/4514409.stm; "Musharraf Hails Blow to Al-Qaeda," BBC News, 27 September 2004, http://news.bbc.co.uk/1/hi/world/south_asia/3692606.stm; "Burqa Trap Set for Terror Suspect," BBC News, 5 May 2005, http://news.bbc.co.uk/1/hi/world/south_asia/4516567.stm.

9. "Riyadh Attack Death Toll Mounts," BBC News, 9 November 2003, http://news.bbc.co.uk/1/hi/world/middle_east/3254385.stm; Frank Gardner, "Saudis Turn up the Heat on Terror," BBC News, 2 August 2003, http://news.bbc.co.uk/1/hi/world/from_our_own_correspondent/3117471.stm.

10. Anthony Horowitz, "The Anti-Guantanamo: Saudi Arabia's Plan to Tackle Terrorism—Nicely," *The Sunday Telegraph,* 13 July 2008, 8–13; "Powers of Persuasion," *The Economist,* 19–25 July 2008, 10 (part of a special report, *Al Qaeda: Down but Not Out*).

11. Thomas X. Hammes (Colonel, ret., USMC), "Countering Evolved Insurgent Networks," *Military Review* 86, no. 4 (July–August 2006): 18–26, esp. 26.

12. For a discussion of the problem, see Marcus Fielding (Lieutenant General, Australian Army), "Regime Change: Planning and Managing Military-Led Interventions as Projects," *RUSI Journal* 151, no. 5 (October 2006): 20–29.

13. Lawrence Freedman, *The Transformation of Strategic Studies,* Adelphi Paper 379 (London: International Institute for Strategic Studies, 2006); F. G. Hoffman, "Combating

Fourth Generation Warfare," chapter 19 in Terry Terriff, Aaron Karp, and Regina Karp, eds., *Global Insurgency and the Future of Armed Conflict: Debating Fourth-Generation Warfare* (London: Routledge, 2008), 177–199, 182; Mackinlay, *Defeating Complex Insurgency;* Montgomery McFate and Andrea Jackson, "The Object Beyond War: Counterinsurgency and the Four Tools of Political Competition," *Military Review* 86, no. 1 (January–February 2006): 13–26, 18–20.

14. Freedman, *The Transformation of Strategic Affairs,* 90.

15. One of the most notable waves of debate was sparked in 2007 by the publication of a critical book serialized as newspaper articles by Sayyid Imam al-Sharif (or Dr. Fadl), a former associate of Al-Zawahiri in Egypt's Islamic Jihad. Fadl was in an Egyptian prison cell, but Zawahiri took his criticism sufficiently seriously to write a 200-page rebuttal entitled *The Exoneration.* By this time, it was becoming clear that many Egyptian militants, including many in prison, were seeking reconciliation with the Egyptian government. At about the same time, another significant militant in Saudi Arabia, Shaikh Salman al-Oadah, also condemned Al Qaeda and bin Laden for the killing of innocents. Lawrence Wright, "The Heretic: How Al-Qaeda's Mastermind Turned His Back on Terror," *The Observer,* Magazine Section, 13 July 2008, 14–49; Abul Taher, "Al-Qaeda: The Cracks Begin to Show," *The Sunday Times,* 8 June 2008, 14.

16. Hoffman, "Combating Fourth Generation Warfare," 182.

17. The initiative was announced in an address by President George W. Bush in the Rose Garden on 24 June 2003, "George Bush's Plan for Peace," *The Economist,* Special Issue on America's World Role, 29 June–5 July 2003, 11–12; "Special Report: The Middle East," *The Economist,* 29 June–5 July 2003, 23–26.

18. Remarks by President Bush at the twentieth anniversary of the National Endowment for Democracy, "President Bush Discusses War on Terror at National Endowment for Democracy," 6 November 2003, www.ned.org/events/anniversary/20thAniv-Bush.html.

19. Francis Fukuyama, "History and September 11," in Ken Booth and Tim Dunne eds., *Worlds in Collision* (Basingstoke, UK: Palgrave Macmillan, 2002), chapter 2, 27–36, esp. 32; Richard Allen Green, "Bush's Language Angers US Muslims," BBC News, 12 August 2006, http://news.bbc.co.uk/1/hi/world/americas/4785065.stm.

20. Kilcullen, "Countering Global Insurgency," 609.

21. Ibid., 609.

22. Ibid., 610.

23. Hussein Agha and Robert Malley, "The Last Negotiation," *Foreign Affairs* 81, no. 3 (May–June 2002): 10–18.

24. Colin Powell, "The President's Budget Request for FY2005," written remarks to the Senate Budget Committee, 26 February 2004, http://budget.senate.gov/democratic/testimony/2004/powell_intlaffairsbudget2005.pdf.

25. "President Bush Discusses Freedom in Iraq and Middle East, Remarks by the President at the Twentieth Anniversary of the National Endowment for Democracy, United States Chamber of Commerce, Washington, DC, 6 November 2002, www.ned.org/events/anniversary/20thAnniv-Bush.html.

26. Ibid., 2.

27. Ibid., 3.

28. Ibid., 5.

29. "Saudis Criticize US Reform Plan," BBC News, 22 March 2004, http://news.bbc.co.uk/1/hi/world/middle_east/3555957.stm.

30. Condoleezza Rice, US Secretary of State, "Remarks at the American University in Cairo," 20 June 2005, www.america.gov/st/washfile-english/2005/june/200506 20111148ESnamfuaKO.1146204.html.

31. The Muslim Brotherhood won 19 percent in Egypt's three-round parliamentary elections and was set to take some 87 seats in the 454-seat National Assembly. President Mubarak's National Democratic Party (NDP) won 70 percent and was set to take at least 314 seats. Eight opposition activists were killed during violence on 7 December 2005 as they clashed with security forces that had cordoned off ten polling stations, reportedly to prevent voting. "Egypt Islamists Make Record Gains," BBC News, 8 December 2005, http://news.bbc.co.uk/1/hi/world/middle_east/4509682.stm.

32. Colin Gray, "Future Warfare: Or, the Triumph of History," *RUSI Journal* 150, no. 5 (October 2005): 16–19.

33. For an example of an attempt to speculate about the future dynamics of interstate conflict, see Jeremy Black, "Into the Future: The Rivalry of Major Powers?" *RUSI Journal* 153, no. 4 (August 2008): 12–17.

34. Ibid., 17.

Bibliography

Agha, Hussein, and Robert Malley. "The Last Negotiation." *Foreign Affairs* 81, no. 3 (May–June 2002): 10–18.
"Agreement Between the United States of America and the Republic of Iraq on the Withdrawal of United States Forces from Iraq and the Organization of Their Activities During Their Temporary Presence in Iraq." www.mnf-Iraq.com/images/CGs_messages/security_agreement.pdf.
Ahmed, Akbar S., and Hastings Donnan, eds. *Islam, Globalization and Postmodernity*. London: Routledge, 1994.
Alderson, Alexander (Colonel, British Army). "Revising the British Army's Counter-Insurgency Doctrine." *RUSI Journal* 152, no. 4 (August 2007): 6–11.
Ancker, Clinton J. (Colonel, ret., US Army), and Michael D. Burke (Lieutenant Colonel, ret., US Army). "Doctrine for Asymmetric Warfare." *Military Review* 83, no. 4 (July–August 2003): 18–25.
Andrade, Dale, and James H. Willbanks (Lieutenant Colonel, ret., US Army). "CORDS/Phoenix: Insurgency Lessons from Vietnam for the Future." *Military Review* 86, no. 2 (March–April 2006): 9–23.
Arnold, Matthew B. "The US 'Surge' as a Collaborative Corrective for Iraq." *RUSI Journal* 153, no. 2 (April 2008): 24–29.
Atwood, J. Brian. Testimony to the Senate Foreign Relations Committee, 23 September 2003, http://foreign.senate.gov/hearings/2003/hrg030918a.html.
Aylwin-Foster, Nigel (Brigadier, British Army). "Changing the Army for Counterinsurgency Operations." *Military Review* 85, no. 6 (November–December 2005): 2–15.
Ayubi, Nazih N. *Overstating the Arab State: Politics and Society in the Middle East*. London: I. B. Tauris, 1995.
Baker, Ralph O. (Colonel, US Army). "A Brigade Combat Team Commander's Perspective on Information Operations." *Military Review* 86, no. 3 (May–June 2006): 13–32.
Barber, Benjamin. *Jihad vs. McWorld: How Globalism and Tribalism Are Reshaping the World*. New York: Ballantine Books, 1996.
Batiste, John R. S. (Major General, US Army), and Paul R. Daniels (Lieutentant Colonel, US Army). "The Fight for Samarra: Full Spectrum Operations in Modern Warfare." *Military Review* 85, no. 3 (May–June 2005): 13–21.
Beinin, Joel, and Joe Stork, eds. *Political Islam: Essays from Middle East Report*. Los Angeles: University of California Press, 1997.

Benbow, Tim. "Talkin' 'bout My Generation? Assessing the Concept of 'Fourth Generation Warfare.'" *Comparative Strategy* 27, no. 2 (April–June 2008): 148–163.

Benchmark Assessment Report, submitted consistent with Section 1314 of the US Troop Readiness, Veterans' Care, Katrina Recovery, and Iraq Accountability Appropriations Act 2007 (Public Law 110-28). 14 September 2007. http://online.wsj .com/ documents/WHBenchmarkreport0914.pdf.

Bennett, Brian. "Who Are the Insurgents?" *Time,* 24 November 2003, 40–41.

Berntsen, Gary, and Ralph Pezzullo. *Jawbreaker—The Attack on Bin Laden and Al-Qaeda: A Personal Account by the CIA's Key Field Commander.* New York: Three Rivers Press, 2006.

Biddle, Stephen. *Afghanistan and the Future of Warfare: Implications for Army and Defense Policy.* Report undertaken for the Strategic Studies Institute, US Army War College, Carlisle Barracks, PA, November 2002. www.strategicstudies institute.army.mil/pdffiles/PUB109.pdf.

———. "The New Way of War?" *Foreign Affairs* 81, no. 3 (May–June 2002): 138–144.

———. "Seeing Baghdad, Thinking Saigon." *Foreign Affairs* 85, no. 2 (March–April 2006): 2–14.

Bird, Tim. "UK Effects-Based Planning and Centre of Gravity Analysis: An Increasingly Dysfunctional Relationship?" *RUSI Journal* 153, no. 2 (April 2008): 46–49.

Black, Jeremy. "Into the Future: The Rivalry of Major Powers?" *RUSI Journal* 153, no. 4 (August 2008): 12–17.

Bluth, Christopher. "The British Road to War: Blair, Bush, and the Decision to Invade Iraq." *International Affairs* 80, no. 5 (October 2004): 871–892.

Boniface, Pascal. "The Specter of Unilateralism." *The Washington Quarterly* 24, no. 3 (Summer 1991): 155–162.

Boot, Max. "The Corps Should Look to Its Small War Past." *Armed Forces Journal* (March 2006): 17–21.

Booth, Ken, and Tim Dunne, eds. *Worlds in Collision.* Basingstoke, UK: Palgrave Macmillan, 2002.

Brassett, James, and Richard Higgott. "Building the Normative Dimension(s) of a Global Polity." *Review of International Studies* 29, Special Issue (December 2003): 29–55.

Bremer, L. Paul. "How I Didn't Dismantle the Iraqi Army." *New York Times,* 6 September 2007, www.nytimes.com/2007/09/06/opinion/06bremer.html.

Bremer, L. Paul, with Malcolm McConnell. *My Year in Iraq: The Struggle to Build a Future of Hope.* New York: Simon and Schuster, 2006.

Brown, Chris. "History Ends, Worlds Collide." *Review of International Studies* 25 (December 1999): 41–57 (Special Issue—The Interregnum: Controversies in World Politics, 1989–1999).

Browne, Des. "Afghanistan: A Comprehensive Approach to Current Challenges." *RUSI Journal* (October 2006): 8–12.

Burke, Jason. *Al-Qaeda: The True Story of Radical Islam.* London: Penguin Books, 2004.

———. "Think Again: Al-Qaeda." *Foreign Policy* (May–June 2004): 18–26.

———. "Dam Holds Back Force of the Taliban." *The Observer,* 28 January 2007, 37.

———. "The New Taliban." *The Observer,* 14 October 2007, 31–33.

Burns, Tom. "Mechanistic and Organismic Structures." Extract 3 in D. S. Pugh, ed., *Organization Theory.* Harmondsworth, Middlesex, UK: Penguin Books, 1971, 43–55 (an extract from his article "Industry in a New Age," *New Society,* 31 January 1963, 17–20).

Buzan, Barry, and Richard Little. "Beyond Westphalia? Capitalism after the 'Fall.'" *Review of International Studies* 25 (December 1999): 89–104 (Special Issue—The Interregnum: Controversies in World Politics, 1989–1999).

Byman, Daniel, Kenneth Pollack, and Matthew Waxman. "Coercing Saddam Hussein: Lessons from the Past." *Survival* 40, no. 3 (Autumn 1998): 127–151.
Calleo, David P. "The Broken West." *Survival* 46, no. 3 (Autumn 2004): 29–38.
Callinicos, Alex. *The New Mandarins of American Power.* Cambridge: Polity Press, 2003.
Cassidy, Robert M. (Lieutenant Colonel, US Army). "Winning the War of the Flea: Lessons from Guerrilla Warfare." *Military Review* 84, no. 5 (September–October 2004): 41–46.
Chandrasekaran, Rajiv. *Imperial Life in the Emerald City: Inside Baghdad's Green Zone.* London: Bloomsbury Publishing, 2006.
Chiarelli, Peter W. (Major General, US Army), and Patrick R. Michaelis (Major, US Army). "Winning the Peace: The Requirement for Full-Spectrum Operations." *Military Review* 85, no. 4 (July–August 2005): 4–17.
Clark, Wesley K. (General, ret., US Army). "How to Fight an Asymmetric War." *Time,* October 23, 2000, 44.
———. *Winning Modern Wars: Iraq, Terrorism, and the American Empire.* New York: Public Affairs, 2003.
Clarke, Richard A. *Against All Enemies: Inside America's War on Terror.* New York: Simon and Schuster, 2004.
Clausewitz, Carl von. *On War.* Edited with an introduction by Anatol Rapoport. London: Penguin Books, 1982 (*Vom Kriege* was originally published in 1832).
Cockburn, Patrick. "A New Dawn? Patrick Cockburn in Baghdad." *The Independent.* Extra Supplement. 15 February 2008, 2–6.
Coffey, Ross (Major, US Army). "Revisiting CORDS: The Need for Unity of Effort to Security Victory in Iraq." *Military Review* 86, no. 2 (March–April 2006): 24–34.
Colvin, Marie (interview with Colonel H. R. McMaster). "Leaving Now Is Not the Way Out of Iraq." *The Sunday Times,* News Review section. 29 July 2007, 5.
———. "Iraqis Lead Final Purge of Al Qaeda." *The Sunday Times,* 6 July 2008, 1.
———. "Al Qaeda Is Driven from Mosul Bastion After Bloody Last Stand." *The Sunday Times,* 6 July 2008, 26–27.
———. "Sunni Sheikhs Turn Their Sights from US Forces to Al Qaeda." *The Sunday Times,* 9 September 2007, 28–29
Comprehensive Report of the Special Advisor Charles Duelfer to the Director of Central Intelligence on Iraq's WMD (the findings of the Iraq Survey Group). 30 September 2004. Addendums to Comprehensive report were added in March 2005, www.cia.gov/library/reports/general-reports1/iraq_wmd_2004/index.html.
Comptroller General of the US Government Accountability Office. *Report by the Comptroller General of the US Government Accountability Office, David M. Walker,* presented before the US Senate Committee on Foreign Relations, September, 2007. http://foreign.senate.gov/hearings/2007/ hrg070904p.html (assessment of the situation as of 30 August 2007).
Cooper, Scott A. "Air Power and the Coercive Use of Force." *Washington Quarterly* 24, no. 4 (Autumn 2001): 81–93.
Cordesman, Anthony. *The Iraq War: Strategy, Tactics, and Military Lessons.* Westport, CT: Praeger Publishers, 2003 (published in cooperation with the Center for Strategic and International Studies, Washington, DC).
———. "An Effective US Strategy for Iraq." Written testimony to the Senate Foreign Relations Committee, 1 February 2005. http://foreign.senate.gov/hearings/2005/hrg 050201a.html.
Cox, Mick. "Empire, Imperialism, and the Bush Doctrine." *Review of International Studies* 30, no. 4 (October 2004): 585–608.

Cox, Robert. "Civil Society at the Turn of the Millennium: Prospects for an Alternative World Order." *Review of International Studies* 25, no. 1 (January 1999): 3–28.
Crane, Conrad C. (Lieutenant Colonel, US Army). "Phase IV Operations: Where Wars Are Really Won." *Military Review* 85, no. 3 (May–June 2005): 27–36.
Cronin, Audrey Kurth. "How al-Qaida Ends: The Decline and Demise of Terrorist Groups." *International Security* 31, no. 1 (Summer 2006): 7–48.
Davis, Anthony. "Afghan Security Deteriorates as Taliban Regroup." *Jane's Intelligence Review* 15, no. 5 (May 2003): 10–15.
A Decade of Deception and Defiance: Saddam Hussein's Defiance of the United Nations. 12 September 2002. www.state.gov/p/nea/rls/13456.htm.
Dekmejian, R. Hrair. "The Rise of Political Islamism in Saudi Arabia." *Middle East Journal* 48, no. 4 (Autumn 1994): 627–643.
Delivering Security in a Changing World. Defence White Paper. December 2003. Presented to Parliament by the Secretary of State for Defence, Geoff Hoon, London, The Stationary Office, 2003. http://merln.ndu.edu/whitepapers/UnitedKingdom-2003.pdf.
Deudeney, Daniel, and G. John Ikenberry. "The Nature and Sources of Liberal International Order." *Review of International Studies* 25, no. 2 (April 1999): 179–196.
Diamond, Larry. "What Went Wrong in Iraq." *Foreign Affairs* 83, no. 5 (September–October 2004): 34–53.
Doctrine Division of the Combined Arms Center, Field Manual 3-24, *Counterinsurgency,* Headquarters Department of the US Army (December 2006).
Dodge, Toby. "Storming the Desert." *The World Today* 58, no. 4 (April 2002): 5–6.
———. "A Sovereign Iraq?" *Survival* 46, no. 3 (Autumn 2004): 39–58.
———. "The Causes of US Failure in Iraq." *Survival* 49, no. 1 (Spring 2007): 85–106.
Doward, Jamie, and Andrew Wander. "The Network." *The Observer,* Focus section, 6 May 2007, 26–27.
Dueck, Colin. "Ideas and Alternatives in American Grand Strategy." *Review of International Studies* 30, no. 4 (October 2004): 511–535.
Elliot, Michael. "If at First You Don't Succeed. . . ." *Time,* 24 November 2003, 38–45.
Fairweather, Jack. "Iraq's Story Is One of Hope and Surprise." *Daily Telegraph,* 23 February 2005, 14.
Falk, Richard. "Legality and Legitimacy: The Quest for Principled Flexibility and Restraint." *Review of International Studies* 31, Special Issue (December 2005): 33–50.
Farrell, Stephen. "Iraqi President Starts Talks to Try to Bring Sunnis Back." *New York Times,* 6 August 2007, www.nytimes.com/2007/08/06/world/middleeast/06iraq.html?scp=1&sq=Stephen%20Farrell,%206%20August%202007&st=cse.
Feil, Scott. "Post-Conflict Reconstruction." Written testimony to the Senate Foreign Relations Committee, 1 August 2002. http://frwebgate.access.gpo.gov/cgi-bin/getdoc.cgi?dbname=107_senate_hearings&docid=f:81697.wais.
———. "Security in a Post Conflict Situation in Iraq." Written testimony to the Senate Foreign Relations Committee, 11 February 2003. http://foreign.senate.gov/hearings/2003/hrg030211a.html.
Fielding, Marcus (Lieutenant General, Australian Army). "Regime Change: Planning and Managing Military-Led Interventions as Projects." *RUSI Journal* 151, no. 5 (October 2006): 20–29.
Flibbert, Andrew. "The Road to Baghdad: Ideas and Intellectuals in Explanations of the Iraq War." *Security Studies* 15, no. 2 (April–June 2006): 310–352.
Freedman, Lawrence. "The Age of Liberal Wars." *Review of International Studies* 31, Special Issue (December 2005): 93–107.
———. "The Third World War?" *Survival* 43, no. 4 (Winter 2001): 61–88.

———. "War in Iraq: Selling the Threat." *Survival* 46, no. 2 (Summer 2004): 7–50.
———. *The Transformation of Strategic Studies.* Adelphi Paper 379. Abingdon, Oxfordshire: Routledge, Published for the International Institute for Strategic Studies (London), 2006, 103.
Friedman, Robert I. *Sheikh Abdel Rahman, the World Trade Center Bombing and the CIA.* Westfield, NJ, Open Magazine Pamphlet Series no. 27 (October 1993).
Fukuyama, Francis. *State Building: Governance and World Order in the Twenty-First Century.* London: Profile Books, 2004.
Gause, F. Gregory III. "Getting It Backward on Iraq." *Foreign Affairs* 78, no. 3 (May–June 1999): 54–65.
———. "The Illogic of Dual Containment." *Foreign Affairs* 73, no. 2 (March–April 1994): 56–66.
Glennon, Michael J. "The New Interventionism: The Search for a Just International Law." *Foreign Affairs* 78, no. 3 (May–June 1999): 2–7.
Goldenberg, Suzanne. "Iraq War Policy Failing, Says Official Report." *The Guardian,* 13 July 2007, 16–17.
Gordon, Michael, R. "The Former-Insurgent Counterinsurgency." New York Times Online, 2 September 2007, www.nytimes.com/2007/09/02/magazine/02iraq-t.html.
Gordon, Michael R., and Bernard Trainor (Lieutenant General, USMC). *Cobra II: The Inside Story of the Invasion and Occupation of Iraq.* London: Atlantic Books, 2006.
Grant, Greg. "US Begins to Counter IED Threat in Iraq." *Jane's Defence Weekly* 42, no. 11 (16 March 2005): 5.
Gray, Colin S. "Clausewitz Rule, OK." *Review of International Studies* 25 (December 1999): 161–182 (Special Issue—The Interregnum Controversies in World Politics, 1989–1999).
———. "Future Warfare: Or, the Triumph of History," *RUSI Journal* 150, no. 5 (October 2005): 16–19.
———. *Another Bloody Century: Future Warfare.* London: Phoenix Paperback, 2006.
Greer, James K. (Colonel, US Army). "Operation Knockout: Counterinsurgency in Iraq." *Military Review* 85, no. 6 (November–December 2005): 16–19.
Grunow, Carl D. (Lieutenant Colonel, US Army). "Advising Iraqis: Building the Iraqi Army." *Military Review* 86, no. 4 (July–August 2006): 8–17.
Halliday, Fred. *The World at 2000: Perils and Promises.* Basingstoke, UK: Palgrave, 2001.
———. "It's Time to Bin the Past." *The Observer,* 30 January 2005, 24.
Halper, Stefan, and Jonathan Clarke. *America Alone: The Neoconservatives and the Global Order.* Cambridge: Cambridge University Press, 2004.
Hammer, Joshua. "Law and Disorder in al-Amarah." *Newsweek,* 24 November 2003, 32–33.
Hammes, Thomas X. www.smallwars.quantico.usmc.mil/search/Articles/Insurgency%20ModernWarfareEvolves.pdf."Insurgency: Modern Warfare Evolves into a Fourth Generation." *Strategic Forum.* Institute for National Strategic Studies, National Defense University, no. 214 (January 2005).
———. (Colonel, ret., USMC). "Countering Evolved Insurgent Networks." *Military Review* 86, no. 4 (July–August 2006): 18–26.
Hamre, John. "Iraq: Next Steps—How to Internationalize Iraq and Organize the US Government Efforts to Administer Reconstruction Efforts." Written testimony to the Senate Foreign Relations Committee, 23 September 2003. http://foreign.senate.gov/hearings/ 2003/hrg030918a.html.
Harkavy, Robert. "Strategic Geography and the Greater Middle East." *Naval War College Review* LIV, no. 4 (Autumn 2001): 36–53.

Harriman, Ed. "Treachery: How Iraq Went to War Against Saddam." *The Sunday Times,* Review Section, 11 January 2004, 1–2.

Hashim, Ahmed S. "The World According to Usama Bin Laden." *Naval War College Review* 54, no. 4 (Autumn 2001): 11–35.

———. *Insurgency and Counterinsurgency in Iraq.* London: C. Hurst, 2006.

Haviland, Charles. "Afghan Bombers Foreigners—UN." BBC News, 8 September 2007, http://news.bbc.co.uk/1/hi/world/south_asia/6985400.stm.

Hawthorn, Geoffrey. "Liberalism Since the Cold War: An Enemy to itself?" *Review of International Studies* 25 (December 1999): 145–160 (Special Issue—The Interregnum: Controversies in World Politics, 1989–1999).

Held, David, and Anthony McGrew. "The End of the Old Order? Globalization and the Prospects for World Order." *Review of International Studies* 24, Special Issue (December 1998): 219–243.

Higgot, Richard. "Beyond Embedded Liberalism: Governing the International Trade Regime in an Era of Economic Nationalism." Paper presented at the Annual Conference of the British International Studies Association, Southampton, 18–20 December 1995.

———. "Contested Globalization: The Changing Context and Normative Changes." *Review of International Studies* 26, Special Issue (December 2000): 131–153.

Higgot, Richard, and Nicola Phillips. "Challenging Triumphalism and Convergence: The Limits of Global Liberalization in Asia and Latin America." *Review of International Studies* 26, no. 3 (July 2000): 359–379.

Hirsh, Michael, Rod Nordland, and Mark Hosenball. "About Face." *Newsweek,* 24 November 2002, 23–27.

Hoffman, Bruce. "The Myth of Grass-Roots Terrorism: Why Osama bin Laden Still Matters" (Review Essay). *Foreign Affairs* 87, no. 3 (May–June 2008): 133–138.

Horowitz, Anthony. "The Anti-Guantanamo: Saudi Arabia's Plan to Tackle Terrorism—Nicely." *The Sunday Telegraph,* Magazine Section, 13 July 2008, 8–13

Hurrell, Andrew. "Legitimacy and the Use of Force: Can the Circle Be Squared?" *Review of International Studies* 31, Special Issue (December 2005): 15–32.

Ignatieff, Michael. "The Challenges of American Imperial Power." *Naval War College Review* LVI, no. 2 (Spring 2003): 53–63.

———. "The Terrorist as Film Director." *The Sunday Telegraph,* Review section, 21 November 2004, 4.

Ikenberry, G. John. "American Grand Strategy in the Age of Terror." *Survival* 43, no. 4 (Winter 2001): 19–34.

———. "American Power and the Empire of Capitalist Democracy." *Review of International Studies* 27, Special Issue: Empires, Systems and States: Great Transformations in International Politics (December 2001): 191–212.

———. "Liberalism and Empire: Logics of Order in the American Unipolar Age." *Review of International Studies* 30, no. 4 (October 2004): 609–630.

Indyk, Martin. "Back to the Bazaar." *Foreign Affairs* 81, no. 1 (January–February 2002): 75–88.

Initial Benchmark Assessment Report, submitted consistent with Section 1314 of the U.S. Troop Readiness, Veterans' Care, Katrina Recovery, and Iraq Accountability Appropriations Act, 2007 (Public Law 110-28). 12 July 2007. http://online.wsj.com/documents/FinalBenchmarkReport.pdf.

Iraq's Weapons of Mass Destruction: The Assessment of the British Government. www.no.10.gov.uk/Page271.asp.

Jenkins, Simon. "By Jingo, Our Brave Boys Are Off to Tame the Afghan. And They'll Fail." *The Sunday Times,* 29 January 2006, 16.

———. "Bush and Blair Have Brilliantly Done bin Laden's Work for Him." *The Sunday Times,* 19 February 2006, 18.

———. "Stop Killing the Taliban—They Offer the Best Hope of Beating Al-Qaeda." *The Sunday Times,* 22 June 2008, 20.

Joffe, Josef. "How America Does It." *Foreign Affairs* 76, no. 5 (September–October 1997): 13–27.

———. "Clinton's World: Purpose, Policy, and Weltanschauung." *Washington Quarterly* 24, no. 1 (Winter 2001): 141–154.

Johnson, Boris. "Out of the Ashes." *The Spectator,* 19 March 2005, 12–13.

Johnson, Scott. "Inside an Enemy." *Newsweek,* 18 August 2003, 16–17.

Joint Doctrine and Concepts Center. *The Military Contribution to Peace Support Operations.* Joint Warfare Publication 3-50 (2nd ed.). Shrivenham, UK. June 2004.

Jones, Seth G. "Pakistan's Dangerous Game." *Survival* 49 no. 1 (Spring 2007): 15–32.

Kagan, Frederick W. *Choosing Victory: A Plan for Success in Iraq—Phase I Report.* American Enterprise Institute, www.aei.org/publications/pubID.25396/pub_detail.asp.

Kagan, Frederick W., and Jack Keane. "The Right Type of 'Surge': Any Troop Increase Must Be Large and Lasting," *Washington Post,* 27 December 2006, reprinted at www.aei.org/pub.ID25356/pub_detail.asp.

Kakutani, Michiko. "From Planning to Warfare to Occupation, How Iraq Went Wrong." *New York Times,* 25 July 2006 (review of Thomas Ricks's book *Fiasco*), www.nytimes.com/2006/07/25/books/25kaku.html?scp=1&sq=From%20Planning%20to%20Warfare%20to%20Occupation,%20How%20Iraq%20Went%20Wrong&st=cse.

Kemp, Geoffrey. "The Persian Gulf remains the strategic prize." *Survival* 40, no. 4 (Winter 1998–1999): 132–149.

———. "Iran: Can the United States Do a Deal?" *Washington Quarterly* 24, no. 1 (Winter 2001): 109–124.

Kent, Randolph C. "International Crises: Two Decades Before and Two Decades Beyond." *International Affairs* 80, no. 5 (October 2004): 851–869.

Kilcullen, David. "Countering Global Insurgency." *Journal of Strategic Studies* 28, no. 4 (August 2005): 597–617.

———. "Counter-insurgency Redux." *Survival* 48, no. 4 (Winter 2006–2007): 111–130.

Kiszely, John. "Learning About Counter-Insurgency." *RUSI Journal* 151, no. 6 (December 2006): 16–21.

Koch, Andrew. "Information War Played a Major Role in Iraq." *Jane's Defence Weekly,* 40, no. 3 (23 July 2003): 5.

Lake, Anthony. "Confronting the Backlash States." *Foreign Affairs* 73, no. 2 (March–April 1994): 45–55.

Lamb, Christiana. "The Bandits Wait for the British." *The Sunday Times,* 29 January 2006, 25.

———. "What a Bloody Hopeless War." *The Sunday Times,* Review section, 10 September 2006, 3.

———. "US Sends in Its Taliban Tamers." *The Sunday Times,* 28 January 2007, 24.

———. "Rogue Pakistan Spies Aid Taliban." *The Sunday Times,* 3 August 2008, 25.

Lamm, David (Colonel, US Army). "Success in Afghanistan Means Fighting Several Wars at Once." *Armed Forces Journal* (November 2005): 25–27.

Lia, Brynjar, and Thomas Hegghammer. "Jihadi Strategic Studies: The Alleged Al Qaida Policy Study Preceding the Madrid Bombings." *Studies in Conflict and Terrorism* 27, no. 5 (September–October 2004): 355–375.

Lowe, Christian. "It Will Be Better When You Leave." *Armed Forces Journal* (March 2006): 45–46.

Ludlow, Peter. "Wanted: A Global Partner." *The Washington Quarterly* 24, no. 3 (Summer 2001): 163171.
Luttwak, Edward N. "Toward Post-Heroic Warfare." *Foreign Affairs* 74, no. 3 (May–June 1995): 109–122.
Maass, Peter. "Professor Nagl's War" (interview with Major John Nagl). *New York Times Magazine,* 11 January 2004, http://query.nytimes.com/gst/fullpage.html?res=9902E6D61531F932A25752C0A9629C8B63&scp=1&sq=the+counterinsurgent&scp=1&sq=Peter%20Maas,%20The%20Counterinsurgent&st=cse.
Mackinlay, John. "Iraq Campaign Failed to Plan For Peacekeeping." *Jane's Intelligence Review* 15, no. 6 (June 2003): 36–37.
———. *Defeating Complex Insurgency: Beyond Iraq and Afghanistan.* Whitehall Paper 64. London: Royal United Services Institute, 2005.
———. "Counter-Insurgency in Global Perspective—An Introduction: Politicians Need to Understand Insurgency." *RUSI Journal* 152, no. 6 (December 2007): 6–7.
Mann, Michael. "The First Failed Empire of the 21st Century." *Review of International Studies* 30, no. 4 (October 2004): 631–653.
Maples, Michael D. (Lieutenant General, Director, Defense Intelligence Agency). "Current and Projected National Security Threats to the United States." Written Statement to Senate Armed Services Committee, 28 February 2006, http://armed-services.senate.gov/statemnt/2006/February/Maples%2002-28-06.pdf.
McCaffrey, Barry. "The War We're Winning." *Armed Forces Journal* (November 2005): 17–19.
McFate, Montgomery. "Iraq: The Social Context of IEDs." *Military Review* 85, no. 3 (May–June 2005): 37–40.
McFate, Montgomery, and Andrea Jackson. "The Object Beyond War: Counterinsurgency and the Four Tools of Political Competition." *Military Review* 86, no. 1 (January–February 2006): 13–26.
McInnes, Colin. *Spectator-Sport War: The West and Contemporary Conflict.* Boulder: Lynne Rienner, 2002.
———. "A Different Kind of War? September 11 and the United States' Afghan War." *Review of International Studies* 29, no. 2 (April 2003): 165–184.
Measuring Stability and Security in Iraq. Report to Congress in accordance with Conference Report 109-72 Emergency Supplemental Appropriations Act 2005, Department of Defense, October 2005, www.defenselink.mil/pubs/20051013_publication_OSSRF.pdf.
Meo, Nick, and Leonard Doyle. "Afghanistan: A Nation Abandoned to Drugs." *The Independent,* 19 November 2004, 1, 4.
Metz, Thomas (Lieutenant General, US Army), Mark Garret (Lieutenant Colonel, US Army), James Hutton (Lieutenant Colonel, US Army), and Timothy Bush (Lieutenant Colonel, US Army), "Massing Effects in the Information Domain." *Military Review* 86, no. 3 (May–June 2006): 2–12.
Miller, Linda. "America After the Cold War: Competing Visions." *Review of International Studies* 24, no. 2 (April 1998): 251–259.
Mills, Greg. "Calibrating Ink Spots: Filling Afghanistan's Ungoverned Spaces." *RUSI Journal* 151, no. 4 (August 2006): 16–25.
Ministry of Defence Operations in Iraq: Lessons for the Future. 2003. Foreword by the Secretary of State for Defence, Geoff Hoon, www.mod.uk/NR/rdonlyres/734920BA-6ADE-461F-A809-7E5A754990D7/0/opsiniraq_lessons_dec03.pdf.
Mueller, John, and Karl Mueller. "Sanctions of Mass Destruction." *Foreign Affairs* 78, no. 3 (May–June 1999): 43–51.
Murden, Simon. *Islam, the Middle East, and the New Global Hegemony.* Boulder: Lynne Rienner, 2002.

Murray, Williamson, and Robert H. Scales (Major General, ret., US Army). *The Iraq War: A Military History.* Cambridge, MA: Belknap Press of Harvard University Press, 2003.

Myers, Richard (General, US Army). "Collective Defence in the 21st Century." *RUSI Journal* 150, no. 5 (October 2005): 12–15.

Nagl, John (Lieutenant-Colonel, US Army). *Learning to Eat Soup with a Knife: Counterinsurgency Lessons from Malaya to Vietnam* (with a new preface on the author's combat experience in Iraq). Chicago: University of Chicago Press, 2005. Foreword by General Peter J. Schoomaker.

———. "An American View of Twenty-First Century Counter-Insurgency." *RUSI Journal* 152, no. 4 (August 2007): 12–16.

The National Security Strategy of the United States. September 2002. Foreword by President George W. Bush. www.state.gov/documents/organization/15538.pdf.

National Strategy for Victory in Iraq. Prepared by the National Security Council, 30 November 2005. www.washingtonpost.com/wp-srv/nation/documents/Iraqnationalstrategy11-30-05.pdf.

Naylor, Sean D. "The Taliban Lost the War in Afghanistan, but Still Bedevils Coalition Efforts to Establish Security." *Armed Forces Journal* (November 2005): 19–23.

Niblock, Tim. *Pariah States and Sanctions in the Middle East: Iraq, Libya, Sudan.* Boulder: Lynne Rienner, 2002.

The 9/11 Commission Report: Final Report of the National Commission on Terrorist Attacks upon the United States. Authorized Edition. New York: W. W. Norton, 2004.

Norwitz, Jeffrey H. "Defining Success at Guantanamo." *Military Review* 85, no. 4 (July–August 2005): 79–83.

O'Brien, Kevin, and Joseph Nusbaum. "Intelligence Gathering on Asymmetric Threats—Part One." *Jane's Intelligence Review* 12, no. 10 (October 2000): 50–55.

———. "Intelligence Collection for Asymmetric Threats—Part Two." *Jane's Intelligence Review* 12, no. 11 (November 2000): 50–55.

O'Brien, Mike (MP). "Morality in Asymmetric War and Intervention Operations." *RUSI Journal* 147, no. 5 (October 2002): 40–44.

Office of the Director of National Intelligence. *National Intelligence Estimate: The Terrorist Threat to the US Homeland.* July 2007 (see Press Releases, 17 July 2007). www.dni.gov/press_releases/20070717_release.pdf.

O'Hanlon, Michael, and Kenneth Pollack. "A War We Just Might Win." *New York Times*, 30 July 2007, Late Edition, Final, Section A, 17, www.nytimes.com/2007/07/30/opinion/30pollack.html.

Ollivant, Douglas A. (Lieutenant Colonel, US Army) and Eric D. Chewning (Lieutenant, US Army). "Producing Victory: Rethinking Conventional Forces in COIN Operations." *Military Review* 86, no. 4 (July–August 2006): 50–59.

O'Neill, Conor. "Terrorism, Insurgency, and the Military Response from South Armagh to Falluja." *RUSI Journal* 149, no. 5 (October 2004): 22–26.

Orsini, Dominique. "Walking the Tightrope: Dealing with Warlords in Afghanistan's Destabilizing North." *RUSI Journal* 152, no. 5 (October 2007): 46–50.

O'Sullivan, Meghan L. "The Politics of Dismantling Containment." *Washington Quarterly* 24, no. 1 (Winter 2001): 67–76.

Qadir, Shaukat (Brigadier, ret., Pakistan Army). "Pakistan's Waziristan Problem." *RUSI Journal* 153, no. 2 (April 2008): 42–45.

Quiggin, Tom. "Marching to War: The Invasion of Iraq—A Plan Fourteen Years in the Making." *RUSI Journal* 148, no. 5 (October 2003): 60–65.

Rashid, Ahmed. "Pakistan Crisis Hits Army Morale." BBC News, 6 September 2007, http://news.bbc.co.uk/1/hi/world/south_asia/6978240.stm.

Rathmall, Andrew. "Reforming Iraq's Security Sector." *RUSI Journal* 150, no. 1 (February 2005): 8–11.
Record, Jeffrey. "Bounding the Global War on Terrorism," written under the auspices of the Strategic Studies Institute, US Army War College, Carlisle, Pennsylvania, December 2003, www.globalsecurity.org/military/library/report/2003/record_bounding.pdf.
Rhodes, Richard. *Dark Sun.* New York: Simon and Schuster, 1996.
Richards, David (Lieutenant General, British Army). "NATO in Afghanistan, Transformation on the Front Line." *RUSI Journal* 151, no. 4 (August 2006): 10–14
Ricks, Thomas E. *Fiasco: The American Military Adventure in Iraq.* London: Penguin Books, 2006.
Ripley, Tim. "Planning for 'Iraqi Freedom.'" *Jane's Intelligence Review* 15, no. 7 (July 2003): 8–11.
———. "Retrain, Remodel, Rebuild." *Jane's Defence Weekly* 41, no. 49 (8 December 2004): 24–29.
Roe, Andrew M. (Major, British Army). "To Create a Stable Afghanistan: Provisional Reconstruction Teams, Good Governance, and a Splash of History." *Military Review* 85, no. 6 (November–December 2005): 20–26.
Rogers, Paul. "Reconsidering the War on Terror." *RUSI Journal* 152, no. 4 (August 2007): 32–35.
Roy, Olivier. *The Failure of Political Islam.* London: I. B. Tauris, 1994.
Rugh, William A. "Time to Modify Our Gulf Policy." *Middle East Policy* 5, no. 1 (January 1997): 46–57.
Salmoni, Barak. "The Fallacy of 'Irregular' Warfare." *RUSI Journal* 152, no. 4 (August 2007): 18–24.
Scales, Robert H. (Major General, ret.). "Culture-Centric Warfare." *Proceedings of the US Naval Institute* 130, no. 10 (October 2004): 32–36.
Schon, Donald A. *Beyond the Stable State.* London: Temple Smith, 1971.
Schroen, Gary. *First Inside: An Insider's Account of How the CIA Spearheaded the War on Terror in Afghanistan.* New York: Presidio Press, 2007.
Scott, Shirley V. "Is There Room for International Law in Realpolitik? Accounting for the US Attitude Toward International Law." *Review of International Studies* 30, no. 1 (January 2004): 71–88.
Scruton, Roger. *The West and the Rest: Globalization and the Terrorist Threat.* London: Continuum, 2002.
Secretary-General of the UN. *In Larger Freedom.* Report for the decision of the Heads of State and Government in September 2005. www.un.org/largerfreedom/.
Sengupta, Kim. "Shia Accuse US Forces of Appeasing Insurgents as Attacks Kill 11 Soldiers." *The Independent,* 7 January 2006, 29.
Serchuk, Vance. "Innovative Teams Are Building Goodwill at the Grass-Roots Level." *Armed Forces Journal* (November 2005): 23–24.
Simon, Steven. "America and Iraq: The Case for Disengagement." *Survival* 49, no. 1 (Spring 2007): 61–84.
———. "The Price of the Surge: How US Strategy Is Hastening Iraq's Demise." *Foreign Affairs* 87, no. 3 (May–June 2008): 57–76.
Simon, Steven, and Daniel Benjamin. "The Terror." *Survival* 43, no. 4 (Winter 2001): 5–18.
Simpson, John. "Can the War in Afghanistan Be Won?" BBC News, 17 June 2007, http://news.bbc.co.uk/1/hi/world/south_asia/6756125.stm.
Sky, Emma. "Iraq 2007—Moving Beyond Counter-Insurgency Doctrine: A First-Hand Perspective." *RUSI Journal* 153, no. 2 (April 2008): 30–34.

Smith, David. "Packed Classes Hint at Peace in Battered Iraq." *The Observer,* 11 November 2007, 19.
Smith, Rupert (General, British Army). *The Utility of Force: The Art of War in the Modern World.* London: Penguin Books, 2005.
Stansfield, Gareth. *Accepting Realities in Iraq.* Middle East Briefing Paper. London: Chatham House, May 2007, MEP BP 07/02, www.chathamhouse.org.uk/research/middle_east/papers/view/-/id/501/.
Stemmet, Andre. "International Law and the Use of Force: Some Post 9/11 Perspectives." *RUSI Journal* 148, no. 5 (October 2003): 24–29.
Stevenson, Jonathan. "Pragmatic Counter-Terrorism." *Survival* 43, no. 4 (Winter 2001): 35–48.
"Strategic Framework Agreement for a Relationship of Friendship and Cooperation Between the United States of America and the Republic of Iraq." www.mnf-Iraq.com/images/CGs_messages/strategic_framework_agreement.pdf.
Sullivan, John P. "Fusing Terrorism Security and Response." In Peter Katona, Michael D. Intriligator, and John P. Sullivan, eds. *Countering Terrorism and WMD: Creating a Global Counter-Terrorism Network.* New York: Routledge, 2006, chapter 17, 272–290.
Taher, Abul. "Al-Qaeda: The Cracks Begin to Show." *The Sunday Times,* 8 June 2008, 14.
Taheri, Amir. "We Don't Do God, We Do Palestine and Iraq." *The Sunday Times,* 12 February 2006, 12.
Tardy, Thierry. "The United Nations and Iraq: A Role Beyond Expectations." *International Peacekeeping* 11, no. 4 (Winter 2004): 591–607.
Telhami, Shibley. "America in Arab Eyes." *Survival* 49, no. 1 (Spring 2007): 107–122.
Terriff, Terry, Aaron Karp, and Regina Karp, eds. *Global Insurgency and the Future of Armed Conflict: Debating Fourth Generation Warfare.* London: Routledge, 2008 (an extension drawn from the symposium "Debating Fourth Generation Warfare" in *Contemporary Security Policy* 26, no. 2, August 2005).
Tripp, Charles. "State-Building in Iraq." *Review of International Studies* 30, no. 4 (October 2004): 545–558.
United Nations Office on Drugs and Crime (in association with the Ministry of Counter Narcotics, Government of Afghanistan). "Afghanistan Opium Survey 2007." August 2007. www.unodc.org/unodc/en/crop-monitoring/index.html.
United Nations/World Bank. *United Nations/World Bank Joint Iraq Needs Assessment.* October 2003. www-wds.worldbank.org/external/default/wdscontentserver/wdsp/ib/2007/12/26/000020953_20071226134206/rendered/pdf/419690english011-assessment01public1.pdf.
UN Secretary-General, High-Level Panel on Threats, Challenges, and Change. *A More Secure World: Our Shared Responsibility,* www.un.org/secureworld.
US Department of Defense. *Report of the Quadrennial Defense Review.* Presented by William S. Cohen, Secretary of Defense, May 1997. www.defenselink.mil/qdr/archive.
van Creveld, Martin. *The Transformation of War.* New York: Free Press, 1991.
Van Natta, Don Jr. "Bush Saw Iraq War as Inevitable." *International Herald Tribune,* 28 March 2006.
Wallace, William, and Edmund J. Degen. "Persistent Security: A Key to Success Anywhere Along the Continuum of Operations." *RUSI Journal* 152, no. 4 (August 2007): 26–30.
Ward, Adam, ed. "Negotiating with the Iraqi Insurgency: Dilemmas and Doubts." *IISS Strategic Comments* 12, no. 1 (February 2006), www.iiss.org/publications/strategic-comments/past-issues/volume-12---2006/volume-12---issue-1/.

Weiss, Linda. "Globalization and National Governance." *Review of International Studies* 25 (December 1999): 59–88 (Special Issue—The Interregnum Controversies in World Politics 1989–1999).
Westerman, Ian. "Pacifying Afghanistan: Enduring Lessons from CORDS in Vietnam." *RUSI Journal* 153, no. 5 (October 2008): 14-21.
Wilkinson, Isambard. "Pakistan Signs Deal with Bhutto Killer." *The Daily Telegraph*, 25 April 2008, 18.
Wilson, Gary I., and John P. Sullivan. "On Gangs, Crime, and Terrorism." *Defense and the National Interest*, 28 February 2007, www.d-n-i.net/fcs/pdf/wilson_sullivan_gangs_terrorism.pdf.
———. "As Gangs and Terrorists Converge." Military.com, 16 March 2007, www.military.com/forums/0,15240,128818,00.html.
Woodward, Bob. *Bush at War*. New York: Simon and Schuster, 2002.
———. *Plan of Attack*. London: Simon and Schuster UK, 2004.
———. "Prisoners of War." *The Sunday Times*, News Review section, 8 October 2006, 1–3 (extracts from his book *State of Denial*).
Wright, Lawrence. "The Heretic: How Al-Qaeda's Mastermind Turned His Back on Terror." *The Observer*, Magazine section, 13 July 2008, 14–49.
Wright, Robin. "America's Iraq Policy: How Did It Come to This?" *Washington Quarterly* 21, no. 3 (Summer 1998): 53–70.
Yaphe, Judith S. "Iraq: The Exception to the Rule." *Washington Quarterly* 24, no. 1 (Winter 2001): 125–137.
Zakaria, Fareed. "Job One: Solve the Sunni Problem." *Newsweek*, 24 November 2003, 21.

Index

Abrams, Creighton W., 45
Abu Ghraib prison, 21,153
Abu Zubaydah, 194
Afghanistan, 18,25, 34, 36, 37, 39, 71, 72, 147, 205; case study of contemporary warfare, 2, 3, 20, 26, 131, 193, 196; post-2002 conflict, 1, 2, 3, 40, 46, 54, 88–109, 192; war of 2001–2002, 1, 3, 4, 40, 45, 50, 51, 53, 59, 73, 81–87, 189
Afghanistan-Pakistan border, 85, 86, 100–102, 104, 108, 109
Afghan National Army (ANA), 92, 93, 99, 106, 107
Agha, Hussein, 200
Agoglia, John, 122
Ajami, Fouad, 120
Algeria, 18, 32, 34, 36, 46
Allawi, Iyad, 125, 160
Allegiance Program, 99, 103, 107
American Enterprise Institute, 78, 176
Amos, James, 173
ANA. *See* Afghan National Army
Anbar province, 143, 151, 172, 173, 177, 178
Annan, Kofi, 70
Annapolis peace talks, 198
Al-Aqsa mosque, 37, 65
Arab-Israeli conflict/peace process, 3, 62, 62–63, 64–66, 68, 73, 200
Arafat, Yasser, 65, 66, 203
Al-Asad, Bashar, 201
Al-Asad, Hafiz, 34
Al-Askari mosque, Samarra, 162

Association of Muslim Scholars, 150, 171
Association of the US Army, 120, 130
Asymmetric actors and threats, 6, 13–15, 17, 19, 206
Asymmetric bargaining war, 20, 26
Atef, Muhammad, 87
Atwood, J. Brian, 145, 146
Aum Shinrikyo, 14
Axis of evil, 73, 74
Aylwin-Foster, Nigel, 153
Ayubi, Nazih, 128–129

Baath Party (Iraq): overthrow and dissolution, 69, 137, 138, 181; role in Sunni insurgency, 152, 153, 156, 171, 172
Badr organization, 162, 180, 181
Baghdad: in post-occupation Iraq, 131, 138, 143, 150, 151, 154, 155, 158, 159, 160, 162, 179, 181; the Surge, 173, 174, 177, 178, 183; US capture in 2003, 120, 123–129
Bahrain, 64, 203
Baker, James, 60
Baluchistan, 101, 104
Baqubah, 143, 178
Barak, Ehud, 65
Barber, Benjamin, 117
Basra, 120, 126, 143, 151, 183
Binalshibh, Ramzi, 194
bin Laden, Osama, 1, 3, 34, 35, 37, 39, 40, 71, 72, 74, 83, 86, 87, 109, 189
Black, Cofer, 82

Blackwater Company, 158
Blackwill, Robert, 157
Blair, Tony, 1, 117, 198
Blitzkrieg, 16, 124
Blix, Hans, 116, 117
Bonn conference and process, 88, 89, 90, 91, 93, 102, 106
Bosnia, 34, 35, 49, 50, 51, 52, 56, 57, 131
Brahimi, Lakhdar, 157, 159, 160
Bremer, L. Paul, 2, 120, 123, 144, 145, 146, 148, 157, 158; decision to dissolve Baath Party, 137, 138; policy on establishing new Iraqi government, 141–142, 149, 150, 156–158, 159, 160, 170; use of force to suppress Iraqi resistance, 158, 159
Briggs, Sir Harold, 45, 46, 47
British Army, 50, 105, 107
Burke, Jason, 37, 100
Burns, Tom, 28
Bush, George H. W., 59, 60, 62
Bush, George W., 11, 15, 72, 73; declares end to major combat operations in Iraq, 128, 152; initiation of regime change in Iraq, 3, 115–118, 135; involvement in Iraq war planning, 121, 136–137; on democratic reform in the Muslim world, 202, 203; role in Afghanistan War 2001–2002, 1, 81, 83; role in Arab-Israeli conflict, 66, 73, 198, 199; role in post-invasion Iraq, 120, 137, 138, 142, 169, 177, 179, 180; speech to the UN General Assembly (12 September 2002), 74; State of the Union speech of 29 January 2002, 73–74; war on terror policy, 1, 3, 25, 43, 73, 74, 190, 192, 198, 199, 205

Caliphate, 38, 39
Callwell, Charles E., 45, 46
Camp David meeting, 15 September 2001, 82
Camp David peace talks, July–August 2000, 65, 66
Casey, George, 177
Center for Strategic and International Studies, 120, 130, 143
Central Intelligence Agency (CIA): in Afghanistan, 68, 69, 72, 82, 83, 84; in Iraq, 122, 123, 124

Chalabi, Ahmed, 120, 122, 123, 138
Chandrasekaran, Rajiv, 2, 123, 138
Chechnya, 13, 35, 36, 39, 199, 205
Cheney, Richard, 74, 120, 136
Chiarelli, Peter W., 173, 174
China, 9, 10, 51, 66, 68, 70, 72
CIA. *See* Central Intelligence Agency
Civil Operations and Revolutionary Development Support (CORDS) program, 94, 173, 179, 199
Clarke, Richard, 72
Clausewitz, Carl von, 5–6, 17
Clinton, Bill, 11, 49, 60, 62, 65, 66, 69, 72, 73
Coalition Provisional Authority (CPA), 120, 123, 137, 138, 139, 141, 142, 144, 145, 146, 147, 148, 149, 156, 158, 159; hand-over to Iraqi government, 149, 150, 157, 160
Cobra II, 121
Cohen, William, 70
Combined Arms Center (Fort Leavenworth, Kansas), 50, 174
Combined Forces Command–Afghanistan, 103
Combined Task Force 7, 145
Concerned Local Citizens (*later* Sons of Iraq), 173, 178
Constellation network, 29–31, 40, 41, 194, 195
Conway, James, 159
Core-periphery organizations, 29, 30, 40, 41
Counterculture movement (of the late 1960s), 29, 31–33
Counterinsurgency (FM 3–24/MCWP 33.3–5), 25–26, 174
CPA. *See* Coalition Provisional Authority
Craddock, John, 108
Crocker, Ryan, 178

Dar al-Islam/Dar al-Harb, 35
Al-Dawa (Iraq), 160, 161, 179, 180, 183
Dayton, Ohio, peace talks, 50
Deobandi movement, 100
DFI. *See* UN Development Fund for Iraq
Diamond, Larry, 149
Diego Garcia, 81
Directorate of Inter-Services Intelligence (ISI), 72

Diyala province, 126, 143, 151, 173, 177, 178
Docherty, Leo, 105
Dodge, Toby, 161
Downing Street memo, 116
Dual containment, 3, 62, 66
DynCorp, 93

East African bombings, 7 August 1998, 37, 71, 72, 82
Effects-based warfare, 4, 16, 21, 40, 43, 50, 54, 57, 124, 127, 128, 130, 131, 175, 181, 193
Egypt, 34, 36, 63, 75, 149, 200, 201, 203, 204, 205
Erdogan, Recep, 118
European Union, 66, 67

Fahd, King, 34
Fahim, Mohammad, 83, 84, 85, 89
al-Faisal, Prince Saud, 203
Falk, Richard, 117, 118
Fallujah, 19, 39, 143, 144, 153, 154, 155, 158, 159, 174, 178
Fardh Al-Qanoon (Baghdad security plan), 177
Fatah, 200
Fedayeen Saddam, 124, 127
Feil, Scott, 130
Feith, Douglas, 122, 123, 130, 137, 138, 145, 156
Foley, Tom, 146
Fourth Generation Warfare (4GW), concept of, 3, 15–21, 25, 27, 31, 107
France, 68, 70, 92
Franks, Tommy, 121, 122
Freedman, Lawrence, 12, 196
Fukuyama, Francis, 199
Full-spectrum operations, 174, 175, 184, 196
Future of Iraq Project, 120

Galbraith, J. K., 28
Galula, David, 45
Garner, Jay, 122, 123, 137, 140, 141, 142
Gaza, 65, 191, 200
Gemayel, Amin, 125
Gereshk, 104, 105
Germany, 88, 92, 93
Glennon, Michael, 51

Globalization, 2, 3, 7, 9–15, 18, 19, 25, 43, 46, 191, 193, 205, 206, 207
Glocal insurgency, 2, 3, 17–19, 21, 25, 27, 40, 41, 43, 45, 59, 71, 135, 193, 194, 195, 196, 199, 205, 206, 207
al-Goud, Shaikh Faisal, 172
Gray, Colin, 6, 7, 206
Great Britain (United Kingdom), 45, 68, 70, 92, 93, 97, 116, 117, 118, 119, 127, 131, 162
Greater Middle East Initiative, 202
Green Zone, 145, 148, 150, 158, 161
Guantánamo Bay, detention facility, 21
Gulf States, 63, 64, 71, 149
Gulf War (1991), 8, 35, 59, 60, 61, 62, 63, 71
Gwynn, Sir Charles, 45

Hadley, Stephen J., 179
Hakim, Mohammed Bakir, 154, 158
Hamas, 18, 65, 191, 200, 203
Hammes, Thomas X., 5, 17, 18, 26–27, 195
Hamre, John, 143, 145
Haqqani, Jalaluddin, 100, 104
Haqqani, Sirajuddin, 100, 104
Hashim, Ahmed S., 2, 35, 139, 151, 155
Hawkins, Steve, 122
Hearts and minds, 46, 47, 48, 49, 54
Hekmatyar, Gulbuddin, 102, 104
Helmand province, 96, 97, 98, 103, 104, 105, 106
Hezbollah, 18, 65, 183
Hierarchical organization, 28, 29, 30, 41, 197
Hizb-i-Islami, 102, 104
Hizb ut-Tahrir, 38
Hoffman, Frank, 196, 197
Hussein of Jordan, King, 34
Hussein, Saddam: capture by coalition, 152; presidential palaces dispute, 69, 70; post-2003 legacy, 129, 135, 136, 151, 155, 159; role in 2003 war, 121, 124, 125, 128; sanctions regime, 67, 68, 69; situation after 1991 war, 59, 60, 148; US moves to overthrow, 9, 62, 69, 70, 74, 75, 116, 124, 125, 137, 142, 144, 189; WMD issue, 61, 62, 70, 74
Hussein, Uday Saddam, 124, 128, 152

IGC. *See* Iraqi Governing Council
Ikenberry, G. John, 9–10
India, 9, 10, 45, 82, 100, 199
Indyk, Martin, 62, 63
Information Operations/Warfare, 16, 20–21, 108, 124, 125, 128, 174, 175, 195, 196, 197
International Atomic Energy Agency (IAEA), 61
International Security Assistance Force (ISAF), 91, 94, 103, 104
Internet, 13, 18, 19, 31, 40, 194
Iran, 10, 82; containment by US, 3, 60–62, 66–67, 75, 190, 191, 201; role in post-2003 Iraq, 139, 149, 151, 162, 184, 200
Iran and Libya Sanctions Act 1996, 66, 67
Iran-Iraq war (1980–1988), 64
Iraq: as case study of contemporary warfare, 1,2, 12, 18, 19, 20, 21, 26, 40, 41, 53, 54, 55, 57, 108, 131, 154, 155, 173–179, 184, 191, 195, 196, 197; effect of invasion in Middle East, 3, 59, 189, 190, 191, 200, 201; post-1991 containment regime, 3, 10, 35, 37, 59–62, 64, 67–71, 73; post-2003 conflict, 4, 19, 45, 46, 52, 53, 129, 130, 135–163, 169–184; post-2003 democratization process, 9, 115, 135, 136, 139, 140, 142, 157, 158, 159, 160, 161, 162, 179, 180–184, 203, 204; US decision to invade, 1, 3, 73, 74, 75, 81, 88, 115, 116, 120, 189; US occupation, 119, 137, 138, 142, 145, 199
Iraq war of 2003, 1, 2, 4, 9, 115, 118, 119, 121, 123–129, 131; legality, 2, 4, 11, 116, 117, 118, 199; war objectives, 74–75, 119, 120
Iraqi Governing Council (IGC), 147, 149, 150, 157, 159
Iraqi Interim Government, 147
Iraq Liberation Act 1998, 69
Iraqi National Accord, 125
Iraqi National Congress (INC), 120, 123, 125, 138
Iraqi Security Forces (ISF), 157, 162, 170, 173, 177, 183
Iraq Stabilization Group (ISG), 157
ISAF. *See* International Security Assistance Force

ISF. *See* Iraqi Security Forces
ISG. *See* Iraq Stabilization Group
ISI. *See* Directorate of Inter-Services Intelligence
Islamic Geopoliticals, 37, 38, 39, 41, 42, 196, 197, 198, 201
Islamic Globalists, 37, 38, 39, 42, 198, 201
Islamic Jihad (Palestinian), 65, 200
Islamic Traditionalists, 35, 37, 42, 196, 197, 201
Israel, 37, 45, 62, 63, 65, 66, 75, 200
Israel-Palestinian conflict, 198, 199, 200, 205
Italy, 92

Jackson, Andrea, 196
Jafaari, Ibrahim, 160, 161
Jahiliyya, 34
Jaish al-Mahdi. See Mahdi Army
Jamiat Ulema-i-Islami, 101
Jawbreaker (CIA team, Afghanistan), 83, 84
Al-Jazeera, 202
Jenkins, Simon, 1, 108
Al-Jihad (Egypt), 34
Joint Task Force IV (JTF-IV), 122
Jordan, 34, 61, 63, 68, 152, 154, 203
JTF-IV. *See* Joint Task Force IV

Kagan, Frederick W., 176, 177
Kagan-Keane report, 176, 177
Karbala gap, 127
Karzai, Hamid, 86, 88, 90, 92, 97, 99, 100, 101, 102, 106, 107, 108
Kashmir, 35, 39, 198, 205
Kabul, 83, 84, 85, 86, 87, 88, 91, 92, 94, 96, 97, 100, 102, 120
Kabul government, led by Hamid Karzai, 91, 93, 94, 96, 97, 99, 102, 105, 106, 107
Kandahar province, 84, 86, 92, 93, 94, 100, 103, 104, 105
Keane, Jack, 173, 176
Kenya, 46
Khan, Muhammad Sidique, 39
Khatami, Mohammad, 67
Kilcullen, David, 192, 199
Kirkuk, 126, 143, 151, 160, 181
Kitson, Sir Frank, 45
Komer, Robert W., 45

Kosovo, 50, 51, 52, 57, 118, 131
Kuwait, 59, 60, 62, 64, 67, 75, 116, 119, 203

Lake, Anthony, 62
Lebanon, 18, 65, 75, 191, 201, 203
Lind, William S., 5, 6, 15, 16–17
London bombings (7 July 2005), 39
Loya jirgah, 88, 89, 90
Luttwak, Edward N., 5, 12–13, 17

Mackinlay, John, 18, 192, 196
Madrid conference (October–November 1991), 62, 63
Mahdi Army (*Jaish al-Mahdi*), 158, 162, 171, 178, 179, 181, 183
Al-Majid, Hussein Kamel Hassan, 61
Malaya, 46, 47, 49, 55, 57; Malaysia, 66
Al-Maliki, Nouri, 161, 170, 179, 180, 183
Malley, Robert, 200
Malthus, Thomas, 206
Mao Tse-tung, 17
Marriot Hotel bombing, Islamabad, 101
al-Mashhadani, Mahmoud, 181
Masoud, Ahmad Shah, 82
Mattis, James, 173
Mazar-i-Sharif, 83, 84, 85, 93, 96
McCain, John, 182
McFate, Montgomery, 196
McInnes, Colin, 12
McKiernan, David, 121
McLaughlin, John, 82
McMaster, H. R., 173
McPherson, Peter, 146
Médecins sans Frontières, 94
Mehsud, Baitullah, 100, 104
Mello, Sergio Viera de, 131, 149
MEPI. *See* Middle East Partnership Initiative
Metz, Thomas, 173, 174
Michaelis, Patrick R., 174
Middle East Partnership Initiative (MEPI), 202
Morocco, 203
Mosul, 126, 143, 151, 173, 177, 178
Mubarak, Hosni, 34, 204
Al-Mujaharoun, 38
Muhammad, Khalid Shaikh, 87, 194
Musharraf, Pervez, 72, 81, 100, 101
Muslim Brotherhood, 34, 191, 204

Nagl, John, 173
Najaf, 158
Narcotics trade, Afghanistan. *See* Opium trade
Nasser, Gamal Abdul, 34
National Assembly (Iraq), 144, 160, 169, 172
National Security Council (NSC), 72, 157
National Security Directive 54, 59, 50
National Security Directive 24, 116
National Strategy for Victory in Iraq, 169
NATO. *See* North Atlantic Treaty Organization
Neoconservatives, 73, 74, 119, 122
Netanyahu, Benjamin, 65
New Zealand, 93
North Atlantic Treaty Organization (NATO), 1, 49, 51, 52, 60, 118; in Afghanistan post-2001, 94, 95, 102, 103, 105, 106, 107, 108, 109, 192
Northern Alliance, 82, 83 84, 85, 86, 88, 99
North Korea, 10
North Waziristan, 100, 101
North-West Frontier Province (NWFP), 100, 101, 108
NSD 54. *See* National Security Directive 54
Nuclear weapons, 3, 7, 8, 10, 117, 206

Obama, Barack, 182
Observation-Orientation-Decision-Action (OODA) loop, 27
Occupied territories, 18, 62, 63, 152
Odierno, Ray, 154, 176
Office of Reconstruction and Humanitarian Affairs (ORHA), 116, 122, 123, 137, 138, 140, 141, 142
Office of Special Plans, 122, 123
Ollivant, Douglas A., 175
Oman, 81, 203
Omar, Mullah Muhammad, 37, 83, 87
Operation Anaconda (Afghanistan), 86
Operation Desert Fox (Iraq), 70
Operation Enduring Freedom (Afghanistan), 85
Operation Infinite Reach (against Al-Qaida), 72
Operation Lion's Roar (Iraq), 178

Operation Medusa (Afghanistan), 105
Operation Vigilant Resolve (Iraq), 159, 174
Opium trade (Afghanistan), 91, 92, 93, 95–98, 103, 105
OPLAN 1003-98, 121
Organized crime networks, 13, 136, 149, 152, 155, 176; third-generation criminal gang, 14, 18, 40
Oslo peace process, 63, 65

Pakistan, 34, 36, 37, 38, 40, 72, 73, 99, 100, 101, 102, 104, 106, 107, 108, 189, 191, 201, 2003, 205; and 2001–2002 Afghanistan war, 81, 84, 85, 86, 87
Pakistani Taliban, 100, 101, 104, 108
Palestine/Palestinian territories, 35, 36, 39, 199, 200, 203
Palestinian National Authority, 63, 65
Peacekeeping: developments in the 1990s, 48–53
Peace Support Operations (PSO), 49, 50, 56
Peng, Chin, 55
Pentagon: planning invasion of Iraq, 81,116, 119–123; role in Afghanistan war of 2001–2002, 83, 84, 85, 87; role in post-2003 Iraq, 129, 130, 136, 137, 138, 142, 143, 145, 146, 147, 156, 157
Petraeus, David, 108, 126, 173, 174, 176, 177, 178
Petraeus-Crocker benchmark reports, 180–181
Philippines, 35, 36, 45, 205
Policy Action Group (Afghanistan), 103
Powell, Colin, 83, 157, 203
Provincial Reconstruction Team (PRT): in Afghanistan, 93, 94, 95, 103; in Iraq, 177
PRT. *See* Provincial Reconstruction Team
PSO. *See* Peace Support Operations
Pushtun tribal politics, 82, 85, 86, 88, 90, 98, 99, 100–102, 103, 108

Al-Qaida: 1, 4, 36, 37, 71, 72, 73, 74, 75, 189, 190, 191, 192, 193; association with Taliban, 34, 37, 38, 71, 72, 81, 82, 83, 85, 108, 109; defeat in 2001–2002 Afghanistan war, 3, 4, 40, 86, 87, 99; diffuse global movement, 2, 13, 17, 19, 25, 27, 34, 37, 40–43, 45, 193, 194, 195, 196; "distant Jihad," 35, 37, 39; effects of 2001–2002 Afghanistan war, 85, 86, 87, 99, 189; narratives, 3, 33–40, 196, 197, 199, 201; potential for glocality, 199, 200, 201, 205
Al-Qaida in Iraq, 18, 21, 40, 41, 154, 172, 173, 178, 181, 195, 197
Qadaffi, Muammar, 69
Qanbar, Abud, 177
Qatar, 64, 116, 122, 203
Quetta, 100, 104
Qutb, Sayyid, 34

Rabin, Yitzhak, 63, 65
Ramadi, 143, 154, 178
Rashid, Ahmed, 101
Reconstruction, Reconciliation, and Assimilation (RRA): 47, 48, 49, 50, 52, 53, 54, 55, 57, 195, 196; closing the RRA gap, 55–56, 106, 107, 109, 169, 170, 171, 179, 181, 184; in Afghanistan, 88, 89, 91, 92, 93, 94, 95, 102, 103, 105, 106, 107; in Iraq, 135, 140, 141, 142, 144, 146, 148, 154, 156, 161, 169, 170, 174, 179, 180, 181, 182; in the war on terror, 201, 204
Record, Jeffrey, 190
Red Cross, 52, 85, 154
Red mosque, Islamabad, 100
Renuart, Gene, 124
Republican Guards, 70, 124–125, 128; Medina Division, 126, 127; Special Republican Guards, 70, 124, 125, 127, 128
Revolution in Military Affairs (RMA), 19, 60
Ricciardone, Frank, 69
Rice, Condoleezza, 157, 204
Richards, David, 105
Ricks, Thomas E., 2, 121, 122, 137
Al-Risha, Shaikh Abdul Sattar, 172
RMA. *See* Revolution in Military Affairs
Roe, Andrew M., 107
Roy, Olivier, 34
RRA. *See* Reconstruction, Reconciliation, and Assimilation
Rumsfeld, Donald, 81, 82, 83, 84, 87,

Index 229

118, 119, 120, 121, 123, 136, 137, 138, 145
Russia, 9, 10, 13, 45, 51, 66, 68, 70, 71, 82, 199
Russia-Georgia war, 206

Al-Sadr, Muqtada, 158
Sadr City, 174, 183
Sadr movement, 158, 159, 180, 183
Salvation Council for Anbar, 172
Samarra, 126, 143, 151, 160, 162
Sanchez, Ricardo, 145, 153, 154, 156, 158
Sangin, 104, 105
Saudi Arabia, 34, 35, 36, 64, 70, 71, 75, 152, 154, 194, 199, 200, 201, 203, 205
Scales, Robert, 20, 173
Schon, Donald A., 27, 28–33, 193, 195
Schwarzkopf, Norman, 60
SCIRI. *See* Supreme Council for the Islamic Revolution in Iraq
September 11, 2001, attacks (9/11), 1, 3, 2, 25, 40, 43, 57, 59, 73, 75, 81, 82, 87, 116, 131, 189, 194, 201; 9/11 Commission, 70, 72
Serbia, 10, 45, 49, 50
Shah-i-Kot Valley, 86
Sharon, Ariel, 65
Shinseki, Eric, 121
Shomali Plains, 84, 85
Simon, Steven, 182
Sistani, Ali, 157, 159, 160, 161
Sky, Emma, 176
Smith, Rupert, 5, 8, 9
Social Network Analysis, 25–33
Solidarism, 11
Somalia, 12, 25, 35, 36, 48, 49, 51, 52, 205
Sons of Iraq, 173
South Waziristan, 100, 101, 104
Spain, 117
Stansfield, Gareth, 163
Sudan, 34, 71, 72
Sullivan, John P., 14
Sunni insurgency, Iraq, 139, 150–160, 162, 171, 172, 173, 176, 195
Supreme Council for the Islamic Revolution in Iraq (SCIRI), 154, 158, 160, 161, 162, 180, 183
Surge, Iraq (2006–), 4, 108, 171, 173–183, 184

Swat Valley, 100, 101, 104
Syria, 34, 63, 68, 70, 75, 152, 154, 190, 191, 200, 201, 203

Tajikistan, 82, 84, 85, 104
Takrit, 126, 128, 143
al-Takriti, Mahar Soufiane, 125
TAL. *See* Transitional Administrative Law
Tal Afar, 174
Taliban: 36, 104; as bargaining adversary, 88, 107, 108, 109, 199; defeat in 2001–2002 war, 3, 4, 40, 73, 85, 86, 87, 88, 89, 95, 189, 203; fighting in the war in 2001–2002, 85, 86; insurgency post-2001, 94, 95, 100, 102, 103, 105, 106; links to opium trade, 95–97; as organization, 18, 40, 107; relationship with al-Qaida, 37, 38, 40, 81, 83, 87, 108, 109; relationship with Pakistani security services, 72, 100, 101; resurgence after 2001, 1, 91, 95, 98–102, 103; US decision to overthrow, 81, 82, 83, 203
Tehrik-e Taliban Pakistan. *See* Pakistani Taliban
Templer, Sir Gerald, 45, 46, 47
Tenet, George, 82
Thompson, Sir Robert, 45, 46, 47
Time-Phased Force Deployment List, 121
Transformation agenda, Pentagon, 87, 121
Transitional Administrative Law (TAL), 157, 159
Tripp, Charles, 150
Turkey, 63, 66, 68, 118, 149, 200
Two Holy Mosques, of Mecca and Medina, 37, 71

UIA. *See* United Iraqi Alliance
UNAMA. *See* United Nations Assistance Mission to Afghanistan
United Iraqi Alliance (UIA), 160
United Kingdom. *See* Great Britain
United Nations (UN), 51, 52, 61, 66; operations in post-2001 Afghanistan, 92, 97; operations in post-2003 Iraq, 131, 146, 147, 148, 154, 157, 160
United Nations Assistance Mission to Afghanistan (UNAMA), 93

United Nations Charter 1945, 11, 81, 118; Article 2(4), 116; Article 51, 81
United Nations Children's Fund, 67
United Nations Development Fund for Iraq (DFI), 147
United Nations High Commissioner for Bosnia, 50
United Nations Monitoring, Verification, and Inspection Mission (UNMOVIC), 68, 75, 116, 117
United Nations Office on Drugs and Crimes (UNODC), 96
United Nations Oil for Food program, 61, 67, 68
United Nations Security Council, 51, 71, 75, 116, 118
United Nations Security Council Resolutions 242 and 338, 63
United Nations Security Council Resolution 687, 61
United Nations Security Council Resolution 986, 68
United Nations Security Council Resolution 1284, 68
United Nations Security Council Resolution 1386, 91
United Nations Security Council Resolution 1441, 116
United Nations Security Council Resolution 1483, 147
United Nations Security Council Resolution 1546, 160
United Nations Special Commission (UNSCOM), 61, 69, 70
United States (US): as global hegemonic manager, 9–13, 14, 25, 34, 35, 37, 51, 59–75, 117, 118, 190, 206; military pre-eminence, 1, 3, 7, 11, 15, 16, 49, 50, 56, 206, 189, 193, 206
USAID, 146
US Army War College (Carlisle Barracks, Pennsylvania), 50, 120, 190
US Army 2nd Armored Cavalry Regiment, 127
US Army 3rd Infantry Division, 121, 124, 126, 127, 128
US Army 4th Infantry Division, 119, 121, 125, 154
US Army 82nd Airborne Division, 121

US Army 101st Airborne Division, 121, 127, 173
US Army 173rd Airborne Division, 121
US Central Command, 85, 108, 121, 122, 138
US Congress, 142, 169, 170, 178, 180
US Department of Defense. *See* Pentagon
US-Iraq "status of forces" agreement and strategic framework, 183
US Marine Corps, 26, 86, 121, 128, 159, 174; 1st Marine Division, 126, 128
US National Intelligence Estimate 2007, 191
US National Security Strategy, September 2002, 202
US Senate Armed Services Committee, 147
US Senate Foreign Relations Committee, 130, 145
US State Department, 93, 97, 120, 122, 123, 146
Uzbekistan, 35, 36, 82, 84, 85, 205

Van Crevald, Martin, 5, 6, 8, 17
Vedrine, Hubert, 67
Vietnam War, 8, 18, 33, 46, 57, 60, 94, 131, 173, 175, 179, 180

Washington, 50, 63, 68, 69, 71, 72, 93, 123, 137, 138, 145, 148, 157, 158, 159, 182
Weapons of mass destruction (WMD), 14, 190
Weapons of Mass Destruction of Iraq, 61, 62, 68, 70, 73, 74, 75, 116, 117, 118, 119; danger of proliferation, 73–74
Wehrmacht (German Army, World War II), 16
West Bank, 64, 65, 200
Westerman, Ian, 94, 95
WMD. *See* Weapons of mass destruction
Wolfowitz, Paul, 137, 145, 147, 156
Woodward, Bob, 2, 82
World Trade Center, 71, 73
Wright, Robin, 71

Yaqoubi, Mustafa, 158
Yemen, 36, 154

Yugoslavia (former), 13, 25, 49, 52, 57

Zardari, Asif, 101
al-Zarqawi, Abu Musab, 40, 154, 194

Al-Zawahiri, Ayman, 34, 37, 39, 40, 71, 87, 189, 194
Zinni, Anthony, 121
Zionist-Crusader alliance, 35, 197

About the Book

Why, despite indisputably superior military might, have the US-led military interventions in Afghanistan and Iraq been so fraught with setbacks? Does it make sense in today's security environment to use military force to achieve strategic objectives? How does the contemporary battlefield function? Addressing these questions, Simon Murden explores the contradictions inherent in attempting to combat global terrorist networks by intervening in complex, local social settings.

Murden proposes two approaches to better understand the nature of contemporary warfare: one focusing on the nature of insurgency and the other on the dynamics of intervention. Applying these approaches to the cases of Iraq and Afghanistan, he offers important conclusions about the shortcomings of US strategy in the global war on terror.

Simon W. Murden is senior lecturer in the Department of Strategic Studies and International Affairs at Britannia Naval College. He is author of *Islam, the Middle East, and the New Global Hegemony*.